In Search of the True Russia

IN SEARCH OF THE TRUE RUSSIA

*The Provinces
in Contemporary Nationalist Discourse*

Lyudmila Parts

THE UNIVERSITY OF WISCONSIN PRESS

The University of Wisconsin Press
728 State Street, Suite 443
Madison, Wisconsin 53706
uwpress.wisc.edu

Gray's Inn House, 127 Clerkenwell Road
London EC1R 5DB, United Kingdom
eurospanbookstore.com

Copyright © 2018
The Board of Regents of the University of Wisconsin System
All rights reserved. Except in the case of brief quotations embedded in critical articles and reviews, no part of this publication may be reproduced, stored in a retrieval system, transmitted in any format or by any means—digital, electronic, mechanical, photocopying, recording, or otherwise—or conveyed via the Internet or a website without written permission of the University of Wisconsin Press. Rights inquiries should be directed to rights@uwpress.wisc.edu.

Printed in the United States of America

This book may be available in a digital edition.

Library of Congress Cataloging-in-Publication Data

Names: Parts, Lyudmila, author.
Title: In search of the true Russia: the provinces in contemporary nationalist discourse / Lyudmila Parts.
Description: Madison, Wisconsin: The University of Wisconsin Press, [2018] | Includes bibliographical references and index.
Identifiers: LCCN 2017046045 | ISBN 9780299317607 (cloth: alk. paper)
Subjects: LCSH: Russian literature—20th century—History and criticism. | Russian literature—21st century—History and criticism. | National characteristics, Russian, in literature. | National characteristics, Russian, in motion pictures. | Nationalism and literature—Russia (Federation) | Mass media and nationalism—Russia (Federation)
Classification: LCC PG2987.N27 P37 2018 | DDC 891.709/3581—dc23
LC record available at https://lccn.loc.gov/2017046045

ISBN 9780299317645 (pbk.: alk. paper)

For my daughters,
Yuliya
and
Adele

Contents

List of Illustrations — ix
Acknowledgments — xi
Note on Translation and Transliteration — xiii

Introduction: Imagining the Provinces — 3

1. Journalism: "We Look for Wealth in the Provinces and Find It There!" — 42

2. Literature: In the Provincial State of Mind — 73

3. Film and TV: "My Country—My Moscow!" — 104

Conclusion: On Cultural Authenticity — 139

Notes — 147
Bibliography — 171
Index — 187

Illustrations

Back cover of *Iaroslavskii Stil'* 3 (2006)	13
Title card for the serial *The Milkmaid from Khatsapetovka*	119
From *The Milkmaid from Khatsapetovka*	120
Title card for *The Milkmaid from Khatsapetovka 2: Challenging Fate*	123
From *Kokoko*	135

Acknowledgments

This project was a natural outgrowth of my work on cultural myths, especially the Chekhov myth where the provinces are such an important constituent. The heightened significance the cultural myth of the provinces has attained in recent times required a study of its own. With the financial support by the Social Sciences and Humanities Research Council of Canada I made several trips to Russia—to work at the Moscow, St. Petersburg, and Voronezh libraries—and to academic conferences in the United States, Canada, Russia, Germany, and Finland.

Many colleagues and friends have provided me with intellectual and moral support as well as invaluable feedback; I am especially grateful to Anne Lounsbery, Mark Lipovetsky, Nancy Condee, Birgit Beumers, Edith Clowes, Susan Smith-Peter, Dirk Uffelmann, Il'ia Kukulin, and Valeria Sobol for so generously offering their expertise and advice. The lively discussions at the conference on regional identities at the University of Virginia, organized by Edith Clowes and Ani Kokobobo, pushed me to clarify the differences between regions and the provinces and how, exactly, Voronezh is not Paris. Likewise, the exchanges at the conference I organized at McGill on the provinces in film helped me to specify the extent to which the village and the provinces have overlapped in the contemporary cultural imagination.

I owe a special debt of gratitude to Krystyna Steiger for editing and proofreading the manuscript and translating innumerable Russian quotes, all with nuance and finesse. Sections of chapter 3 appeared in earlier drafts, in *Slavic Review* 74, no. 3 (fall 2015) and *Zeitschrift für Slavische Philologie* 68, no. 1 (2011). I would like to thank the editors and anonymous readers at the journals and at the University of Wisconsin Press for their very helpful comments.

My greatest and most constant source of support has always been my family, Vladimir Parts and our daughters, Yuliya and Adele, who never ask me what I write about but are always willing to listen.

Note on Translation and Transliteration

All translations are mine unless noted otherwise. I have followed the Library of Congress system for transliteration of quotations and of Russian titles and proper names in the notes and bibliography. I anglicized Russian proper names throughout the main text and preserved the conventional spelling of well-known names.

In Search of the True Russia

Introduction
Imagining the Provinces

> The rawness of the backwoods and the rottenness of the center—such are the poles of Russian life.
>
> N. Berdyaev, 1918

A hundred years ago the philosopher Nikolai Berdyaev described "the geography of the Russian soul" as dominated, and oppressed, by the vastness of the Russian land.[1] He considered the traditional division of this immense space into the center and the provinces to be gravely misleading, particularly as it related to the intelligentsia's quest for the authentic Russian spirit: "People of the cultured and intellectual centers too often think the essence of the spiritual and social life of the nation lies somewhere out in the depths of Russia." Armed with preconceived notions of what constitutes the essence of Russianness, they expect to find it in Russia's far-away corners. Berdyaev suggests discarding this false dichotomy in favor of developing, on equal terms, the moral and cultural potential of all of Russia, beginning with the individual soul: "The true center is neither in the capital, nor the provinces, in neither the highest, nor lowest stratum, but in the depths of each individual."[2] In today's Russia, as has been true over the past two centuries, the undeveloped provinces and the "rotten" center remain the two opposing poles of "the geography of the Russian soul." The philosopher's advice remained unheeded over the course of the twentieth century; in fact, since the end of the Soviet Union, "the capital versus the provinces" as the binary opposition at the heart of Russian culture has acquired new significance and emerged at the forefront of public discourse. Today's intellectuals of the center have recommenced the search for the spirit of Russianness in the far depths of provincial Russia while their provincial counterparts actively engage in elaborating the idea of the provinces as the home of enduring values and the Russian national spirit.

This book focuses on the provinces as the imagined locale of authentic Russianness. The role of provincial Russia as the realm within which to contemplate the country's past and future, the problems of identity and authenticity, and other recurring yet seemingly unresolvable issues places the provinces at the core of Russian cultural mythology. The myth of the provinces provides the contemporary cultural elite with a semiotic apparatus for formulating Russia's new postimperial identity. Contemporary cultural production locates true Russianness outside of the newly prosperous, multiethnic, and westernized Moscow. In mass culture, the traditional privileging of the center over the backward provinces gives way to the view of the provinces as a repository of national traditions and moral strength. Conversely, high literature and art-house films provide an alternative, harshly critical image of the provinces. In both cases, a particular concept of Russianness is negotiated in which the provinces play a central role.

How is it possible that the provinces of the Russian classics—those cheerless little towns, plagued with boredom and insecurities—so often figure in today's literature and film as locales in which the Russian national idea perseveres and takes shape? The contemporary shift toward a predominantly positive view of the provinces occurs when they become incorporated into the discourse of nationalism. Within this discourse, the fundamental "provinces versus the center" binary intersects with the equally fundamental opposition in Russian symbolic geography of "Russia versus the West." In the semantic field in which these two binaries overlap in post-Soviet culture, the provinces versus capital opposition becomes a thematic and ideological alternative to Russia's perpetually problematic relationship with the West. In light of this development, I examine the provincial theme in post-Soviet journalism, literature, and film as a cultural representation of Russian nationalism.

Focusing on the provinces in contemporary nationalist discourse provides a means of redirecting discussions of Russia's national identity away from the psychologically unsatisfying opposition of Russia versus the West, which invariably centers on Russia's response to its loss of imperial might and prestige. This approach offers instead a hermetic national model that serves a dual purpose: it replaces the superior Other of the West with a more ambiguously defined Other of the provinces while also positing a dynamic of benevolent leadership *within* the new national borders. Ultimately, the focus on the provinces offers a model of national identity based on "us versus us" rather than the traditional oppositions of "us versus them."

A cultural myth is an ideological construct. It is a type of discourse, a message that is determined by historical conditions; it signifies whatever the contemporary consumer, conditioned as she is by history, sees as significant; it "cannot possibly evolve from the 'nature' of things."[3] It is a mode of explanation that arranges visions of the past so as to confirm those of the present. At times of major historical shifts, such as the revolutionary decades of the early twentieth century and of the post-Soviet period, the cultural myth ensures cohesion for a culture that is undergoing a process of reexamination.[4] By definition, a cultural myth has little to do with reality and everything to do with the way the cultural elite—the intelligentsia—constructs their interpretation of reality.

Defining the provinces as a cultural myth requires some clarification. We know, for instance, that the provinces exist—populated by millions, discussed by economists and politicians, and portrayed by writers and film directors. And yet, actual Russian towns, big and small, have very little to do with the cultural myth of the provinces as it has developed over the past two centuries. Like all cultural myths, the provincial myth reflects not the reality of the provinces but rather a certain perception of this reality, conveyed by the intelligentsia by means of the press, literature, and (since their inception) cinema, television, and the internet. Historians and sociologists study the regions—that is, the "actual" provincial locales one can visit—in terms of their history, customs, landscape, and administrative and political structures.[5] Scholars of literature, film, and culture, meanwhile, examine the provinces "as text"—that is, they look at the ways in which authors construct the provinces and work them into Russian symbolic geography, in their literary, filmic, or scholarly endeavors.

Today, the cultural myth of the provinces is complex and continues to combine two opposing views of Russia's noncapital space as both a stifling environment (as depicted in the prose of Gogol, Chekhov, and

Sologub) and an idealized repository of "Russianness." What prevails in contemporary cultural mythology, especially in mass culture, is precisely this second, heretofore only minimally elaborated view of the provinces, which must embody, in concentrated form, all the components of a positive national identity: magnanimity, kindness, soulfulness, and generosity. Provincial Russianness is posited as a means of countering the arrogance, callousness, and egoism of both the West and westernized Moscow. In effect, the provincial myth has been coopted into the discourse of nationalism, thus ensuring that most portrayals of the provinces, both positive and negative, can be understood as making a statement about the Russian national character. In this role, the myth has been producing multiple cultural texts that expound on the role of the provinces in generating a new geography of the Russian soul.

I begin by tracing the history of the provinces as a concept and outlining the salient features of the provincial myth. My main focus, however, is on the post-Soviet period, which witnessed changes to that myth that were of a magnitude unprecedented in the history of Russian culture.

Definition

The term "the provinces," *provintsiia*, was introduced into the Russian language at the end of the seventeenth century, during Peter the Great's administrative reforms. These reforms were intended to regulate the capital's relationship to other cities in terms of economy, trade, and taxes—that is, to effect "the replacement of a geographic area by an administrative unit."[6] Thus was formed a system of regional hierarchy comprising a *guberniia*, an *uezd*, and a *provintsiia*. In 1775, Catherine II restructured the system, eliminating the province as an administrative unit; by and large, the *guberniia* subsumed the territory of the province, and the term *provintsiia* ceased to exist. Consequently, the words *provintsiia*, *provintsial*, and *provintsial'nyi* were free to acquire a new function in the Russian cultural imagination: as markers of the cultural myth that organizes the vast space of the Russian empire into the basic binary opposition of the center versus the provinces. As Lyudmila Zayonts observes in her analysis of the concept of *provintsiia* and its history, losing its referent allowed the word "to exist as an open lexical form, generating its own text-producing space."[7]

Introduction

Even by the late eighteenth and early nineteenth centuries, neither *provintsiia* nor *provintsial* ("a provincial") had entered the dictionaries or acquired any negative connotations. The readership of the day was preoccupied with literary depictions of the landed gentry who, freed from obligatory state service by Catherine's "Charter of Nobility" (1785), took up permanent residence on their country estates.[8] These largely pleasant portrayals of country life yielded to stories of tragic displacement following the Emancipation of the Serfs in 1862.[9] More to the point, at about the same time that the country landowner engaged in husbandry was being cast in a positive, Rousseauian light, "the provincial" began to assume negative connotations as someone backward and unrefined. Thus, the countryside carried the highly appealing markers of purity and nature, but the provincial town was associated with boredom and crudeness. In other words, two different binaries were at play: the capital versus the provinces (*stolitsa–provintsiia*), which generally defined the periphery in negative terms, and the capital versus the village/countryside (*stolitsa–derevnia*), which construed the countryside in the lyrical terms of "sentimental pastoralism."[10] The two cultural concepts—the provincial town and the country estate—engender different types of plotlines and belong to different symbolic geographies; however, both acquire significance and meaning only in relation (and contrast) to the capital.

While "village," "landowner," and "peasant" all occupied an important and clearly defined place in the nineteenth-century Russian cultural imagination, the same cannot be said of the concept of the provinces. The latter term was so broad in its meaning as to encompass diverse ideas about the whole of the country situated outside the capital. By the mid-nineteenth century, the word had found its niche, and the provinces (not the countryside) now stood for the whole of Russia: "Regional hierarchy dissolves in the unified provincial space. The Empire breaks down into the capital and the provinces. All of Russia's space, with the exception of its two capitals, is seen and referred to as the provinces [*provintsiia*]."[11] Thus the word firmly entered the language of Russian literature and culture as a mythologeme within the realm of *symbolic* geography rather than in the administrative or scientifically geographical sense. Provinces thus conceived could only be imagined, not visited; they possessed no inimitable names or characteristics and could be situated anywhere at all between the center and the exotic periphery.[12] Provinces in this sense constituted unstructured space outside the capital, the locus of biases, fears, and illusions. Provincial space could be construed either as backward and devoid of hope and vitality or, conversely, as the abode of enduring values and the national spirit.

Dictionary definitions reflect this shift in meaning from administrative unit to mythologeme and illustrate how the word *provintsiia* and its derivatives—*provintsial, provintsial'nyi,* and *provintsial'nost'*—acquired stable, negative connotations. Vladimir Dal (1863) defines *provintsiia* in neutral terms, as analogous to the other administrative units of *guberniia, oblast', okrug,* and *uezd*. Dal's definition of "a provincial" as someone who lives "not in the capital" but in a *"guberniia, uezd, zakholust'e"* is slightly less neutral, since *zakholust'e*, meaning "the sticks," is clearly a pejorative term. Twentieth-century sources, including the authoritative dictionaries by Ushakov (1940) and Ozhegov (1949), note the foreign origins of the word and define it in the very general terms of being "noncapital": "generally—an area of a country, as distinct from the capitals." The negative definitions apply only to the adjective "provincial" (*provintsial'nyi*): "metaph. Backward, naive and ignorant." Post-Soviet dictionaries replicate the above definitions but include the connotations of "backwardness" for both the noun ("A locality situated at a distance from the capital, the sophisticated metropolis. Used as a symbol of stagnancy, backwardness") and the adjective ("inherent in the provincial. Backward, naive and ignorant").[13]

"Provincial" was effectively banned from Soviet official language, both as a word and a concept; it was replaced by the neutral designation of "periphery," in reference to a distant place where "people work as hard, harmoniously, and selflessly, as in the center."[14] After the 1917 revolution, scholars observe, "the history of the provinces ended, and the history of the periphery and [the] deep country [*glubinka*] began."[15] Both "periphery" and "deep country" are singular nouns; thus their grammatical form emphasizes the homogeneous, undifferentiated nature of this space. By contrast, the prepositional plural form of the term *na mestakh*, meaning "on the local level," implies subordination to a central power. Distinctions aside, however, the neutral "periphery," the spatially curious *glubinka* (literally, "the depths"), and the hierarchical *na mestakh* share one quality: they are unassociated with any preceding cultural discourse and, therefore, are not value-laden. They do, however, feature consistently in the official journalistic discourse of Soviet newspapers, whose emphatically neutral designations are counterbalanced in the vernacular with such odd-sounding toponyms, real

Introduction

and concocted, as Chukhloma, Mukhosransk, Uriupinsk, and Katsapetovka.[16] The negative connotations attached to the provinces have been so persistent through most of the twentieth century as to taint even the intended "neutral" status of their replacements. Aleksei Yudin traces the negative connotations acquired by "periphery" over the course of the twentieth century, for which reason, he concludes, in the post-perestroika period the "new euphemism for the neutral definition of areas removed from the capital is the word 'region/s.'"[17]

Thus, the negative perception of the provinces, equated (until recently) mostly with backwardness and inadequacy, has proven remarkably unyielding.[18] The provinces, as they have been imagined in the Russian cultural tradition, lack many things—access to culture and the latest in fashion and political news; taste and originality of thought; prospects for a successful career or marriage; and even self-respect. Readers of nineteenth-century literature are familiar with portrayals of a stifling provincial atmosphere characterized by narrowmindedness and a penchant for gossip. According to this vision, intellectual life in the provinces merely echoes, faintly and often ridiculously, the truly progressive intellectual thought of the center, and provincial cultural events are typically second-rate. The governing emotional state of provincial life is boredom, and its color—gray. Provincial urban space is uniform and unimaginative, and its streets are typically muddy, full of large puddles, or thick with dust.

The most important thing to remember about the provinces as described above, however, is that they are thus perceived from the perspective of the center—the place that presumably possesses everything the provinces lack. The recurring dichotomies that organize the provinces–capital opposition include those of nature versus culture, static versus dynamic, and even (in auditory and visual terms) quiet and monotonous versus noisy and motley.[19] These are easily recognizable attributes; what makes them especially interesting, however, is the ability of a cultural text to reverse the positive/negative value of each. Defined negatively, provincial life signifies a lack of culture as well as stagnation, boredom, imitativeness, and a narrow-minded worldview. Viewed positively, the same features are reinterpreted as the opportunity to enjoy life at a slower pace and to engage in reflection. From this point of view, provincials are closer to nature and possess stronger ties to the country's land and history. Most importantly, because provincial residents are not as susceptible as residents of the capital to the whims of fashion, their way of life preserves national cultural traditions. Thus, the provincial inferiority complex is often accompanied by its compensatory opposite, which presents all attributes of provincial life as superior to the center. Such reversals occur regularly on a small scale. During historical periods of sweeping change these changing attitudes mark significant cultural and ideological shifts.

Redefinition

Since the provincial topos constitutes "an object of ideological reflection,"[20] it acquires particular importance in times of cultural and political shifts. Between the two revolutions in the early twentieth century, the positive view of the provinces briefly gained prominence in the discourse of *passéism* (the nostalgic privileging of the past over the present), fueled by the image of the provinces as a pure, uncontaminated place, a repository of the national tradition and cultural wealth. Zayonts observes that the consideration of provincial spaces "moved from the narrative realm into the sphere of cultural-historical inquiry" in the 1910s.[21] During this period, central periodicals published a great number of materials about, and from, the provinces, and when the provinces became an object of examination, "all non-capital culture was nominated a kind of 'national conservancy area,' where any object could become an artifact."[22] Passéism thus created a particular view of the provinces "as a cultural and historical reserve, in the depths of which, as F. Sologub would later write with longing, 'there was so much hidden—pure powers and prophetic dreams.' A stable complex of representative literary allusions from Pushkin to Chekhov completed the picture."[23] Important cultural personae, art historians, and artists embarked upon trips to the provinces and published their studies of provincial architecture and artifacts. The provincial discourse acquired its own publication venues: magazines, such as *Russian Olden Times* (*Russkaia starina*), and encyclopedias, such as *Great Russia: Geographical, Ethnographic, and Cultural Profiles of Contemporary Russia* (1912). A bookstore named the Provincial Colleague (Sotrudnik provintsii) opened in Moscow, and numerous ethnographic expeditions presented their findings for discussion in public forums.[24]

Alexander Etkind describes the intensification of interest in subordinate territories—in this case, Russia's own lands (which he defines as internal colonies)—as a characteristic of colonialism in an era witnessing the decline of an empire. "Russian Populism—the rapturous deference to the exploited peoples on the eve of the fall of the empire—is functionally equivalent to Western Orientalism, as described by Edward Said: a heightened interest of imperial centers in their colonies, which is motivated by the need for knowledge-as-power and simultaneously by feelings of guilt."[25] Early twentieth-century passéism too viewed "exotic" customs and works of art through the prism of its Orientalist interpretative paradigm. Like all cultural myths, the constructed image of the provinces—poetic and inviting—had no relation to reality. Rather, it responded to the needs of the cultural elite of the center.[26] Born of the Zeitgeist and characterized by an acute awareness of imminent change, the provincial myth was in demand. The burst of nostalgia, foreshadowing and anticipating the end of an era, necessitated the creation of a stable image of the outgoing reality.

The wave of passéism that engendered the renewed interest in the provincial myth in the post-Soviet period is similarly prompted by major sociopolitical changes and fueled by nostalgia; it is a widespread cultural trend with various cultural manifestations, from commercial cinema to academic conferences. Until the post-Soviet period, the subject of the provinces rarely cropped up, except in history books and philological studies of the nineteenth-century classics. However, since at least the early 1990s onward, most discussions of Russia's political and cultural development assigned the provinces a major role. In the year 2000, during one of the numerous forums on the theme of Russian provincial culture, the Perm philologist Vladimir Abashev, himself an active participant in this discussion,[27] observed: "Oddly enough, the discussions of the provinces arose ubiquitously precisely when the [Soviet] empire ceased to exist. In the topical discourse of the seventies you almost never came across the term. Yet since the end of the eighties, up to this very day, there's been a deluge [of] articles, conferences, scholarly works, and it's all still gaining momentum."[28] Thus, the provinces came to constitute an object of ideological reflection precisely when the nation had to adjust to its new borders and its new relationship to the world. The new geopolitical map of Russia—its actual geography—required a new corresponding "symbolic" geography—namely, the "geography of the Russian soul." The provinces' role on this symbolic map is crucial, as the home of the true Russia, both past and future.

The rehabilitation of the provinces and all things provincial begins with the very words *provintsiia* and *provintsial'nyi*. In keeping with their renewed positive associations, a high number of regional newspapers have been retitled as the *Provincial News/ Tidings/ Chronicles (Provintsial'nye novosti/ izvestiia/ khroniki)*.²⁹ The Provintsiia publishing house distributes its weeklies throughout twenty-five regions in Russia, and two major journals, *The Russian Provinces (Russkaia provintsiia)* and *Russia's Provinces (Rossiiskaia Provintsiia)* launched between 1991 and 1993. Collections of work by provincial writers and artists, released mostly in their home towns (but also in Moscow), have entered the mainstream.³⁰ Examples include exhibitions in Moscow galleries entitled "Provincial Artists" and anthologies of short fiction by provincial women.³¹ For the same reasons that, at the outset of his political career in Moscow, Boris Nemtsov asserted himself as a provincial, far-removed from the political intrigue of the capital,³² a popular female singer titles her album *A Provincial Gal (Provintsial'naia devchonka)*. The joint-stock companies Provintsial (Kursk) and The Provinces (Piatigorsk) boast quality, local dairy products; across the country, similarly named small businesses offer various goods and services, from cleaning products to home repair; and The Provincial Lady dating service claims to represent modest, virtuous "truly Russian" women. The Provinces real estate agencies open offices in Kurgan, Arkhangelsk, Vologda, and Rostov-on-Don; Your Provinces sells real estate in Moscow Oblast, and My Provinces in Yaroslavl. The city's Provincial Collection fashion festival (since 2002) presents a Provincial Chic line of clothing; Voronezh, home to its own fashion festival, Guberniia Style (since 2005), nominates itself the capital of provincial fashion; and since 2014, the Viatskoe history museum complex in Yaroslavl Oblast has hosted a festival called The Provinces Are the Soul of Russia.

An analogous proliferation of the word *provintsiia* is evident in discourse of a more academic nature. Since 2004, the Kul'tura television channel has broadcast a series entitled *Provincial Museums of Russia*, while in 2006 a documentary journalism series entitled *Letters from the Provinces* gave the following description of its subject matter: "about the cultural life of the Russian provinces, about the people, who are preserving the national culture, about tradition, [and] the customs of the peoples of Russia." In academia proper, a great number of conferences, conference proceedings, and collections of articles reflect an intense interest in this subject. Examples include *The Social History of the Russian Provinces* (Yaroslavl University, 2006–11); *The Spiritual Life of the Provinces. Images. Symbols. Worldview* (Ulyanovsk University, 2003); and *The Life of the Provinces as a Phenomenon of Spirituality* (Nizhniy Novgorod University, since 2003). In 2006, a major scholarly journal,

Introduction

Back cover of *Iaroslavskii Stil'* 3 (2006). Report on the Provincial Collection competition. The caption reads "Professional School 31, 'Provincial chic.'"

Otechestvennye zapiski, devoted an issue titled "Anatomy of the Provinces" to the topic. The name of the opening piece, "And the Last Shall Become the First," could serve as the motto for the trend within provincial studies of approaching the provinces neither as geopolitical entities nor sites of local history, but rather as a subject requiring highly abstract terms of nationalist discourse such as tradition, spirituality, and cultural heritage.

A large number of these publications record, without analyzing, the shift toward reimagining the provinces in positive terms and presenting a uniform and passionate apology for the provinces. What strikes one most is the consistency with which the idea of provinces is reduced to the notions of spirituality, memory, and tradition, as in the examples below:

> Despite all the negative, emotional connotations [assigned to] the concept of "the provinces," what remains entrenched in the mass consciousness *for* the provinces is their image as the binding constant of the national idea. The provinces' potential is in the spiritual and cultural sense. Here is where the national-historic memory has

not yet been lost.... The provincial world... is inextricably bound to the Russian [world].³³

Russian provincial culture can be considered an option for the preservation of the national cultural heritage.... The most important qualities and characteristics of the whole of Russia's culture still remain deeply rooted in the expanses of the provinces.³⁴

The determinate complex assigned to provincialism of predominantly negative meanings which, in the contemporary context, are actively desemanticized, forfeit their evaluative function, and accumulate new topical shades of meaning and interpretations. From here on out, being provincial doesn't signify being uncultivated, inferior, inept but, rather, authentic, unique, sober-minded.... It's no longer about rural pastorals, but about mobilizing the cultural potential of the provinces for the rebirth of all of Russia.³⁵

Questions may arise as to the logic behind this revision, particularly with regard to precisely how the last became first, what would convince a woman to dress in "provincial chic," and what justifies the provincials' pride in being provincial. As the examples above demonstrate, the positive conceptualization of the provinces occurs within the discourse of the national idea, as the emphasis shifts from the notions of inadequacy to those of historical memory, cultural heritage, and the provinces' potential to regenerate the entire country. As a result, the provinces of post-Soviet times are imagined as the place of tradition and spirituality—the place that holds the key to Russia's rebirth as a country with strong national roots and an equally strong idea and spirit.

Cultural myths are not constricted by reality; rather, they possess the power to shape our view of it. Thus, myths constitute the very basis of national identity creation. Authors who depict the provinces in negative terms and assign a bleak vision of Russia's social and political situation to its heartland contribute to the same discourse of national identity as those who idealize the provinces. In both cases, the provinces serve as an organizing myth of Russian nationalist discourse. It is precisely because the "good" provinces (as the locale of authentic Russianness) have been claimed by the nationalists that the negative portrayals of the provinces and provincials are inevitably seen as a response to this idealization and an alternative view of Russia's past and future.

The nationalists imagine—and praise—the simple way of life, loyalty to tradition, soulfulness, and purity they associate with provincial Russia; their opponents portray stupefaction, degradation, and poverty. This pessimistic view is all the more pronounced when the same setting doubles as the locale where mass culture and commercial cinema situate their positive and uplifting visions. Both groups may exaggerate, yet both employ the myth of the provinces in commenting on the current state of the Russian nation.

The discourse of nationalism—that is, the body of texts engaged in the intellectual inquiry into the problems of nationalism and national identity—encompasses various political and ideological stances. Within this discourse, a popular author's approach to the issue would diverge from that of a scholar, film director, or politician. Nevertheless, they all participate in the same intellectual inquiry. As participants in this discourse in today's Russia, nationalists are opposed not by internationalists or globalists, and certainly not by Russophobes, but by those predominantly liberal thinkers who see nationalism as a conservative, pro-government, and essentially anti-democratic force that is conducive to (and often used to justify) xenophobia and totalitarianism. Ultimately, the fact that these participants conceive variously of what constitutes a nation, and often subscribe to different political views, is of secondary importance. What matters is that the provincial myth facilitates discussions of the subject and is therefore crucial to discerning the problems associated with Russian nationalism today.

Nationalism and Cultural Myths

Nationalism has not always had the bad name it has today. It serves to provide large civic or ethnic communities with an inalienable sense of identity and belonging that overrides the categories of class, education, or wealth. If a community is to develop an identity, it must possess the means with which to describe and discuss it; these are usually found in narratives of celebrated origins and a glorious, common destiny—in other words, stories that legitimize nationalism by rooting it in history and projecting greatness onto the nation's future. It is only when nationalism becomes militant, and justifies aggression toward other communities, that it is viewed negatively. However, this general and rather optimistic picture explains very little about why the latter scenario is so often the case and how particular stories achieve the status of national myths. Studies of nationalism throughout the twentieth century suggested a number of ways to analyze its development and role in the events that have been reshaping the world: wars and revolutions, the spread of fascism, anticolonial movements, and the formation of new states after the crumbling of old Empires.

While scholars of nationalism rely on various combinations of political, economic, ethnic, cultural, and religious approaches to their subject, all acknowledge the paramount role of culture in expressing and promoting the nationalist sentiment. Ernest Gellner points out the limitations of equating nation with state and nationalist sentiment with the political; he also discounts the view that nations are organically developing ethnic or linguistic communities that somehow achieve statehood. For Gellner, nations are the products of nationalists, and not the reverse; both are products of industrialist cultures. In his view, nationalism acquires political legitimacy "when general social conditions make for standardized, homogeneous, centrally sustained high cultures, pervading whole populations and not just elite minorities."[36] Gellner does not specify the means whereby high culture shapes national sentiment; however, other scholars have focused precisely on the particular role of cultural factors in the process of creating a nation. Benedict Anderson posits such cultural products as print-capitalism, in general, and educational institutions as factors instrumental in modifying people's perception of their place in society relative to others. These new ways of imagining communities have replaced the premodern conceptions linking "fraternity, power and time meaningfully together."[37] Similarly, Homi K. Bhabha treats the concept of nation "as a form of narrative-textual strategies, metaphoric displacements, subtexts and figurative stratagems." He focuses on the ambivalent cultural language of nationalism and catches cultural authority "in the act of 'composing' its powerful image."[38]

Bhabha states that nations "lose their origins in the myths of time,"[39] while Anthony D. Smith calls nationalism itself "one of the most popular and ubiquitous myths of the modern times."[40] National identity, he argues, is a "collective cultural phenomenon" that is broader than nationalism.[41] Smith posits that ethnic identity, as a constituent element of national identity, gives cohesion to the myths, memories, and symbols of the nation. Ethnic groups and nations, both, must have a name, a common myth of descent, a shared history and culture, a territory and a sense of solidarity. Nations, however, must also have a sense of political community.

Scholars of Russian nationalism have responded to the challenges of theorizing nationalism in general while also analyzing its development in a vast, multinational and multiethnic Empire whose territory straddles Europe and Asia and whose rulers, bureaucratic apparatus, intelligentsia, and peoples coexist less than peacefully in an increasingly complex network. Thus, neither the socioeconomic, the cultural, nor the ethnic approach alone can adequately serve an analysis of the development of the Russian national identity.[42] As argued by Geoffrey Hosking and Vera Tolz, among others, the main problem with Russian nationalism lies in the stymied formation of ethnic Russian identity that is subsumed within a larger imperial identity.[43] Similarly, as Terri Martin observes, the Soviet Union attempted to advance a single, overarching Soviet identity to transcend all others, although, somewhat paradoxically, this process involved implementing affirmative-action-like measures that successfully institutionalized ethnicity.[44]

These and other in-depth studies address the complex relationship between the imperial and national ideologies in the Russian Empire and the Soviet Union, emphasizing the relationship between the imperial center and its border peripheries—some of which have become independent states since the fall of the Soviet Union—and between the ethnic core and other ethnic groups and nationalities. By contrast, the provincial myth does not concern interethnic relationships, colonial peripheries, or exotic others. Rather, it concerns the relationship between two loosely defined groups of Russians: those of the capitals and of the provinces. The symbolic geography of the provincial myth is simple to the point of austerity: it comprises the capital and the rest of the country. The capital represents political, administrative, cultural, ideological, and symbolic aspects of center's superiority in relation to the provinces. Thus, despite having developed alongside Russia's other foundational narratives, the provincial myth is decidedly unique.

Russian national myths are stories of a glorious past and a unique destiny; they explain, justify, or distract from whatever comprises a popular understanding of Russianness and determines the Russian state's policies at home and abroad, in any given historical period. Orthodoxy has always been a crucial element of Russian nationalism, as have the ideas of Pan-Slavic Messianism.[45] Powerful secular myths feature great rulers and warriors, such as the Varangian princes;[46] Princes

Dmitry Donskoy, Alexander Nevsky, and Vladimir Monomach; Peter the Great;[47] and such intellectual figures as Mikhail Lomonosov,[48] who westernized Russia by shaping and directing its political, scientific, and cultural development along the recognizable lines of a European power. Stories of great military victories have proven instrumental to national self-definition to the extent of having underpinned Russian national mythology well into the twentieth century.[49] The myth of the Cossack provided an appealing image of a warrior hero who is quintessentially Russian but, at the same time, geographically removed from the center of culture. The Cossack emerged as an image of both the Other and the Self that, as Judith Kornblatt demonstrates, helped "Russians understand themselves in a native context, and not simply as slower stepbrothers of the West, enslaved by the European customs."[50] The twentieth century contributed the myths of Arctic exploration and the Soviet Space program.[51]

Unlike these great stories, the myth of the provinces has no heroes—neither princes, generals, warriors, scientists, nor explorers. However, like the Cossack myth, it assigns a certain vision of Russianness to a large group that, most importantly, it locates outside the cultural center. Because of their cultural and physical distance from the center, both the Cossacks and the provincials are regarded as custodians of the religious and cultural purity of ancient Rus' and the integrity of the mysterious "Russian soul." The provincials comprise a much larger and more amorphous group than the Cossacks of real life or myth. Like the Cossacks, however, they represent both Self and Other; hence, they simultaneously attract and repel.

Constructing an image of the Other is a crucial element of all identity formation; the majority of Russian cultural myths presume, at least implicitly, the image of a hostile, mysterious, or superior Other whom Russian national heroes either subdue, conquer, emulate, or eclipse. Foreigners, particularly stands-in for "the West," have always figured as Russia's most significant and troubling Other.[52] In this configuration, the West is a loosely defined, catch-all term for most of Europe and, increasingly, the United States. In other words, the West is everything that is not Russia (except the East), just as the provinces are everything that is not the capital (except the exotic). The only geography capable of accommodating these definitions is a symbolic one. In nationalist discourse, therefore, both the West and the provinces function as cultural myths that can easily and usefully be manipulated and filled with any content.

Introduction

The Ternary Model of "The Provinces–the Capital–the West"

The cultural representations of the provinces have ranged from negative to idealized over the past two centuries. These shifting meanings associated with the provinces in turn affect the perception of the other element in the capital versus the provinces binary. When the provinces are construed as a backward swamp, the capital is the locus of meaning and progress; when the provinces function as the abode of spirituality and moral wealth, the capital becomes a corrupt metropolis. The nightmarish, depressing small towns depicted by Gogol and Chekhov can only be construed as such in opposition to the capital, even if both entities are equally ideological constructs. Anne Lounsbery argues that this same interdependence also characterizes the way Russian thinkers have defined their country in comparison with the West, by either proclaiming or denying its superiority. These two relationships follow the same model.[53] Thus, the concept of provinciality, with the attending concepts of inauthenticity and backwardness, is central to Russia's self-identity as "a provincial" in Europe. This recurring perception of Russia's position as provincial, and therefore either inferior or superior in relation to the West, guarantees the problem of the provinces a central position in the ongoing discussion of Russian identity.

The provinces function as the symbolic locale where major Russian cultural myths are negotiated and, most importantly, a national idea is articulated. The post-Soviet focus on the provinces is similar to the passéism of the previous century; however, it possesses an added incentive: the acutely perceived need to redefine Russian culture as self-sufficient, with its own center–periphery dynamic beyond the Russia–West opposition, which disadvantaged Russia. Consequently, these two major binaries of Russian culture—the provinces versus the capital and Russia versus the West—amalgamate into a ternary structure, in which the Russian capital is situated *between* the West and the Russian provinces. If, in relation to Europe, Russia represents the backward provinces, then from the opposite perspective, Moscow is the center in relation to its own noncapital space, which is culturally and administratively subordinate. The division into capital and provincial space in Russian culture creates an *intranational* parallel to the *transnational* model of Russia versus the West. In both cases, cultural myths are at work; however, the relations that emerge permit the discourse of national identity to exceed the strict parameters of the Russia versus the West opposition and attempt to develop an alternative, and nonconflicting, conception of national identity. To this end, not the Russia-West binary but the ternary the provinces-the capital-the West, must serve as the reference model.

To varying degrees, the ternary model can be traced to numerous literary texts of the nineteenth century, including those traditionally examined as developing the binary model of the capital versus the provinces. In Gogol, the provinces endeavor to imitate the capital, which, in turn, imitates Europe, thereby generating a sequence of poor copies. In Tolstoy's *Anna Karenina*, the symbolic sequence of Levin's estate-Moscow-Petersburg-Vronsky's "English estate" constitutes a coherent transition from positive to negative. In *Demons*, as Lounsbery demonstrates, Dostoevsky situates Russia "in a provincial relationship to European culture, as is illustrated by the radicals' wholesale acceptance of imported ideas."[54] That the action in the novel takes place in a provincial city emphasizes the remoteness from "the source" and, hence, the unoriginality of Russian revolutionaries' radical ideas. That the inhabitants of the provincial town are more susceptible to the influence of ideas from the center, both Russian and foreign, reveals the nature of this dependency—that is, the perception of the provinces as a place where the purpose, meaning, and relevance of life can only derive from without. This underscores the dangers of Russian provincial thinking, of the inferiority complex, which is a mere step away from dogmatic adherence to "demonic" Western ideas.

In the mid- to late-nineteenth-century provincial tale, where provincialism forms the very basis of the plot—however limited by generic conventions and the already established literary image of the provinces—the protagonist from the center is often distinguished not only by the sheen of the capital, but also by his European mannerisms and tastes. Thus, in Maria Zhukova's "Nadenka" (1853), Lemetyev returns to his native town from the capital as a "guest" from Petersburg. He is estranged from the provincial city by his "capitalness" alone; however, his Anglophile tendencies give Lemetyev a "double-," or "*super*-capitalness" (*superstolichnost'*), as articulated by Irina Savkina,[55] achieved by the added European element. This "super-capitalness" would indeed be superfluous if it did not correspond to the logic of the ternary model of the provinces-the capital-Europe, in which the capital, per se, is incapable of securing the significance and centrality of the protagonist.

Like that of village to center, the relationship of provinces to center is determined by cultural rather than physical distance. Its construction, labeling, and ongoing manipulation, constitute one of the most productive themes of Russian classical literature. Etkind defined the relationship between the Man of the Common People and the Man of Authority and Culture as constituting the "metanarrative of numerous classical texts."[56] The Russian Man of Culture has defined his national essence within the bounds of these two hierarchical systems, comprising his own people and other national cultures. Within the parameters of the discourse of national identity, he is both subordinate and subordinator, looking condescendingly at the provinces from the capital but looking up to Europe.

In examining the provinces as "one of Russian literature's governing tropes,"[57] Lounsbery demonstrates how both the backward provinces and the capital fall short of meeting the high standards imposed by the West: "The Russian capital, always trying to catch up to and imitate Europe, might be seen as no less provincial than the provinces in relationship to the real center, which was Europe."[58] Gogol undermines the provinces-capital distinction by repeatedly demonstrating the fundamental "alikeness" of the provincial town N. and the capital, St. Petersburg: both lack authenticity and a positive identity; both can be defined only in terms of the extent to which they differ from their professed model, Europe. The discomforting realization of Russia's provinciality ensures that "the provinces continue to be figured as an unanswered question" of Russian identity.[59]

The Russian provinciality that was a worrisome, even terrifying, possibility for nineteenth-century thinkers is interpreted by contemporary nationalists as a source of hope. Herein lies the primary difference between the traditional hierarchies of the provinces-the capital and Russia-the West, and the ternary structure generated by the provincial discourse in post-Soviet Russia: while the elements are unchanged, the hierarchy has been reversed, whereby the provinces are often posed as superior to the capital and, perhaps, even to the West. This claim to superiority is based on the notion of *authenticity*, which has been reconceptualized in ideological rather than aesthetic or ontological terms. Regarded as a repository of the Russian national essence, the provinces surpass the capital in being true to the national character, which in turn is theorized as morally superior to the character of Westerners. This trend is especially apparent in the anti-Western sentiment cultivated by the official propaganda of Putin's Russia. The heightened interest in all things provincial reflects the Russians' need to reorganize the country's symbolic geography as one that allows them to perceive of the West as tainted and unappealing (or at least irrelevant) while the provinces represent everything that assures Russian superiority.

Nationalism and *Ressentiment*

That Russia's national self-definition has often been expressed within the framework of the Russia versus the West opposition is a truism. Liah Greenfeld investigates the development of the concepts of nation and national character in Russia as a process of assimilating the Western idea of nationality, which trumps the categories of class and rank. Toward the beginning of the nineteenth century, as part of this process, the image of the West was formulated in Russia as both model and rival: "The moment the West was acknowledged as the model—and this happened simultaneously with the first, tentative flirtation with national identity—the degree to which this identity was psychologically gratifying hinged on the outcome of the competition with the West."[60] As Greenfeld demonstrates, the realization that equality with the West proved impossible, and that "having the West as a model must inevitably result in self-contempt,"[61] brought about the rejection of the very idea of the West as a model for Russia. The paradox (and persistent problem) of Russian national self-definition is that the West, reviled or revered, remains a model. Moreover, since Russian intellectuals borrowed the Western concept of national character along with the Romantic idea of the folk as its bearer, the West remains the source for the very terms and categories of the discourse of nationalism.

The outcome of Russia's competition with the West was the realization, given the terms and conditions determined by the West, that Russia was unequipped to compete. This realization in turn engendered a grievous sense of inferiority and a more or less conscious revolt. Greenfeld examines this revolt in the terminology of the Nietzschean concept of *ressentiment* while Boris Groys applies to it the terms of psychoanalysis, referring to the conflict between the unconscious (Russia) and the conscious (the West).[62] *Ressentiment* and existential envy are not limited to an expressed antipathy toward an offending object; these feelings can also bring about a system of values that can relieve the sense of cultural inferiority. In the case of Russia, such feelings have given rise to a national model based upon the self-perception of Russia as standing apart from the West, occupying a superior position. Groys describes virtually the same process, examining the history of Russian national

Introduction

philosophy from Chaadaev to Bakhtin as the appropriation of the Western concepts of otherness and the creation of a model of Russian national character as the Other to the West. Its primary elements are those that stand in contrast to the fundamental constituent element of the image of the West: rationalism. Thus, rationalism is opposed by the mystical soul, individualism by communalism, spiritual impoverishment by spirituality, mercantilism by honorable impracticality, and so on.

Gogol may have been ambiguous about Russia's position in the world, but the famous Chichikovian troika, whose wheels may not make it to Moscow, proceeds onto a symbolic and mythopoeic path, whereby it flies beyond the borders of Russia as the other nations part before it, "with a sidelong glance." Gogol's troika intimidates Europe.[63] In contrast, Dostoevsky declares in his Pushkin Speech that Russia's historical mission consists in Europe's salvation. Despite their differences, both writers' visions are based upon a fundamental opposition between Russia and Europe, the idea that in terms of the only truly meaningful criteria Russia surpasses Europe, and the view that Russia should abandon its blind compliance with Europe's objectionable path. Both Gogol and Dostoevsky voice patriotic sentiment through expressions of disaffection with the familiar hierarchy of nations that clearly favor the West over Russia. This is exactly the kind of sentiment that leads to *ressentiment* and to attempts to reconsider the hierarchies: since Russia cannot compete with Europe in the European categories of advancement, modernization, or social and cultural development, the qualities of religiosity, spirituality, and the sense of a historical mission (which they attribute in their historiosophical conceptions to the Russian people) move to the forefront, presenting themselves as unconditionally more important.

Ressentiment is a feeling of being wronged that cannot be remedied by action. As Nietzsche explains, "when the *ressentiment* itself becomes creative and gives birth to values," it is the sentiment of "natures that are denied the true reaction, that of deeds, and compensate themselves with imaginary revenge."[64] Sociologists and psychologists understand it as characteristic of low-status individuals or social groups who experience anger and hurt but are unable to either assuage those feelings or exact revenge. It could act as a self-destructive force or an impetus for action and change, from civil action to revolutions.[65] Some scholars describe these processes in terms of Social Identity Theory (SIT) as outlined by Tajfel and Turner in the 1970s, according to which members of low-status groups have three potential ways of coping with their group's negative self-perception: by becoming members of a higher status group (social mobility); by enacting real change in the group's relative status (social competition); or by changing the evaluative criteria, thereby allowing their group to claim superiority (social creativity).[66] Olga Malinova discusses the development of Russian nationalism as the progression through stages during which different strategies of *ressentiment* prevailed. Thus, the nineteenth-century Westernizers championed the adoption of Western values and practices, thereby envisioning the path of social mobility for Russia; the Slavophiles preferred to reinterpret "the differences for the benefit of Russia in the logic of the social creativity strategy." In the early twentieth century, there was a period during which social competition (that is, the "pursuit for advantage where possible, without striving for convergence") seemed attainable, but the Iron Curtain ensured that nationalist rhetoric became firmly attached to the language of absolute differences.[67] When it became clear, post-perestroika, that parity with the more advanced, Western societies remained out of reach, "social creativity," that is, reformulating the criteria whereby advancement is evaluated, remained the only alternative. While this account simplifies the views of large groups of thinkers who emerged from different periods and schools of thought, it reveals an important trend uniting them. To the extent that the coping strategies of Social Identity Theory can be applied to such vast groups of individuals as nations, the "social creativity" strategy of *ressentiment* is the nationalist's refuge in that it allows for disengagement from verifiable reality and calls instead for an act of creating or imagining a world organized according to criteria and values that suit the creator.

Since the emergence in the public sphere of the concept of national identity, the creative reevaluation of what constitutes advancement and accounts for a nation's relative standing in the world has been the preferred strategy of Russian nationalist discourse. Today as always, it works to define the Russian national character by means of negative comparison with its Others, most often the West. State propaganda has been explicitly engaged in the project. A prominent political scientist and head of the Council on Foreign Defense Policy, Sergei Karaganov, observes in the official newspaper *Izvestiia*: "Russia, in the process of searching for and regenerating herself, began to propose a viable and appealing model of behavior and set of values to the majority of the world."[68] Karaganov explicitly defines the values of national sovereignty, and the willingness to defend it by force, as proper, "old-fashioned" morality. He calls the rejection of consumerism a "non-Western" position and sees the whole of Russia's political and ideological platform as

"Russia's challenge to the West." He summarizes and reiterates the prevailing mode of contemporary nationalist discourse thus: to ensure that Russians perceive of their country as a leading power, they must evaluate its standing based on values that differ from the Western ideals of economic prosperity, democracy, tolerance, and pluralism. The alternative value system emphasizes moral aspects, such as "traditional Christian ethics," "honor, national dignity, and valor," which have been rejected and betrayed by Europe.[69]

In other words, Russia's challenge to the West lies not in the arena of verifiable achievements but in the realm of such abstractions as behavioral norms and moral values. This perspective is highly typical of contemporary nationalism and enjoys considerable resonance in the population. Summarizing the 2003 public opinion polls by the "Levada-Center"—a major independent sociological research organization—Lev Gudkov records a persistent view of the West, especially the United States, as standing in opposition to the Russian moral core: "If the USA is a rich society, then we're poor; if Americans are primitive, vulgar, devoid of genuine high culture, [and] material-minded, in a nutshell, a culturally undeveloped country, then we, by contrast, are vital, 'spiritual.' Russians have behind them 'supreme culture,' literature, art, music, a 'millennial history,' and so on."[70]

Of course, all nationalisms are based on sentiments and make claims that cannot be scientifically verified. Gellner observes that "nationalist ideology suffers from pervasive false consciousness. Its myths invent reality."[71] Scholars trace the various ways in which Europe defined itself against its Eastern Others, including Russia.[72] Thus, the Russian nationalists' dependence on the Other as a point of contrast is a universally common technique: "othering" is essential to all social, political, and national identity formation. The process of defining and nominating Others always involves a discussion of values. In addressing French nationalism, Tsvetan Todorov centers his discussion of human attitudes toward differences on the question of values. "If I am a nationalist," he points out, "I proclaim that the values of my own country, whatever they may be, are superior to all others." The "other" countries and cultures can be defined only in terms of how different, or similar, they are to one's own; in any case, "the entities compared, 'ourselves' and 'the others,' remain purely relative."[73] Thus, self-definition by way of what one is not belongs to what Todorov calls "the proper uses of Others." Russian nationalist discourse is therefore not particularly unique either in the nature of its elements or even in the intensity and aggressiveness of its proponents.

The Missing *People*

Contemporary nationalists know what constitutes the positive attributes of Russianness; but like their nineteenth-century predecessors, they need to designate a bearer of these characteristics. If the majority of Russian intellectuals are (and have always been) indebted to the West (the embodiment of everything alien to the Russian spirit) for their ideas, philosophies, and the very terms in which to discuss them, they cannot possess true Russian characteristics. In the mid-nineteenth century, the Slavophiles found in "the people" the ideal entity that could embody these values, and so they nominated "the Russian peasantry" as "the standard bearer of nationality."[74] Today, the provinces are cast in the same role.

"The people" comprised "the essential element of the Slavophile's utopia"[75] and were discussed in the elevated, albeit abstract, terms of preserving traditions and withstanding external influences. This utopia was situated in the past of pre-Petrine Rus', conceived of as an idealized society—centered on the peasant commune—which lived according to traditions and principles of collectivity. The writer Konstantin Aksakov, a particularly ardent representative of the Slavophile "folk-mania,"[76] repeatedly set up an opposition between (on the one hand) an educated public whose entire existence was based on borrowed ideas and values and (on the other hand) "the people," who preserved authentic Russianness. "The common people are the bedrock of the country's entire social structure. And the source of its material wealth, and the source of its external power, the source of its inner strength and vitality, and ultimately, the whole country's idea, abide in the common people."[77] The peasant commune was particularly appealing to Slavophiles, who conceived of it as an embodiment of principles of common ownership and a way of life that stood in direct opposition to Western individualism.[78] Russia's educated and westernized circles could not compare with this standard; thus, their alienation from the people became a pressing problem in Russian thought. Clearly, the Slavophiles envisioned "the people" as a cultural myth, imagined and defined in contrast to the educated classes and, by extension, the West.[79] Russian literature is rife with portrayals, albeit not uniformly positive, of memorable representatives of the people—from Karamzin's "poor Liza" to Tolstoy's, Turgenev's, and Chekhov's peasants. Yet with all their appeal and credibility, these characters merely represent the authors' interpretations of the cultural myth of the peasantry. The peasants, like all subaltern groups, remain silent, no matter how many highly eloquent and well-meaning people speak for them.

Like the Slavophiles, Fyodor Dostoevsky was deeply disturbed by Russia's infatuation with Europe. In his travelogue *Winter Notes on Summer Impressions* (1863), he bemoans the fact that the educated elite became foreigners in their own land, and he directs his ire at Russians' "slavish kowtowing to European forms of civilization." However, when Dostoevsky calls for "faith in one's own national strength," or expresses belief in "a kind of chemical combination between the human spirit and its native land," he offers no clarification of what constitutes this strength and bond.[80] The people remain undefined bearers of the equally undefined national idea. Dostoevsky's *Notes* constitute an exercise in replacement: what should be his impressions of foreign places are in fact discussions of the Russian national idea, by comparison and contrast with what he describes as the West. They are also an exercise in *ressentiment*: he berates the educated elite for imposing European ideas and standards on Russia, thereby asserting Russia's inability to stand up to comparison. Dostoevsky refuses to hold up the West as a model and proceeds to denigrate it; only half in jest, he suggests that condemnation of the West is the Russian patriot's duty: "to love one's country means to vilify foreigners."[81]

The peasant commune and the people in general consistently serve as an argument against Western influences in the considerations of Russia's unique path. The remarkable thing is the extent to which these words, uttered over a century-and-a-half ago, resonate with present-day pronouncements on the provinces as the place where "the national-historic memory has not yet been lost" and "the most important qualities and characteristics of the whole of Russia's culture still remain deeply rooted," guaranteeing their potential for "the rebirth of all of Russia." The contemporary provincial myth presents the provinces as a sacral place, "the territory of truth and mystery . . . where eternal values and absolute meanings are stored."[82] Like the peasant commune of old, the provinces are construed as authentically Russian and therefore superior, both to the capital and the West. Although nationalists today are fond of quoting the Slavophiles, the point here is not that contemporary considerations of the provinces explicitly emulate Slavophile ideas. The point is rather that both ways of thinking respond to the need to imagine a designated bearer of the national idea that exists apart from the "rotten," westernized center. Both formulate Russian identity within a symbolic geography, in which the West and the Russian people (the imagined national core) stand mutually opposed. The *people*—precisely because, as an abstraction and a cultural myth, the concept is immune to historical realia—remain the custodians of the Russian spirit, in opposition to Western aberrations. However, their habitat is no longer necessarily the peasant hut or the village.

Ivan Aksakov offered an interesting view of the provinces as the middle ground between the people—conceived of as true Russians—and members of educated society, who amount to foreigners in their own land: "If the provinces, instead of being a servile copy and mimicking those who, in their turn, mimic an alien model, tried harder to strengthen their ties to the traditional way of life, to which, naturally, they are closer than [they are] to that of the capital, they could take on fundamental importance in the matter of true Russian education. . . . Provincialism could occupy its rightful place in developing all of the individual facets of the many-faceted Russian spirit!"[83] Aksakov envisions the provinces as capable, if only potentially, of being delivered from their own provinciality—of switching paradigms, so to speak—and aligning themselves with an unequivocally positive entity, the people. Clearly, for nineteenth-century Russian nationalists, the village-provinces distinction was important; but it ceased to be functional in the twentieth century. In the Russian classics, the village is the abode of the peasant, whose role as the bearer of the Russian national spirit offsets, at least to some extent, his impoverished material surroundings. By contrast, twentieth-century village life assumed the decidedly negative connotations of conflict, tragedy, and decay. Collectivization—the forced organization of peasant households into collective farms—put an end to the peasant commune. The presumed beneficiaries of the Bolshevik revolution were not peasants, but workers. The official language of Soviet industrialization and urbanization reconceptualized peasants into a labor force and renamed them *kolkhozniki*.[84]

The positive hero of early Soviet literature, as Katerina Clark demonstrates, is not a "spontaneous" peasant but a revolutionary worker, often charged with the task of bringing the peasant from elemental spontaneity to revolutionary consciousness.[85] The Socialist Realist Kolkhoz Novel "fabricated" a new village that lived by, and strived for, the ideal of the future. Meanwhile, the Village Prose of the 1980s, characterized primarily by nostalgia for the loss of traditional village communes, looked to "the radiant past."[86] In developing the themes of home, tradition, nature, and memory, the Village Prose writers turned to rural Russia in search of a better past, an idealized vision born of nostalgia rather than real experiences.[87] The fundamental theme informing Village Prose was the Russian countryside in crisis as the abode of tradition, and its main protagonists were the elderly. Today, the notion of *narod* as "the folk" is no longer associated with the countryside, and in the urban space of contemporary culture, what represents the opposition to the authoritative center is the provincial town, or more accurately, the provinces as myth. As cultural constructs, both "the village" and "the provinces" collapsed in the twentieth century into one noncapital space. The provinces have absorbed the positive connotations of the village, as developed in Russian classical literature, but not the negative meanings prevalent in twentieth-century culture, as a place of conflict and decay.[88]

The two terms often function as synonyms. In fact, in a recent (and very typical) internet publication on the subject of the provinces as the savior of Russia, three terms—"the people," "the provinces," and "the village"—are used interchangeably: "Today it is impossible not to feel how 'mysteriously and invisibly' 'a redeeming upheaval' is brewing in the nation's depths [*v narodnoj glubine*] and paving the way for the people's voluntary return to the provinces [*v provintsiiu*]. It is important that this long-awaited return of the people to their little motherland [*v maluiu rodinu*] be supported in every way—both materially and ideologically—by the state since, clearly, a city dweller will not be able to cope with the problems of the village [*s derevenskimi problemami*]."[89]

The statement is part of the author's ruminations on the dangers of the westernized consumerist society of the urban centers, especially Moscow, where "the enormous mass of people, predominantly cosmopolitan and easily seduced by popular promises of the good life, 'as in the West' [*kak za granitsei*], is becoming easy prey for external manipulation." The Russian provinces, or the village, which "is emerging as a huge asset for the whole world" and "holds the sacred power to self-generate human life," is the only place where the human soul can today find "refuge and salvation"; it constitutes "the only renewable source of healthy, national strengths." This combining of two different paradigms is symptomatic of the highly abstract nature of both concepts: devoid of any specificity, they are interchangeable as long as they function in the discourse of nationalism as the counterpoint to Western corruption.

This is the nature of nationalist discourse in general: it is not bound by social and historical reality; in fact, as Nancy Condee points out, it strains "to the breaking point evidentiary information and usher[s] us instead into the realm of conjecture, where data and imagination utterly fail to account for each other."[90] One of its tasks is to preserve and, if necessary, to construct a nation's origins and traditions. These traditions "are always already there: eternal, essential, transparent, organic and (most importantly) immune to further analysis."[91] Since myth is instrumental in legitimizing social structures and in maintaining social identities, it plays a central role in discourses of nationhood.[92] All national stories rely on visions of the past and their legitimizing power. The "Golden Age" myth, as Anthony Smith demonstrates, is necessary "to create a convincing representation of the 'nation,' a worthy and distinctive path must be rediscovered and appropriated. Only then can the nation aspire to glorious destiny for which its citizens may be expected to make some sacrifices."[93] This focus on the origins and therefore on the temporal aspect of the national idea is common to all nationalisms. The Russian tradition, too, firmly ties together temporal and spatial perspectives with notions of a utopian golden age of the national spirit and the cultural myth of its bearers. When the village and the provinces are posed as imagined locales, remote in both time and space, they invite not analysis, but myth construction.

Post-Soviet Nationalism and the Provinces

The collapse of the Soviet Union, together with the subsequent disintegration of the economy and the loss of Soviet-imperial international prestige necessitated, above all, the creation of a new *post*-imperial collective identity. Russian culture of this period becomes the domain for the elaboration of a concept of national identity in a country that had been an empire throughout the course of its entire history. It is now a federated state, in need of a national conception, capable not only of consolidating the numerous ethnicities inhabiting its territory into a "people of Russia" (*rossiiskii narod*) but also of situating in this as yet nonexistent community the Russian ethnic majority. Emil' Pain attributes the rise of xenophobia and ethnonationalism in the past two decades to the "typical psychological complexes of post-imperial conditions, associated with the distress of the ethnic majority's adaptation to its new spatial body, as though it had shrunk, following the collapse of the Union."[94] Thus, the process of forming the ethnic and civic conceptions of a "nation," and of forging a distinctly "Russian path," is consistent with a subsequent rise of xenophobia and anti-Americanism—that is, it

Introduction

occurs within the already familiar framework of opposition to Others, including the West.[95]

The nationalistic extremism of the 1990s, often regarded by commentators as a frightening parallel to prewar Nazi Germany,[96] remained a marginal phenomenon of the post-perestroika period. But in the 2000s, the pathos and terminology of extremism entered the discourse of official ideology, wherein the concepts of a national idea, and a national path to its development, became instruments of state nationalism, in an initiative to "consolidate Russian society around the federal establishment."[97] The primary components of this initiative are the creation of a positive collective identity and its attendant definition of the Other. The nationalist pathos and rhetoric of *ressentiment* penetrate all cultural and social discourses in today's Russia, from television serials to school textbooks. In the rhetoric of official documents, historical research, school textbooks, television programs, and other media, a positive identity is based on the greatness of Russian history, spirituality, the religiosity of the Russian people, and the distinctive character and uniqueness of the Russian path. Implicit in this composite of ideas, with its persistent emphasis on apartness and difference, is the tendency toward self-determination through opposition to external forces. The history of the Russian nation comes across as "the story of its greatness and humiliations, its heroism in the eternal battle against its enemies."[98] Its patriotism thus becomes a "concept [that] is dependent on revealing the capabilities for collective survival in an aggressive environment."[99]

Acknowledging the inability to "catch up" to the developed nations in the process of modernization summons up a morbid and unacceptable sense of inferiority, which must be justified and mitigated. Commenting on the effect of this rhetoric on the new generation, Lev Gudkov writes: "It is not surprising that by the end of the 2000s it is precisely the youth who take the strong antimodern position: anti-Western, nationalist and xenophobic attitudes, on the one hand, and a willingness to support a higher authority (the rejection of political alternatives and choices) on the other."[100] Russia's economic problems and the peculiar nature of its democracy are discussed as phenomena that are directly linked to the problems of national distinctiveness and the inappropriateness of Western models. The rational, individualistic, and depraved West cannot serve as a model for Russian society because the spiritual essence of the Russian people is irreconcilable with that soulless world. The breakdown of the economic reforms in the transitional period is considered by analysts as proof of the unsuitability for Russia of Western economic models; curtailing its democratic institutions as their own version of "democracy" is justified by the fact that "Russia has 'her own' path to democracy."[101] A growing number of Russian economists call for the rejection of Western models and for the cultivation, instead, of "a Russian economic model," which takes into account traditions, economic principles, and Russia's uniquely specific character.[102]

The anti-Western rhetoric of difference and antagonism intensified in the mid-2010s, beginning with Russia's annexation of the Crimea and its intervention in Ukraine, followed by the sanctions imposed by Western countries. In its essence, though, the rhetoric remains unchanged: since the collapse of the Soviet Union, Russia has attempted to define its relationship to the West on its own terms, to deflect the *ressentiment*, and to find a viable alternative model. The discussion, however, progressed from consideration of whether Russia should follow Western social and economic models to the rhetoric of war, couched in a tone of hostility that harks back to the language of the Cold War. The journalist and TV personality Maxim Shevchenko summarizes the official national platform thus: "We're not Europe? Well, thank God! Russia is one of last bastions of man and mankind." The article thus titled takes the age-old animosities to the extreme: while Russian nationalists have traditionally defined the West as alien to the Russian character, present-day extreme nationalists go so far as to deny the Westerner any shared human qualities: "In all likelihood, we and most Western people belong to differing humanoid species, outwardly similar, but fundamentally different on the inside." As Shevchenko sees it, the problem lies not merely in the nature of the West as rational, egotistical, and driven by material interest, but in its betrayal and perversion of the basic, universal human values (even though his only example is Western tolerance of homosexuality). "This is war," he says, and Russia is the world's last hope. It will save Europe from itself in that "the ideology of opposition toward this evil of the new liberal totalitarianism will develop and be formulated right here, in Russia."[103]

Pyotr Akopov, another prominent journalist and editor of the *Political Journal*, expresses typical concern over Western influences following the disintegration of the Soviet Union: "The genuine colonization of Russia by the West has begun. What's more, its main agents weren't even foreigners, but homegrown 'Europeans.' They've blindly implanted all the Western models, from the constitution to advertising, concerned not with whether they suit Russia, but with how well they assure domination by the newly established 'elites.'"[104]

Of particular interest in these statements is that they operate according to a ternary model: the West, intent on subjugating Russia; the Russian Europeans, who are its agents; and Russia proper, always on the defense, and defined only by what it is not and should not be. Within this model, any attempt at a positive definition of Russia is restricted by the built-in rationale of opposition and conflict. In this version of the ternary model comprising the West–the capital–the provinces, the capital is defined as home to the westernized, educated elite. The capital is thus positioned between two opposing entities: the West and the true Russia.

On the other side of the political spectrum, the "Russian Europeans," or the "global Russians," as the liberal media project *Snob* designates its target audience, comprise a disparate group, forced to defend themselves against accusations of a lack of patriotism and equally unable to formulate a viable alternative national idea. The prominent literary critic Natalia Ivanova argues that, for this reason, "the literary nationalist discourse, largely coinciding, today, with the new-imperial political discourse of the current Russian government, not only advances the patriotic rhetoric, but also attempts to expropriate culture itself." She sees the provinces as a particular object of the nationalists' attention as they "[scratch] away at the provinces' provincialism, reassuring [the provincials] that backwardness is in fact accomplishment."[105]

Thus appropriated by nationalist discourse, the provinces mark the rhetorical ambiguity therein: the nationalists' dual claim of victimhood on the global scene, and, within Russia, of the capital's hegemonic power over the provinces. Condee discusses this conceptual "slippage" as "two different rhetorical projects: on the one hand, emancipation from the hegemonic culture; on the other, exaltation at a hegemonic victory over the minority culture."[106] The minority culture here is that of a different ethnic group, but the same logic informs the relationship of the capital with the provinces. The gaze from the Russian center encapsulates both projects: directed outward, it sees Russia as an object of colonizing practices, interpreted as interference in political and cultural matters; directed inward, it posits the Russian provinces as objects of a sympathetic, but nevertheless objectifying, gaze. The provinces constitute ideal objects for the exercise of hegemonic power and, in fact, the only entity available for subjugation by Russian nationalists following the disintegration of the Empire. In other words, the Russian elite may feel wronged by the West; however, even after the Empire's demise, they are able to find an object for their hegemonic posture. This is precisely how the

Russian provinces become conceptualized as the Other, but unlike the hostile Other of the West, or the resisting Others of the former Soviet republics, the provinces are both different and essentially the same—safely removed in time and space but not so distant as to preclude reconciliation.

This oscillation between demeaning and idealizing the provinces could be described as a recurring shift between an Orientalist view of the provinces—reducing them to either an object of ridicule or an unspecified locale of pure national origins—and an Occidentalist view of the capital as a corrupt city of sin. The Orientalist view, the hegemonic gaze from the center that creates and objectifies the provinces, resembles the manner in which the Western gaze created and controlled the Orient in Edward Said's classical discussion of "Orientalism's insensitive schematization of the entire Orient."[107] This gaze imposes on its subject its very otherness, strangeness, and exotic nature, which it purports to analyze and explain. The provinces, as they have been imagined in Russian culture, have served as the Other to the center: they act either as the capital's outlandish imitation or as its wholesome, more authentic version. This is the Other that Bhabha describes as "at once an object of desire and derision, an articulation of difference contained within the fantasy of origin and identity."[108] Abashev emphasizes the same inherently hierarchic dynamic in suggesting the provinces exist merely as an element of a power structure: "The provinces—that's the capital's term for the marginal territories, [under] the gaze (and edictal gesture) from the center, and from the top down. The term can be scornful, condescending and even moving to tears, [but] it doesn't alter the disposition of the relations. . . . After all, the provinces are not an entity, but merely an attribute of the imperial spatial structure."[109]

Occidentalism, on the other hand, reverses the gaze, imposing objectification and reduction on the West and perceiving it as a "rootless, cosmopolitan, superficial, trivial, materialistic . . . civilization."[110] The Occidental perspective is not limited to marginalized groups in the Third World; it often characterizes urban intellectuals, who feel displaced in the world of rationality and mass commerce and turn to the idealized, if often imagined, spiritual past of their nation. This reliance on cultural constructs, on essentializing broad phenomena for the purposes of containment and control, allows Orientalism and Occidentalism to coexist in the discursive space of nationalism: both rely on images of the Other to support the construction of identities.

Introduction

The official legitimization of the provincial myth is supported by empirical data revealing that the majority of the government's support comes from small, impoverished towns that are dependent on government subsidies. Lev Gudkov interprets public opinion polls as suggesting that the focus on the regions signals the government's realization of its having lost the support of the relatively prosperous, educated population of large urban centers.[111] For many in the provinces and the capital alike, the devastating effects of the 1990s economic reforms appeared directly related to the application of Western economic and political models. Not surprisingly, public opinion polls reveal large-scale nationalistic and anti-Western attitudes: those by the All-Russian Public Opinion Research Center (VTsIOM) indicate that "non-Russian" is highest on a list of negative terms including "capitalism," "communism," and "the West."[112] Indeed, the surveys indicate that capitalism and even democracy are concepts with little appeal to Russians.[113] In summarizing his analysis of the surveys in 2009, N. P. Popov writes that "more and more people think the West is interfering in Russia's advancement to greatness." He further notes that "the accomplishments and advantages of the Russian national character, compared to the national traits of the West, continue to remain an important component of the Russian national idea.... The fundamental distinction between the Russian national character and the qualities of Westerners, according to popular opinion, is the magnanimity, goodness, warm-heartedness and generosity of Russians, as opposed to the greediness, egoism... cunning [and] callousness of Westerners."[114] Among the negative traits inherent in Westerners, "money-hunger, arrogance, egoism and heartlessness" are foremost, according to Russian evaluations. Upward of half of those surveyed see the fundamental qualities of the Russian people as "kindness, honesty, sincerity" (41 percent) and "soulfulness, generosity and decency" (26 percent).

However, the same surveys reveal that the Russians who so advantageously distinguish themselves from Westerners and possess "typically Russian" positive qualities live outside of the Russian center. And they do not like Muscovites: a 2012 survey shows that two thirds of Russians dislike residents of the capital, and almost half think that Moscow prospers at the expense of the regions.[115] The surveys by the All-Russian Public Opinion Research Center reveal high levels of hostility toward Muscovites (24 percent in 2004, 63 percent in 2006, and 59 percent in 2013).[116] Internet sites and blogs indicate that the residents of the Russian heartland think Moscow has amassed the country's assets, along with its economic and cultural resources, and lives at the expense of other regions. They consider Moscow a "non-Russian" city due to its growing number of migrant workers and describe Muscovites with the same negative epithets as they do Westerners: "narcissistic, arrogant, and greedy,"[117] "proud and arrogant," and "greedy, and avaricious."[118] Moscow residents respond in kind, relying, in their characterizations of the provincials, on the traditional notions of inadequacy in education, taste, and manners.[119]

Of course, these figures tell us very little about the real qualities of residents of Moscow or the provincial Saratov, Voronezh, or Tver. "Soulless" Moscow is as much of a cultural myth as the "soulful" Russian provinces.[120] The very intensity of this exchange of perspectives, however, affirms Moscow's change of status, from the symbolic and metonymic representative of Russia to becoming increasingly identified within the conceptual sphere of the Other. Moscow has become for the rest of the country what the West has always been—an object of envy, desire, or even resentment. By replacing the traditional hierarchies with those that allow them to reimagine the features of the provinces in positive terms that set them apart from the capital, the provincials view and express their relationship with the capital in terms of *ressentiment*.

Consequently, the relationship between the provinces and the capital duplicates that between Russia and the West, though with a crucial difference: unlike the Western Other, the provincial is familiar and controllable. Designated as the Other, the provincial can elicit both contempt and veneration; he can be discursively molded into the object of hegemonic control and Orientalist desire or embody the dream of the Golden Age and the guarantee of a radiant future. Both the pro-government intelligentsia and the political opposition turn to the idea of the provinces to comment on Russia's state of affairs. Yet, crucially, all conceive of the opposition to the center—the provinces as much less contentious than the opposition of Russia and the West. Representatives of opposite ideological camps seem to share an understanding that the antagonism implied by this binary is potentially easily dissipated, as in a family feud or a quarrel between friends. This relationship has at its disposal all the mechanisms of social identity—social mobility, competition, and creativity. Thus, a provincial can integrate into Moscow life in a way that Russia could never envision itself integrating into the "family" of Western nations. Provincials can lay verifiable claims to a superior "quality of life," and any number of debatable claims to "moral superiority."

Introduction

The three elements central to the Russian national idea—the provinces, the capital, and the West—remain locked in a symbolic configuration, in which they are ranked according to a value system born of *ressentiment* and the desire to reimagine a symbolic geography of the world that would accommodate a "psychologically satisfying" national identity.

This ternary structure dramatically reimagines the relationship of its component parts within the new symbolic geography by incorporating the strong anti-Western sentiment cultivated by Russian official propaganda and the view of the provinces as the repository of the Russian moral code. The West should be seen not as exemplary but as corrupt and either dangerous or irrelevant; the capital—as infested with Western agents; and the provinces—as embodying those features of Russianness that assure Russia's unique and foremost position in the world. By proposing a national identity derived not from "us versus them" but rather from "us versus us," the ternary structure promotes a dynamic of benevolent leadership within the new national borders.

The provincial myth is not the only myth informing the narrative of Russian identity, and focusing on the relationship with Others, both internal and external, is not the only viable approach to Russian nationalism. Nevertheless, these dichotomies have played an essential role in Russian national identity formation for more than two centuries. The symbolic status of the provinces has always been linked with that of Russia as a whole; thus, the changes in their status and function in the post-Soviet period provide important insights into what constitutes national identity today and how Russians envision the symbolic geography of their world. To discuss the Russian provinces today, as always, is to discuss Russia's national character, its pride and insecurities, and its visions of the past and future.

In outlining the development of the provincial myth and the shifts in meaning of the provinces in contemporary culture, I have relied thus far on philosophers, scholars, politicians, and even dictionaries, all of which establish a background for the analysis of the ways in which various cultural texts represent and advance this change. The subsequent chapters provide a detailed analysis of the provincial topos and myth in journalism, literature, and film, respectively. Across media and genres, similar patterns emerge: regardless of whether the authors earnestly elaborate the vision of the provinces as the abode of authentic Russianness or deconstruct the myth's clichés and ideologies, the provincial myth serves as a framework in which to discuss the "Russian national idea."

In choosing my texts, I faced a problem familiar to all scholars of cultural mythology: the question of whether any number of examples, however instructive, form a sufficient evidentiary basis for inferences on such a broad subject. In journalism, there are numerous examinations of the Moscow–provinces relationship, authored by provincial cultural and political figures. In literature, a wide array of characters explore the symbolic and physical configuration of Russian geography. In film and on TV, the provincial, particularly the provincial girl, has become a stock character. In all media, the recurrence of particular topics, character types, and plot elements generates reflections upon what it means to be a provincial, what qualities provincials bring to Moscow, what it takes to be successful in today's Russia, and, by extension, what it means to be Russian. I therefore selected what I considered the most illustrative examples from various media and genres, including scholarly treatises and newspaper editorials as well as literary and cinematic works of "high" and mass culture to cover a representative time span. My goal is to present texts that are both striking and typical and engage explicitly with the provincial myth and the discourse of nationalism.

The next chapter looks at the ways in which the cultural and political elite of the Russian provinces reconfigure the "center versus periphery" paradigm to their own ends. This chapter thus gives voice to locations that, as part of the noncapital space have always been the objects of imperial description and objectification. Although not silent per say, these locales must contend with a discourse that is construed for them by observers from the center. The texts examined are examples of journalism from outside Russia's capitals: several general interest newspapers and popular weekly magazines and three journals: *The Russian Provinces* (Tver), *Russia's Provinces* (Naberezhnye Chelny) and *Guberniia Style* (Voronezh). These publications' editorial policies, mission and philosophy statements, opinion articles, and interviews with important personae feature provincial cultural, political, and business leaders actively promoting the "provinces is our everything" attitude. Their statements demonstrate a growing resistance to the Orientalist position of the center, evident in these publications' frequent Occidentalist, anti-Moscow rhetoric. These sources also explicitly allude to Russia's provincial relationship vis-à-vis the West in the context of their reevaluation of provincial Russia's role in Russian state- and nation-building. This reconceptualization of the provinces unfolds through a shift in emphasis:

Introduction

from dependency on the center to self-efficiency, and from notions of backwardness to those of authenticity and tradition-based strength.

The city of Voronezh serves as my case-study for the following reasons: a large provincial city in the Russian heartland, it is in many ways a typical provincial locale but finds itself in the somewhat paradoxical position of being promoted by city officials as "the capital of the provinces." In attempting to develop the Voronezh image and brand, officials face the problems typical of all identity projects and branding enterprises in the Russian provinces: in order to develop a unique identity for the city they must counteract the long-standing perception of the provinces as a vast and homogeneous realm with places barely distinguishable from one another. Even when the provinces are endowed with positive associations and viewed as the repository of true Russianness, the problem remains: as a set of abstract categories the cultural myth of the provinces cannot accommodate the development of concrete regional identities and thus continues to deny specificity to provincial locales.

Chapter 2 deals with the literary works of the post-Soviet period that directly address the theme and myth of the provinces. The authors of these works represent diverse geographical, generational, and ideological positions, but all of them develop visions of the Russian provinces that are much less optimistic and unequivocal as those advanced by provincial journalists and scholars. Moreover, their focus is precisely on the clichés and limitations of the provincial myth as it evolved in post-Soviet times, such as its tendency toward binary constructions, simplifications, and sweeping generalizations.

Two novels of the 1990s, *Lines of Fate or Milashevich's Trunk* (1985-92), by Mark Kharitonov, and *Letter from Soligalich to Oxford* (1995), by Sergei Yakovlev, belong to the early stage of contemporary interest in the provinces. Kharitonov's *Lines of Fate*, awarded the first Russian Booker Prize in 1992, introduces, meticulously develops, and essentially deconstructs all the issues central to the privileging of the provinces in contemporary Russian cultural discourse, thus exposing them as at best ideologically charged and at worst tools of self-deception. Yakovlev's novel operates within the ternary structure of the provinces-the capital-the West: having spent some time in Oxford the protagonist sets out to rebuild a run-down house in Soligalich in the English fashion. This attempt, and failure, to transplant a little of the English tradition and solidity onto the Russian soil is both real and symbolic, allowing the protagonist to address questions of Russian national identity and Russia's position vis-à-vis the West. The small provincial Soligalich and Oxford enter into an opposition of their own, one that Yakovlev superimposes on the familiar dichotomies of the provinces versus the capital and Russia versus the West.

Alexei Ivanov's novels *The Center for Supplementary Fornication* (*Bluda i Mudo*, 2007), *The Dog-Headed* (*Psoglavtsy*, 2011), and *Community* (*Kom'iuniti*, 2012), along with Zakhar Prilepin's novel *Sankya* (2006), address the provinces versus Moscow dichotomy directly while also touching on the topic of patriotism. These works emphasize the notions of spirituality, tradition, and moral strength associated with the provincial myth as a component part in the "national idea" discourse. Dmitri Bykov's short story "Mozharovo" (2007) focuses on the otherness of the provinces, taking the theme to extremes by depicting provincials as monsters who can appear in human form, Bykov comments on the process of othering that helps deny Others their very humanity—something we have witnessed in the radical nationalists' writings on the West.

The last chapter presents the films of the first decades of the twenty-first century, both art-house and mainstream, that are either set in the provinces or depict provincials who set out to "conquer" Moscow (with an important subset, here, of films and TV serials about "provincial Cinderellas"). My analysis comprises the following diverse group of cinematic texts: the TV series *Lines of Fate* (Meskhiev, 2003) and *The Milkmaid from Khatsapetovka* (Gres, 2006), the TV "limited series" *Wide Is the River* (Poltoratskaya, Nazirov, 2008), and the films *Gloss* (Konchalovsky, 2007), *Yuryev Day* (Serebrennikov, 2008), *Once Upon a Time in the Provinces* (Shagalova, 2008), *About Love* (Subbotina, 2010), and *Kokoko* (Smirnova, 2012). I have not limited my choice to works of great stature or significance. Although some of these films have been noted by critics, others might be of limited interest to scholars of Russian cinema. Still, popular cinema and TV reflect with some accuracy the cultural discourses of their time in terms of plot development and character types. Most importantly, each of the selected films articulates explicit commentary on the provinces versus center opposition. The focus on the provinces may prove misrepresentative, as in the first episodes of Daria Poltoratskaya and Stanislav Nazirov's *Wide Is the River*; or the topic may be subsumed by a different theme, as in Avdotia Smirnova's *Kokoko*, but it is always present, motivating the characters and shaping the audiences' expectations.

In these films, both the provincials and the people of the center face the hierarchical shifts and changing perceptions of what constitutes superiority (moral and otherwise) as they negotiate contrasting views of their locales. The idea of the provinces as a microcosm of Russia has been firmly established, with variations depending on the underlying ideology. In contrast to the positive vision of the provinces prevalent in mainstream cinema, the art-house directors depict the moral, ideological, and political crises, thereby offering a depressing picture of the Russian condition. These authors go beyond actualizing the metaphor of the dark corners of life: they portray the provinces as reality proper, raising its horrors to the level of the grotesque and challenging the status quo favored by mass culture. In the topography of these films, the provinces, the capital, and the West are semiotic markers in a symbolic chain of mutual *ressentiment*, of apophatic definitions incapable of offering a stable positive representation of Russia.

The journalistic, literary, and cinematic treatments of the provincial myth develop and deconstruct the hermetic national model of "us versus us" in the imaginative space of the post-Soviet symbolic geography. In this search for Russia's identity, the role of the provinces is crucial: regardless of its disparate articulations, the provincial topos serves in every case to introduce the many unresolvable, yet recurring, issues of Russia's past and future, including what it means to be Russian and where "true" Russians can be found.

1

Journalism

"We Look for Wealth in the Provinces and Find It There!"

> Love Voronezh. Moscow can wait.
> Downtown.ru, 2011

In 1991, when the map of the Soviet Empire transformed almost overnight, as it seemed to many, into the map of an area with more than a dozen independent states, each of the newly independent peoples faced the task of firmly defining a national identity to go along with their new territorial status. For the people of Russia, whose national identity had been subsumed within an imperial whole, the task of developing an ethnic identity presented particular difficulties. While the people of Ukraine or Kazakhstan celebrated gaining a country, Russians felt the loss of an empire. Most studies of post-Soviet Russian nationalism focus on the relationships between numerous ethnic groups within Russian borders and consider the tensions between the Russian population and migrant workers from the newly formed states, as well as Russia's relationship with these states (namely, Central Asia, the Baltics, Georgia, and Ukraine).[1] Fewer studies have addressed the multiple localities within the Russian Federation that found themselves with a record level of autonomy after the fall of the Soviet Union. These are the predominantly Russian-populated regions, or provinces, that in the 1990s attempted to use their autonomy to assert control over their natural resources, industry, and governance. In subsequent decades, the central government reestablished its financial and administrative control over the regions. However, this first, post-Soviet decade witnessed a cultural development that has continued to date: the physical regions' status notwithstanding, within Russia's symbolic geography the provinces of cultural myth have consistently claimed their status as unique and powerful.

As multiple provincial localities reformed their economic and political organization, they also engaged in the process of conceptual and symbolic self-definition. This bi-directional process unfolded thus: the cultural elite of the center produced a nationalist discourse that imagined the provinces as the habitat of true Russianness. The cultural and political elite of the Russian provinces, meanwhile, responded with their own texts, celebrating their newly acquired independence from the center and their pride in being provincial. In most cases, these provincial figures exploited "the provinces are our everything" idea to further their political or business agendas. In this chapter, I examine the newspapers and popular weekly general-interest magazines of the Russian heartland along with three journals: *The Russian Provinces* (Novgorod), *Russia's Provinces* (Naberezhnye Chelny), and *Guberniia Style* (Voronezh).[2] I pay particular attention to each publication's first year in circulation, especially inaugural issues outlining editorial policies as well as mission and philosophy statements. The various editorials, essays, and interviews with important political and cultural personae reveal a unique blend of immediate responses to, and (nonacademic) analyses of, the cultural myth of the provinces and its role in the new Russia's discourse of national self-definition.

In the 1990s, the reconfiguration of Russian symbolic geography coincided with the rehabilitation of prerevolutionary concepts and values. This *passéist* impulse brought both the concept of the provinces and the word itself, *provintsiia*, to the forefront of sociocultural discourse. The word is now perceived as linked to the past and "to the memory of culture, [that] points to prerevolutionary history."[3] Among the indications of this reevaluation is the wave of renaming regional newspapers and magazines to include references to the provinces in their titles. Monica Spivak presents an overview of how the word functions in the mass media and the realms of marketing and advertising; she cites a long list of titles such as *The Provincial News* (*Novosti* or *Vedomosti*), *Provincial Chronicles, Provincial Stories,* or *The Golden Provinces* (Izhevsk), *The Business Provinces* (Kaluga), and *The New Provinces* (Murom), to name only a few. Most of these newspapers and weeklies are strictly local publications whose titles may or may not specify the town or city of publication itself; many of them remain under the control of regional political powers. Most significantly, these publications reflect little interest in either the cultural concept or the myth of the provinces; rather, their stated emphasis is on local news, politics, and business. Thus, the inclusion in their titles of *provintsiia* reflects little more than the word's heightened cultural and ideological appeal. Simply stated, for the media owners, "provincial" becomes a more prestigious synonym for "regional" and "local."

The term's positive connotations have also proven to be profitable; one sees the proliferation of business and show-business enterprises cashing in on its appeal, with bookstores, artists' exhibitions, volumes of poetry, food companies, and marriage agencies using "provincial" in their names.[4] Thus, politicians hailing from the provinces, including the late Boris Nemtsov, position themselves as uncorrupted provincial outsiders;[5] singers give their albums titles such as *A Provincial Girl*; advertisers promote the purity of provincial dairy products; and marriage agencies such as "The Provincial Lady" in Chuvash tout the quality of their brides. In everyday discourse, "provincial" may still be equated with "second-rate"; however, as a marketing and ideological tool, where it reflects the discourses of national and regional identity and is coupled with anti-Moscow rhetoric, its meaning is unequivocally "first-class."

Local periodicals renamed with reference to the provinces invariably carve out space in their inaugural issues to justify their new titles as reflecting both their sense of pride in being provincial (and thus truly Russian) and their focus on all things local. The issues often begin with a mission statement directly addressing the role of the provinces in Russian culture and economy. Within months, however, the ambition wanes and/or disappears altogether. Ultimately, few publications remain devoted to the subject of the provinces, and those that do engage explicitly with the discourse of nationalism. Thus, local periodicals fall consistently into two categories: the truly local news publications, with little interest in such abstract categories as nationalism, and those nationally oriented periodicals devoted to the provinces that explicitly engage in the discussion of the provincial myth within the discourse of nationalism.

Two important journals, *The Russian Provinces* (*Russkaia provintsiia* [Novgorod, 1991]) and *Russia's Provinces* (*Rossiiskaia provintsiia* [Naberezhnye Chelny, 1993-96]) are faithful to their titles in subject. They comprise reportage, commentary, criticism, essays, and fiction (along the lines of *The New Yorker*) and provide real-time reactions, along with nonscientific (yet intelligent) analysis; thus, both journals serve as indicators of discursive practices in the public sphere.

Though situated and printed in Moscow, *Russia's* (*Rossiiskaia*) *Provinces* was a nationwide bimonthly, published by the Multi-Purpose Cooperative Prikamye in Naberezhnye Chelny—a major city in Tatarstan on the river Kama, the largest tributary of the Volga. Its September 1993 inaugural issue opens with a short editorial by Vadim Churbanov—editor-in-chief, Professor of Philosophy, and then-vice-president of Moscow's Russian State Library. Remarkably dense, this short piece begins with a comment on the 1990s status quo as "the days of woes and troubles" and designates the provinces as the source of national salvation, now as ever, throughout Russian history. Churbanov maintains that Russia survives not "according to precepts [determined by] the philosophy kings of the capital [*umstvuiushchikh stolichnykh pravitelei*], but [thanks to] the wisdom and deeds of the people who populate [the] vast lands called the provinces." In this juxtaposition of the provinces with the capital, the latter, as an adjective, acquires negative connotations: most nationwide publications are truly "of the capital" in spirit and their professed values, whereas *Russia's Provinces* would give voice to the true Russia. He also emphasizes the fact that the journal is published and funded by provincial organizations alone.

Churbanov draws on the authority of Russian writer and historian Nikolai Karamzin in affirming that "Russia's strength is in its provinces" and identifying their "natural wealth, traditions, talent, endurance, industriousness, and conscience" as the sources of this strength.[6] He also equates the journal's addressees, the provincial intelligentsia, with the true Russian people and promises that the journal will not promote any political party or tendency. The editorial contains the key elements comprising the provincial myth—namely, the idea of the provinces as the repository of cultural riches and national character; the emphasis on Russian's ability to endure hardship, coupled with the reference to Russia's uniquely troubled history; and finally, the argument that the capital is part of the problem rather than the solution. The entire first issue of the journal adheres to the editorial's agenda by means of well-written materials, such as rational reflections, free of emotional outbursts and overtly nationalist sentiment, and measured responses to detractors of the provinces in the spirit of calm retrospection, as in Yuri Milovanov's "Level with the Capital: Notes on the Worries of the Provincial Intelligentsia,"[7] which traces the Rostov-on-Don intelligentsia's shift in attitude toward the capital.

Milovanov discusses a provincial *intelligent*'s disenchantment with the center and his subsequent quest for an identity free of its influences. He addresses Moscow's loss of political and cultural authority and the provincial intelligentsia's efforts to find new bases for identity and markers of prestige. The article comprises six subsections, each with its own particular focus, as articulated in the respective headings: "Authority: Moscow-Capital"; "Crisis: 'They Don't Even Know What They Want'"; "Disintegration: Moscow Only Cares About Itself"; "'We Are Different': The Provinces' Wealth Is in Their Own Values"; "'Enough of Feeding Them': Will the Provinces Survive Without Moscow"; "'And Other Personae': Moscow Can Reinstate Its Authority Only through Cultural, not Political, Dialogue with the Provinces." Having discarded the labels of "marginal" and "inferior," and in the absence of a familiar "unified system of values,"[8] the provincial intelligentsia are thus portrayed as uneasy but optimistic about situating themselves on the same symbolic level as their Moscow counterparts, if not higher.

There is a distinct compensatory logic in this and similar ruminations. The provincial intelligentsia feel they have been marginalized, turned into objects of disrespect and ridicule; now, when "the time of Moscow's cultural paternalism has come to an end,"[9] they are ready to fight back. The process involves working out a "new provincial physiognomy," one free of the provincials' complexes, capable of offering Russia new "interest and hope."[10] Significantly, the binary nature of this identity formation remains in place, albeit in reversed hierarchy: the old value dynamic has changed, but the relationship between the provinces and the center is still best described in terms of mutual *ressentiment*. Milovanov's proud affirmation "We are different [*drugie*]" evokes both meanings of the word *drugie*, asserting that the provinces are unlike Moscow and also that they constitute its Other.

In an interview appearing in the same issue, the academician Nikita Moiseev contemplates the subject in like terms, stating that "Russia's fate is being decided in the provinces," and "[The provinces] should not put the fate of Russia in the unreliable hands of Moscow."[11] Similarly, Moscow University philosophy professor Aleksandr Panarin speaks of "'the retaliation of the provinces' and the growing prestige of the provincial way of life." "The provinces," he asserts, "possess the resources most difficult to obtain [*defitsitnye*], which include, above all, their unspoiled nature and unspoiled morality."[12]

The enthusiasm with which the central and provincial elite perform the transvaluation that always accompanies the discourse of *ressentiment* emphasizes both the persistence of the logic of *ressentiment* and the need for an Other as conditions of self-representation. The discourse of otherness remains a constant throughout the journal's duration. Also unchanging is the persistent conceptualizing of the provinces as the repository of moral and cultural wealth, the place where the best features of Russianness have been preserved. The first issue of 1996 published an interview with Valentin Rasputin entitled "Tell Everyone That Russia Is Alive," in which the famous writer is presented with the following statement: "They say [*govoriat*] the Russian provinces, our countryside, have lost that which made it different from, and better than, the center. There is no more of the former purity of morals, the former way of life.... It is as if [*kak budto*] Russia had no place from which to resurrect itself."[13] The very form of the question—an indeterminate subject (*govoriat*), coupled with "as if"—implies and invites disagreement with the statement itself, and the subject, which Rasputin readily provides.

Two pages further on in the same issue, the popular theater and film actor Yuri Solomin is presented with the same statement, albeit more ambivalently phrased: "In recent years a fashionable opinion has been that [*budto*] only the provinces can revive Russia; as if [*budto*] only they have preserved the business acumen, integrity, national traditions, and a treasure trove [*kladez'*] of talent."[14] This version of the statement betrays an underlying cynicism, absent from the first; the "as if" (*budto*) seems to imply a certain skepticism toward the exaltation of the provinces, particularly by suggesting it is a matter of "a fashionable opinion." But Solomin is not distracted by the implication; rather, he pays tribute to the people of the provinces as "unselfish workers in the arts and education—artists, musicians, local historians, collectors, unselfish oddballs [*chudaki-besserebreniki*]."[15] Ultimately, both the opinion voiced by the journalists and the retorts by these prominent cultural personae are fashionable and widely accepted—to the extent that their turns of phrase come across as trite, even to those who contemplate them. The uniform choice of themes and images in addressing the subject is remarkable and suggests they all rely on the cultural myth of the provinces as a stable construct, with a fixed set of images and vocabulary. As individuals, they may be sincere in their responses; however, they draw less on personal experience and observations than on cultural mythology.

Naturally, *Russia's Provinces* devoted space to other written matter, such as book reviews, segments on local history (*kraevedcheskie*) as well as art, a regular section entitled "Pushkin Is Our Everything," and interviews with prominent figures. The latter include such highly ranked officials as the head of the Department of Culture and a governor, both of whom, likely constrained by the journal's nonpolitical stance, sound somewhat unfocused but nevertheless enthusiastic about the provinces' cultural and economic potential. The Head of Samara's Regional Department of Culture muses, "You know, this is an amazing thing in Russia: it often happens that somewhere in Orenburg, Omsk, or Samara one finds creative people of a magnitude that Moscow or St. Petersburg could only dream about."[16] Again, one is struck by the uniform rhetoric of these essays and interviews: a writer, an actor, a philosophy professor, an editor, an administrator, and a rank-and-file *intelligent* seem to draw from the same pool of value-charged adjectives. As if reading from the same script, they distinguish the provinces from the center (in other words, they define them as Other); they refute Moscow's authority and ability to lead Russia out of its crisis; they insist that only the provinces can bring about Russia's revival; and they support the argument by associating the provinces with "truly Russian national characteristics" embodied in the notions of preservation, purity, and traditionalism.

It is also noteworthy that this bland and uniform image, phrased in the familiar vocabulary of the cultural myth of the provinces, has almost no local markers. The provinces exist as a vast homogeneous space; the mention of three separate geographical locations in the last quote— "somewhere in Orenburg, Omsk, or Samara"—only emphasizes their interchangeability. Even when the subject is a particular and unique landmark, the author, having described the efforts put into renovating a monastery or a nature reserve, slips into the same generalizing rhetoric. In a 1995 issue, Sergei Popadiuk writes enthusiastically about community efforts to create a nature reserve near Uspensky Monastery in Sviyazhsk, a town on an island on the Volga. He concludes with a statement abounding with the same hackneyed images of "the invigorating wave of spiritual energy" that, having originated in the provincial Sviyazhsk, could rejuvenate the whole of Russia.[17]

The last example reveals a newly emerged commercial aspect to the rhetoric associated with the provinces. Having found a commercial application for the discourse of difference and *ressentiment*, the provincial elite subtly shift the focus from the rather abstract and unsellable "spiritual purity and wealth" to the concrete and marketable images of unspoiled nature, clean air and water. This tendency, then unique to *Russia's Provinces*, becomes more prominent in regional periodicals of the 2000s as they begin actively to promote local tourism.

Though defunct since 1999, *Russia's Provinces'* short, six-year lifespan as a highbrow, emphatically nonpolitical publication remains impressive in light of its lack of advertising. Also to the journal's credit was its nonxenophobic stance. The opening editorial explicitly addresses "the globally unprecedented, colorful variety [*mnogotsvet'e*] of [Russia's] deeply rooted ethnic groups with a common historical destiny and a common future" and designated "all the peoples of Russia" as the journal's intended audience. The "inclusive" policy of *Russia's Provinces* constitutes its most striking distinction from its contemporary with a near-identical title, *The Russian (Russkaia) Provinces*.

The Russian (Russkaia) Provinces (1991–2002) was distributed in three large regions—Novgorod, Tver, and Pskov—until 1997, at which point the journal achieved national recognition. Every issue comprises works of prose and poetry by provincial authors, reviews of exhibits by provincial artists, a large section on religion, essays on famous writers and artists (Chekhov, Levitan, Platonov) with ties to a certain provincial region, and a local history section with the value-charged title "Motherland Studies" (*Rodinovedenie*). The back cover announces the forthcoming issue's publication date and bears the journal's credo: "We look for wealth in the provinces and find it there!"

In 2000, the journal lost its national status; in the issue announcing its distressing demotion to a regional publication, limited now to Tver, the unapologetically nationalist orientation of *The Russian Provinces* is manifest from its very opening piece—namely, Stalin's famous "Toast to the Russian People at the Reception in Honor of the Red Army Commanders, Given by the Soviet Government in the Kremlin on May 24, 1945": "I would like to propose a toast to the health of the Soviet people, and above all of the Russian people. I drink above all to the health of the Russian people because they are the most outstanding of all the nations that constitute the Soviet Union. I drink to the health of the Russian people, because, during this war, they have earned universal recognition as the guiding force of the Soviet Union among all the peoples of our country. I drink to the health of the Russian people, not only because they are the leading people, but also because they possess a clear mind, a staunch character and endurance."[18]

The last page of the same issue is devoted to an emotional statement from the editor and, as a testament to the journal's planned perseverance, a list of its proposed content, comprising "stories of Russian life: of Russian courage, of Russian endurance, of Russian history, and of Russian values."[19] His repetition of "Russian" is rhetorical, serving less to emphasize the specifically Russian content of these stories than to suggest that "Russian" stories of bravery and endurance are somehow fundamentally different from those "not Russian."[20] It functions, then, to establish boundaries between all things Russian and the rest of the world—including, one must assume, the country's various other peoples, who, in a similar context just two decades earlier, would have been "one" with "true" Russians as "Soviets."

The editor's description of the content intended for the *Russian Provinces'* limited regional circulation clearly emphasizes the same values as those attributed to the Russian people by Stalin fifty-five years earlier: exclusivity among other ethnicities,[21] bravery, and endurance. Both texts rely on familiar features of Russian nationalist discourse: assertions of difference coupled with *ressentiment*, a strong tendency to couch identity structures in binaries, and a portrayal of the constitutive features of the Russian national identity (bravery and endurance) as reactions to enemy attacks and hardships.

The same absence of a positively defined national idea characterizes much of the official nationalist discourse. Eliot Borenstein comments on a similarly redundant, incantation-like repetition of the adjective "Russian" in the names of political parties in the mid-1990s, and he suggests they function less to affirm their patriotic platforms than to assert Russia's very existence as a sovereign country. More specifically, the names perform "the circular function of (re)affirming the country's existence and the population's residency in it. [They] provide an opportunity to say the country's name and thereby, once again, confirm its existence.... as if they are trying to call into existence a desired state of affairs, as in an incantation or magic spell."[22] Borenstein concludes that these repeated assertions of identity preempt any attempt to analyze it. Indeed, while all discourses of national identities rest on what is presented as a nation's unique distinguishing features, the kind of identity one finds in most statements by Russian nationalists lacks specificity. As an attributive of endurance, bravery, civilization, or culture, the adjective "Russian" alleges difference but fails to describe it; thus, no specific and unique identity can be articulated, apart from that of being the Other to Russia's detractors. By contrast, the rhetoric of provincial nationalists appears to offer something concrete: those qualities of the national character that have been lost by the center but are preserved in the provinces. However, these, too, are defined apophatically and within the framework of the customary binaries, as a reaction to (hostile) surroundings. Above all, the provinces are the Other to the center.

The emergence of the two journals with almost identical titles in the early 1990s, coinciding with the Russian cultural and ideological elite's first attempts to articulate Russia's postimperial identity, was no coincidence. Rather, these journals participated in this endeavor, aiming to capture, analyze, and perhaps perpetuate the shift in the perception of the provinces. Many other publications also reflected this shift, albeit somewhat mechanically. They merit attention nevertheless, precisely because their formulaic efforts at an alignment with the provincial identity question affirm the pivotal role in the discourse of post-Soviet identity played by the cultural myth of the provinces.

Typically, the periodicals affirm their "provincial pride" in their inaugural issues, quoting important cultural figures and claiming meaningful connections to famous personages born in the region or town. The first issue of the weekly newspaper *The New Provinces* (Murom, October 1995) begins thus: "By our very title we would like to express our disengagement from purely political topics, because the provinces retain a stronger immunity to this 'disease of the big cities.'"[23] In the same issue, a column entitled "Of the Provinces and the Provincials" juxtaposes statements by the academician Dmitri Likhachev with those by the local tour guide S. Maslennikova. Likhachev is quoted as saying, "We expect the renewal of our life [to emerge] specifically from the provinces. We believe in the provinces and in everything Russian [*vse to russkoe*] they have retained." According to Maslennikova, the provinces are "not a geographical but rather a moral category." "The provinces," she continues, "are as strong as its people (all great people were born in the provinces) and by their unique feeling of love for the motherland."[24] There is no further mention in this or any other issue of the provinces as a concept; rather, true to its stated focus, *The New Provinces* is devoted henceforth to local news and politics. Similarly, having explained its choice of title in the inaugural issue, Sergiev Posad's *The Provincial Woman* (*Provintsialka*, [1995–) proceeds to focus on women. Other such local newspapers include *Provincial—Express* (Kimry, 1996–), *Provincial Thought* (Stavropol, 1994–), and *The Provincial Chronicles* (Vyksa, Nizhniy Novgorod district, 1991–).

The more recent *Ivanovo Provinces* (Shuia, Ivanovo district, 2002–), formerly *City News*, explains that their change of title "means that the editorial office will inform Shuia residents of all the interesting and important events taking place on Shuia land." *The Provincial Word* (Gvardeisk, Kaliningrad district, 2002–) promises, in its first issue, to be a "forum for open and honest exchanges of views on the affairs and concerns of the district."[25] Its third issue includes a page-long interview with a deputy district councillor, entitled "The Country is as Strong as its Provinces," in which he discusses the district's problems and concerns without once addressing the concept of the provinces. In conclusion, the interviewer does pay lip service to the matter by asking whether "the provincial hearth is forever doomed to ask for kindling." "Yes," replies the councillor, "but the important fact is that Russia realizes the importance and the position of municipal powers in the country's power structure. That they realize that Russia is as strong as its provinces."[26] The hackneyed statement that opens and concludes the interview with a local politician reinforces the fact that the local provincial governments, and their provincial constituents, acknowledge and exploit the prestige of "the provinces" in word but exhibit no interest in its conceptual implications.

Unlike *The Russian Provinces* and *Russia's Provinces*, these local periodicals do not engage explicitly in the discourse of national self-definition. Nevertheless, their choices of title, and scant but uniform justification thereof, reflect two important outcomes of the provincial discourse over the past two decades. First, distrust of the capital has increased in the wake of a decentralizing economy, in which Moscow's control over the regions' economic and cultural development has diminished. Second, reevaluations of the provinces have provided their political and cultural elite with a readymade lexicon of positive connotations, which they can exploit to various ends. The very existence of such a lexicon affirms the changes to the country's symbolic geography and affirms the authority of the provinces in an emerging hermetic national identity model. The provinces thus emerge as a contender in Russian culture and ideology for the role traditionally assigned to the West, as the Other.

Thus, both sides of the provinces–capital binary opposition are in the process of being redefined.

The Capital of [Blank]

Just as the symbolic authority of Moscow has eroded over the past two decades, so has the capital's "literal" authority as the site of cultural and economic superiority. The continuous fragmentation of the concept of the capital is evident in the numerous and multiplying designation of locales across Russia as "capitals." The privileging of a city or a town can sometimes be justified by geographical and administrative realities, as when Yekaterinburg is proclaimed the capital of the Urals, Novosibirsk—of Siberia, or Vladivostok—of the Far East. However, such designations are often far from obvious and sound arbitrary, if not forced. Most originate on the official websites of various towns and form the cornerstone of the speeches by city officials.

In the mid-2000s, the Culture, Youth Policy, and Mass Communication Ministry of the Perm Region (*krai*) launched a number of cultural initiatives, such as the programs Perm is the Cultural Capital of the Volga Region (*kul'turnaia stolitsa Povolzh'ia*) 2006 and Perm—Domain of Culture (since 2007).[27] The latter includes an annual contest by the Perm Region's Ministry of Culture for the title of Cultural Capital of the Perm Region, the details of which are featured in the special jubilee issue of the journal *The Perm Period*.[28] As the journal celebrates the Perm Region Jubilee (five years since the merger of Perm Oblast and Komi-Permyak Autonomous Okrug), the image of the *krai* emerges as an independent entity, almost a country, with its own center, history, industry, resorts, and even capital city. However, as three towns or villages are awarded the title of Cultural Capital of Perm Krai annually, the list of capitals grows longer every year.

Just as the Perm projects are initiated and financed by the *krai*'s administration, most other cities receive their "capital" titles though official initiatives. The Nizhniy Novgorod—Capital of the Volga Region program was launched by a special committee comprising the presidential envoy to the Volga Federal District, the mayor of Nizhniy Novgorod, and the governor of the Nizhniy Novgorod region. A report published by the Institute of Scientific Information on the Social Sciences of the Russian Academy of Sciences maintains that "the program is designed not just to revitalize the city, but also to evoke a certain attitude toward it, to adjust its image. Over the past few years, the issues of creating a positive image of Nizhniy Novgorod have attracted the attention of both city officials and the general public. In addition to the program 'Nizhniy Novgorod—Capital of the Volga Region,' the city participated in, and won, the 'Capital of Culture 2006' competition as a result of efforts to establish the city as a cultural center."[29]

The city of Voronezh is referred to as the capital of the "Black-Soil Region" (*Chernozem'e*) in multiple contexts—from tourist guides to news reports and the city's own social networking site.[30] The Spartakiada Gazprom 2011 website describes the town of Saransk, the capital of Mordovia, as the Volga Region's "sports capital."[31] The official site of Dimitrovgrad in the Ulyanovsk Region promotes the town's title as Cultural Capital of the Volga Federal District—2004 and touts its success in winning the 2010 regional competition for projects furthering the development of youth policy and pointing to its status as pilot site for the Youth Capital of the Ulyanovsk Region project.[32] Moreover, BBC Russian reports that Ulyanovsk's administration "has developed a special-purpose program, which is trying to establish the regional center as 'the aviation capital of Russia.'" The same article also suggests, however, that the proliferation of capitals, mentioned above, is merely "an image moment for leadership in the region."[33] Regional leadership does indeed capitalize on the discourses of regional identity and the provincial myth. As Moscow's actual authority wanes, and the very concept of the center even as a symbolic authority grows less viable, any politician claiming a given region's independence from—and even supremacy over—Moscow stands to gain a strong foothold there.

Lurkmore, a humorously inclined, Wikipedia-style web encyclopedia of "contemporary culture, folklore, and subcultures, as well as everything else" begins its entry for "Capital" with "almost any city in this country." It goes on to list city after city, and their numerous respective designations as "capital of —," as in the case of Balabanov, Kaluga Region, whose status ranges from capital of the Urals to the capital of matches.[34] In the spirit of satire, no one takes these designations seriously, though the growing list of "capitals" serves as a reminder that the actual capital has lost its traditional position of authority and prestige. In and of itself, however, the "capital" designation retains its prominence in the rhetoric of city officials, travel agents, journalists, and advertisers; it is a label that promises to add prestige to a given locale and boost its economy by attracting tourists. In other words, the "capital" designation is pivotal to the discourse of regional identity.

Regional Identity, Sausage, and the Little Motherland

"Regional Identity" is the cornerstone of provincial self-definition; the concept has become the topic of multiple scholarly inquiries in the first decades of the twenty-first century. It comprises the region's local history, culture, and natural resources as well as its prospects for future development. The discourse of a region's identity distinguishes its own centers (regional, district, etc.) and peripheries. The resulting imagery is thus circular, functioning according to the "*matreshka* principle," whereby the image of the capital and its surrounding noncapital space is repeated, on a diminishing scale, by countless regional centers within their corresponding district centers, within which are found ever smaller towns, each with their own noncenter spaces. Hence, the very notion of the center is destabilized and acquires new meanings and values.

In a recent, detailed empirical study of regional identity in European Russia, the geographer Mikhail Krylov examines, in addition to regional differences, "a special internal vision of territories as a unique cosmos, a combination of external and internal perspectives."[35] Krylov defines regional identity as a "systemic set of cultural relations, connected with the concept of 'Little Motherland' [*malaia Rodina*]."[36] The complex of ideas the Little Motherland represents includes "local specificity and geographical individuality," as reflected in the local populations' "*ideas and self-consciousness.*"[37] He concludes that "the set of internal images, symbols, and myths"[38] comprising regional identity is well developed, holds positive connotations, and is relatively independent from other, external definitions of the same regions. Krylov's extensive study of multiple regions in European Russia (Vologda, Voronezh, Yaroslavl, Kostroma, Tver, Saratov, Samara, and Belgorod regions) leads him to conclude that regional identity includes love for the motherland as one's birthplace (local patriotism) and is rooted neither in an inferiority complex nor in aggression toward other regions or the capital. Regional identity is thus shaped by local factors alone.

Krylov uses a nondiachronic framework to analyze the concept of regional identity, examining only its contemporary manifestation. Other studies of regional identity note that it gained importance in the post-Soviet period as other kinds of identities grew less satisfying. Leonid Smirniagin, for one, points out that in the Soviet Union, the Soviet identity dominated all other affiliations, including regional identity. He attributes the success of Soviet identity relative to specifically regional identities to a deficient "sense of place" in Russian culture, or its "nonspatiality" (*vneprostranstvennost'*). All the more remarkable, he states, is "how rapidly, with the beginning of perestroika, the regional (or even strictly local) identity has assumed a key position among the most important kinds of personal identity."[39] Following the Soviet Union's collapse, regional identity replaced political, professional, and even ethnic identities, all of which at the time failed to orient the individual in a changing world. Nadezhda Zamiatina, too, sees the growing importance of the regional identity as an outcome of the shift from Soviet geography's construction of the center-periphery relationship to post-Soviet situation when decentralization allowed the provinces to attempt self-description and representation.[40]

Similarly, Semyon Pavliuk notes that "the sense of place," repressed in the Soviet Union, acquired new significance in the post-perestroika years, with the development of regional independence and identity. He points out that most Soviet newspapers bore nondescript titles with few local markers and reported the same, mostly central and world news, using similar vocabulary. Citing a popular Soviet song, he even agrees to some extent that in those days a person's only address was "not a house or a street" but the Soviet Union.[41] Pavliuk's case study comprises the newspapers published in Torzhok, an ancient town in the Tver region, between 1985 and 2001. He briefly outlines the progression from the nonspatial (*vneprostranstvennye*) nature of the coverage in 1985, which included no local news, to the brief appearance of materials devoted to local problems during the immediate post-perestroika years, and finally, to the well-balanced coverage of the town's regional and nationwide news by 2001. Pavliuk notes the publication, during the later years of his study, of a considerable amount of material devoted to local culture, reflecting pride in Torzhok's history and natural resources.

Zamiatina approaches her analysis of regional self-representation, based on official websites of several regions, in a similar fashion. She observes the general tendency to redefine the center-periphery relationship by changing the very meaning of the word "center" to denote not the concrete capital, but a place of cultural, historical, and economic significance. Zamiatina explains, however, that "as soon as one accepts the logic of the center versus periphery opposition and applies a method of ranking, every region automatically becomes someone's center (be it the Volga area, West Siberia, or Russia in general) and someone's (Moscow's, the West's) periphery."[42] The traditional hierarchy is thus undermined and the concepts of center and periphery destabilized. Nonetheless, the inherently binary nature of all identities (on the one hand), together with the changing concept of center (on the other hand), has resulted in the emergence of intriguing shifts in Russian symbolic geography.

While regions across Russia undoubtedly differ, their regional identity projects are fundamentally similar in that they emphasize shared values rooted in place of birth, true Russian traditions, and unspoiled nature. These identity projects are invariably discussed in implied (or explicit) contrast with the capital, which presumably lacks these provincial values. Discussions of the elevation of provincial identity are also imbued with a palpable sense of pride over the reappropriation of material and cultural products, including such basics as food, which until recently had gone to Moscow.

Not surprisingly, this factor is of great consequence to the regions. In a country plagued by constant shortages under Soviet rule, food becomes a persistent theme, reflected in the recurrence of such announcements as "our stores now offer the same variety of food as Moscow stores." The editorial statement in the first issue of Sergiev Posad's *Provincial Woman* begins with "Dear Girlfriends" (*podrugi*) and explains their choice of title thus: "We contemplated the name for a long time. We realize that the word 'provincial' has carried, until recently, a somewhat negative connotation. But our lives have changed. We no longer rush around Moscow, perspiring, angry, weighed down with grocery bags. We now travel to the capital on business or just to [go to] the theater. We realize that we can recover from the metropolitan bustle and grime only in our cozy little town. I think many people now realize that the road to future reforms in Russia is largely dependent on the provinces."[43] The smooth segue in this passage from "we no longer have to schlepp food from Moscow" to "we will effect true reform" is at once remarkable and typical. Also typical is that Moscow's economic and cultural appeal and control—or lack thereof—are reduced to two recurring images: food and the theater.

In an interview in Volgograd's *Provincial News*, Oscar-winning film director Nikita Mikhalkov also addresses the political, economic, and cultural diktat of the center by lumping together food and the theater. He begins his argument as to why "Russian problems can be only solved by the Russian provinces" (the interview's title) with the same point: "I think today we're witnessing a very important metamorphosis. In the beginning, everyone looked up to Moscow and expected directives and orders from the Center. And the Center amassed all kinds of powers. Five–ten years ago, we went to Moscow for sausage, but now Tula has its own sausage, and for less than in Moscow. We went to Moscow to visit the Bolshoi Theater, but now it is virtually closed to domestic audiences. Today, [we see] emerging a national regional identity and the concept of the little motherland."[44] Apparently, then, sausage, theater (a catch-all for culture in general), and national identity are inextricably linked within the framework of provincial discourse.

Let us not look down our noses at sausage: Russian literature has endowed it with heavy symbolic meaning in such seminal texts as Yuri Olesha's *Envy*, Mikhail Bulgakov's *Heart of a Dog*, and Alexander Solzhenitsyn's *One Day in the Life of Ivan Denisovich*. In the provincial myth, sausage serves as the stand-in for economic and cultural independence. In popular discourse, having their own sausage gives provincials the sense of having freed themselves from Moscow's economic and political rule. Scholars advance the same argument with the contention that the regional economic independence is a prerequisite for self-governance and that both processes underlie the development and articulation of regional identities.[45]

Until perestroika, Moscow's dominion over both "sausage" and culture, when the provincial talent migrated to the capital, could be described as a relationship of a metropole to colonized territories: the center established political and economic control over the territories in order to gather wealth, resources, and profits for its own purposes. This constitutes a colonial situation of economic and cultural control, the reaction to which is predictably postcolonial in rhetoric: the provincial elite attempts to restructure the relationship with Moscow, by means of the concepts and vocabulary typical of post-colonial discourse. They challenge the established hierarchies of the center—the provinces opposition, and in addition to claiming the independence from the center, they claim superiority over it. Ultimately, however, they exploit the familiar dichotomy rather than dismantle it.

I use the term postcolonial strictly as it relates to the power relationship between entities from the viewpoint of a self-perceived object of such colonizing practices as political and economic control and exploitation. Most scholarly analyses of Russia by means of the critical apparatus of postcolonial studies focus on the relationship between the Russian center and the multiple ethnicities of the Russian and Soviet empires. By contrast, the provinces comprise those nonexotic lands with a predominantly ethnic-Russian population; thus, a postcolonial analysis of the center–province relationship would focus not on issues of ethnicity, but on the dynamics of domination as determined by centralized control over economy and culture. Alexander Etkind defines the relationship of Russia's imperial center to the Russian heartland as one of internal colonization, or "the culture-specific domination inside the national borders, actual or imagined,"[46] due equally to the colonization process of imposing control and the center's relationship with the lands and peoples of Siberia as well as southern Russia and Central Asia. This relationship implies an imagined geography and "a metaphorical landscape that represented not geographical fixity, but the fixity of power."[47]

David Chioni Moore describes the postcolonial as "characterized by tensions between the desire for autonomy and a history of dependence, between the desire for autochthony and the fact of hybrid, part-colonial origin, between resistance and complicity, and between imitation (or mimicry) and originality."[48] Like that of other postcolonial entities, the Russian provinces' reaction to the weakening of central control in post-Soviet times has developed by questioning the seemingly fundamental geographical, cultural, and political hierarchies. The predominant theme in provincial publications of the 1990s is that Moscow has lived off the provinces both economically and culturally, and the situation must be remedied by changing the relationship from one of dictate to one of dialogue. Such is the nature of postcolonial discourse when the formerly colonized assert cultural and economic independence from the center, reinterpret their past relationship, and propose new terms for its development. Viatcheslav Morozov points out that "Contemporary interpretations of postcolonial agency describe it not as directly confronting colonialism, but rather as re-appropriating and restructuring the whole discursive space in which domination is possible."[49] This is precisely what provincial journalists and politicians do: without changing the elements of the discourse, they restructure it, replacing dependence and inferiority with autonomy and superiority. This discourse is one of emotion, concerned less with logic and rational analysis than with assuaging, through transvaluation, the sting of provincial *ressentiment*.

Identity into Brand

With regional self-definition well rooted in both concept and practice by the 2000s, local publications retained their pointedly provincial titles but shifted their thematic focus from promoting the need to assert the economic and cultural authority of the provinces to catering to the needs of their local and regional media. Pride in one's birthplace, embodied in the expression "Little Motherland," now served a predominantly commercial purpose. Many periodicals placed article-length advertisements into sections with titles such as "Loyalty to Tradition" or "Discover Your City."[50] In one instance, an ostensibly historical account of a local heritage building is, in fact, an advertisement for the pharmacy situated on its ground floor, while another advertises local businesses and services. Similarly, the content of most provincial publications often includes a token salute to inquiries regarding local history (*kraevedenie*), though most of the issue is devoted to advertisements in the guise of interviews and articles.

Promoters of local tourism capitalize on the now securely positive connotations of the provincial discourse as they advertise various Russian destinations—from nature reserves to historic sites—appealing as much to the readership's ideas of recreation as to their patriotic sentiments. The advantages of local tourism are clear: it boosts the economy of provincial cities and generates the funding of "travel-worthy" sites and vicinities, thus assuring increased tourism in the future. Moreover, businesses that appeal to the readership's sense of patriotism gain a marketing tool, and politicians score extra points by publicizing their endeavors to develop a region's cultural, natural, and economic resources. Thus the website of the "Ethnomir" museum-park near Kaluga not only promotes what the museum itself has to offer, but also promotes cultural projects sponsored by the regional government and provides materials on the spiritually regenerative effects of traveling within Russia with an eye to its history.[51]

These marketing strategies fall under the rubric of "regional branding," a concept and practice that is gaining acceptance in Russia. Regional identity and city branding are both products of the process of reevaluating, and redefining, the provinces—the former as a set of internal images and myths, and the latter as tangible, reproducible texts, directed outward to potential investors and tourists. The marketing term "branding" applies to various techniques intended "to improve the image of a region, and raise its commercial, investment, and social attractiveness,"[52] whereby places that "can be constituted through a plethora of images and representations . . . are communicated to potential target markets and audiences."[53]

When a team of branding specialists sets to work on developing a city's brand, they attempt to formulate its unique "story." In order to develop "coherent strategies with regard to managing [the city's] resources, reputation, and image,"⁵⁴ the team must distinguish the most representative and viable attributes of its internal images and transform them into a "brand image," perceived as positive by its residents, potential investors, and tourists. N. Abalmasova and E. Pain include branding in the broader concept of "symbolic management," used "for creating the positive image of a region designed for an outside audience—buyers."⁵⁵

Thus, to create a city brand is to give shape to existing, positive associations that distinguish it from other cities and burnish its image relative to the competition.⁵⁶ And this is precisely where provincial cities face their most daunting challenges: until recently the cultural myth of the provinces held mostly negative connotations and assigned no individuality to provincial places. Anne Lounsbery observes that, since Gogol's day, the provinces have been perceived not only as backward but, more importantly, as uniform: "the provincial admits of no real variation, no individuality. Here is where the seemingly unreal quality of N actually points to a certain social and historical reality: by making the provincial city's lack of defining features one of its defining features, Gogol is ascribing negative moral value to the physical characteristics of Russia's provincial towns."⁵⁷

The towns of N, S, or "***ov" in nineteenth- and early twentieth-century Russian literature refer simultaneously to no particular place and to all provincial places: all towns are presumed to look and feel the same. To some extent, this is true. Those towns erected after Catherine II's administrative reforms, without the defensive walls of medieval town-fortresses, were modeled after the capital at that time, St. Petersburg. Thus, "*guberniia* centers were smaller copies of the capital, and *uezd* centers—its miniatures."⁵⁸ The subordinate nature of provincial life was, therefore, literally built in. In her analysis of nineteenth-century picture postcards, Alison Rowley points out the "interchangeability of the images" on postcard representations of Russian provincial towns, especially those of monuments and public gardens. Equestrian statues everywhere are similar; but the planting of public gardens across the empire imposed "a centralized Europeanized vision onto the diverse Russian landscape"⁵⁹ and contributed to standardized urban planning and the resulting sense of "sameness" typical to all provincial locales.

This proliferation of St. Petersburg replicas, whereby a small "model provincial city" is patterned on a bigger provincial city, modeled, in turn, on St. Petersburg, "which looked, or aimed to look, like Europe,"⁶⁰ explains the inclusion of imitativeness among the representative features of provincialism: only similar objects can be compared within the same system of values. The countless, often comical, portrayals in nineteenth-century literature of the efforts by provincials to imitate the capital merely justify the perception of provincial backwardness.

The sense of sameness grew more pronounced still during the Soviet period, with the uniform arrangement of administrative buildings, Houses of Culture, and multistoried apartment blocks typifying the Soviet urban landscape. Local identification in the Soviet Union was further suppressed by a new system of administrative-territorial division, which ignored the historical geographical demarcations and instead "cut up the country's living body [*rezala po zhivomu*]."[61] The official media portrayed the country as "something huge, and divided into a multitude of almost identical units with similar problems, goals, and aims."[62]

The same problem persists today: despite significant efforts by the provincial political, business, and cultural elite to create distinct and unique regional and city identities, provincial locales continue to coalesce into a nondescript, "noncapital" realm. Indeed, the provinces' symbolic nature is intrinsic to the challenges of regional self-representation, which, in turn, must operate within the symbolic geography of Russian nationalism. In developing a brand—that is, an attractive, sellable identity—a provincial town or region (*oblast'*) must first counteract the persistently negative connotations of the provinces in Russian culture before it can establish an image that strikes a balance between the local/concrete and the national/symbolic. Given the provinces' new role in the discourse of nationalism, however, this negative association yields to the perception of provincial Russia as a repository of the best features of the national character. Once the notion of true Russianness is introduced, this discourse enters into the broader discourses of Russian identity and nationalism, wherein "the local" disappears and the logic of cultural myth dominates. The provinces of myth have no local markers and no sense of place. To fulfill their role as the symbolic locale of true Russianness, the provinces must remain the amorphous space outside of, and opposed to, the capital.

Thus, the primary obstacles in constructing a provincial city's identity involve the questions of how to: create a sense of place; grant the uniqueness of a recognizable brand to a place whose characteristic feature is its very indistinguishability from other such places; and invest with meaning that which has always been characterized by a lack of it.

Case Study: "How is Voronezh not Paris?"

The internet meme "Bomb Voronezh," popular since at least 2008, appears in a number of images that feature Vladimir Putin saying: "If NATO invades Syria we will bomb Voronezh," and in a newer version: "If they introduce new sanctions, we will bomb Voronezh."[63] Thus, the meme describes an act that intends to harm or spite someone, but harms the perpetrator more than the intended target. The origins of the meme are not entirely clear,[64] but the role in it of Voronezh is evident: to distinguish Russia's most typical locale. To bomb Voronezh, and not Moscow, is to harm Russia proper, as opposed to Russia's capital, which no longer carries that connotation.

My interest throughout this study has been in the Russian heartland, the nonexotic noncapital, the bland, depersonalized provincial "town of N"—in this case, Voronezh. I focus on Voronezh for the following reasons: it is a large provincial city in the Russian heartland, the true provinces, as demonstrated by the internet meme above; it hosts a journal with an agenda similar to that of *The Russian Provinces* and *Russia's Provinces*; and at least some of its officials are actively engaged in establishing and promoting its somewhat paradoxical status as the capital of the provinces.

Unlike some provincial cities, Voronezh faces an uphill battle in its quest for Russia-wide and world status: it possesses very few cultural myths, identity markers, or recognizable brands. The numerous claims to fame of the nearby Tula region, for instance, include Kulikovo Field, Leo Tolstoy's estate Yasnaya Polyana, Tula weapons, Tula gingerbread, and the Tula samovar. Voronezh could exploit its own history as the birthplace of the first Russian fleet, the poet Aleksei Koltsov, and writers Ivan Bunin and Andrei Platonov. It could also tout itself as Osip Mandelstam's place of exile and the source of a famous block of rich, black soil that traveled to the 1889 Paris World Fair. Rather than promote these facts, however, Voronezh's image-makers have elected instead to create a completely new identity for the city. This has resulted in a set of conflicting images and messages, fueled by a combination of nationalist and Occidentalist rhetoric. Whether or not a coherent story emerges from these efforts, granting meaning to the provincial void, is yet to be determined.

The journal *Guberniia Style: The Russian Provincial Journal of Literature and Journalism*, was founded in 2006. To the same extent that *The Russian Provinces* and *Russia's Provinces* were products of the 1990s status quo, *Guberniia Style* is a product of the 2000s, by which point the discourse of the provinces, as the storehouse of Russia's cultural, moral, and economic potential, has sufficiently developed. Most of the journal's materials comprise regional studies and literary works about and of the provinces. Each issue begins with a short editorial; the first of these, entitled "The Russian Renaissance," opens several issues in modified form and formulates the journal's mission thus: "Our magazine is for the Russia of the future. We will behold the approaching global perspectives from the depths of the Russian provinces. We will create our own factory of thoughts and ideas based on the intellectual and spiritual experience of the generations living in provincial Russia. . . . We will uncover the layers of the cultural and spiritual treasures of the Russian provinces."[65] On their own, "spiritual treasures," and even the preservation of traditions, make for esoteric concepts. Within the context of the provincial discourse, however, they carry specific connotations, primarily as the spheres in which the provinces triumph over Moscow. *Guberniia Style*'s inaugural issue addresses these concepts explicitly, whereby it best illustrates my point, that the provincial discourse is invariably nationalist.

Editor Nikolai Sapelkin's introduction to the issue's first section, "Guberniia Argues" (*Guberniia sporit*), outlines some of the assumptions and problems to be discussed: "The spiritual strength, intellectual potential, and defensive power of Russia are in its provinces (*v ee glubinke*). A cure for its diseases is also there. Today, as Russia searches for its own way into the future, now drifting toward the global community, now considering isolationism, we provide a provincial perspective on these challenging Russian problems."[66] The section includes a report on "The Future of Russia," a roundtable discussion moderated by Sapelkin—comprising local representatives of Russia's major political parties, a regional Duma member, and a priest—devoted to Russia's defense capabilities and demographic situation. In concluding the heated exchanges on such topics as patriotism, migration, abortion, and the problems facing today's youth, Sapelkin raises a question heretofore not explicitly addressed: "If Russians were to suddenly scatter throughout the world, or stay in their own country but within a global society without borders, would it be possible to distinguish a Russian from [someone] of another ethnic background? What are, or may become, the features that determine our ethnicity?"[67] Predictably, the participants affirm these as language and ethnic self-identification, religion, and a uniquely Russian spirituality. Sapelkin thus closes the roundtable by returning to the issue of national identity because in all discussions of

Russia's past and future, the "provincial perspective" inevitably involves the issue of nationalism.

The same section includes "The Russian Face of Patriotism"—an essay by Vladimir Bondarenko, literary critic and editor-in-chief of the newspaper *The Day of Literature*.[68] The rhetoric in this unapologetically xenophobic version of Russian nationalism is typically Occidentalist and steeped in *ressentiment*:

> Russian civilization, by its very existence—is a challenge to Western civilization. The matter is neither in our aggressiveness, our expansionism, nor in our wealth or intelligence. It is not even in the nature of our ideology or political system. Whether we are a monarchy, a republic, the Soviet power, or presidential rule—all that is secondary to Western civilization. And it is also not about the Chechens, Tatars, Jews, or any other peoples of Russia. Anti-Semitism appeared not in Russia but in enlightened Europe; it is not in Russia where they paid cash, per Native American scalp, but in the United States. But as long as we exist as the other type of civilizational development . . . our otherness will irritate the Western world. Alas, this is our historical fate. . . . Conservative challenge—that's our way in the world. It is our alternative to economic pragmatism.[69]

Characterizing the West as pragmatic and hypocritical is a staple of Occidentalist discourse, as is positioning Russia as the Other to the West. Otherness is conveyed as a quality intrinsic to the Russian character and independent of the nation's political or economic realities; it is almost mystical in nature. Also typical is the definition of patriotism—less as love for one's country than as distaste for its assumed detractors. To state that Russia's mission is to be different from the West neither helps define the Russian character nor suggests any practical solutions to its problems.

Bondarenko's extremist stance is balanced by an academic overview of the various manifestations of patriotism by Moscow political scientist Sergei Markedonov's "Russian Question," cautioning against the dangers of ethnic extremism. Thus, *Guberniia Style* maintains a relatively neutral position; its leanings toward ethnic nationalism come through in the recurrent editorial framing of materials in terms of provincial discourse, with its inherent nationalist element.

Occidentalist discourse is further characterized by a negative view of the capital. This position provides the basis for denying Moscow its status as Russia's symbolic center. *Guberniia Style* goes one step further, by reconfiguring the center-periphery opposition in order to exclude Moscow altogether, as evidenced by Sapelkin's mission statement: "We do not focus our projects on Voronezh or Moscow, but rather we try to make them as international as possible. We deliberately exclude the capital, because the capital of any large country is cosmopolitan in nature. . . . Moscow is like a big meat-grinder; it crushes people and averages them out [*usredniaet*]. There are in the provinces a great number of interesting topics, events, and phenomena that get lost in a globalizing world. We decided to focus on these topics in the Russian provincial journal of literature and journalism, *Guberniia Style*."[70] Sapelkin clearly articulates the Occidentalist view of Moscow as a soulless, cosmopolitan metropolis, feeding on the individuality of the provincials; as such, it can no longer serve as the nation's organizing symbol. By the same token, even by pointedly excluding Moscow from his journal's sphere of interests, Sapelkin continues to define Voronezh in terms of the Moscow-provinces binary. The concept of the capital has always been crucial to regional self-identification; Zamiatina observes that a relational position to Moscow once numbered among a given region's positive attributes, among them easy access to the capital, branches of Moscow institutions, and the possibility of exporting local produce to Moscow. Having lost its positive value, Moscow ceases to be the primary point of reference; in addition, any foreign city is now considered "a more prestigious consumer of goods, or neighbor," than Moscow.[71]

Thus, in an interview entitled "How is Voronezh not Paris?" (Chem Voronezh ne Parizh?), first published online in *Chef* magazine (2007) and then reprinted in *Guberniia Style* (2010), Sapelkin sees nothing unusual in pairing the capital of the Black-Soil Region with the capital of France: "Take Voronezh. It is no worse than Paris. It is just that the capital of France is better promoted [*raskruchena*]; a large proportion of the city's budget is spent on its image. Voronezh has its own certain something [*svoiu osobinku*], but does not advertise, does not promote it. . . . This requires the joint efforts of the administration, and business."[72] Sapelkin's statement invites a number of questions, from that of how one promotes (*raskruchivaet*) a provincial city or a region, to why he breaks out of the traditional capital-provinces binary, eschewing the Russian capital as a point of reference and proceeding to compare his city to the "capital of the world," Paris. To some extent, the foreign reference point reflects the relative ease with which Russians now travel abroad. Yet I contend that it also reflects the attempt to envision new centers of symbolic authority and replace one that no longer seems acceptable. For the provincial elite, the relationship with Moscow is a complicated one, founded on the uneasy dynamic of Orientalist and Occidentalist attitudes. Meanwhile, Moscow's exclusion in favor of a foreign point of reference, such as Paris, makes room to assign prestige to the region within new, completely imagined, systems of reference and hierarchies. Since this new geography doesn't rely on any kind of scientific data and is entirely symbolic, how, indeed, is Voronezh different from Paris? Or Houston? Or Amsterdam?

A city brand is always removed from geographical and cultural reality. Rather than reflect a given city, a brand bundles and transforms its cultural, historical, natural, and architectural phenomena into a slogan and/or logo designed to convey a coherent story. Paris is a great example of the contrast between the geography of a city and its "metageography," defined as the mental images that people associate with a given place.[73] Paris of the popular image may not be fully supported by physical, cultural, and geographical data, but it exists nevertheless because, as the geographer Dmitri Zamiatin points out, "the transition from the physical and cultural layers to the metageographical layer" occurs as a result of a long-term branding process, both spontaneous and organized.[74] Ostensibly, there is no particular reason for Paris's great popular appeal. However, a 2008 study of the correlation between the wealth of assets and the "brand power" of the ten biggest cities in Europe ranked Paris first in both categories.[75] In other words, a brand may be a construct, often merely an "aspiration that has yet to be realized,"[76] but its longevity requires a cultural and geographical basis. To imagine Voronezh, a city without any significant assets, in a position to rival Paris requires a very different sense of identity building, and of geography as another construct—a symbol susceptible to reimagining and reconstructing.

This symbolic geography is best envisioned alongside the postmodernist view of the world, where everything is a text, reality is a construct, the notion of "truth" is undermined and replaced by that of multiple truths, and, by analogy, the concept of a center is replaced by that of multiple centers. In a world thus mapped, Voronezh (or any other city) is indeed independent of Moscow and on equal footing with world capitals.

The *Guberniia Style* journal shares its title with an annual fashion festival (since 2002); its goal is to establish Voronezh as Russia's fashion capital and potential rival to Paris. The festival is a joint project of the National Academy of the Fashion Industry, the Ministry of Industry and Trade of the Russian Federation, and other national organizations. Participants are young designers from Russia, Ukraine, and sometimes other nations; jury members have included the maître of Russian fashion, Viacheslav Zaitsev, and prominent fashion industry figures from China and France. The organizers hold an annual roundtable discussion entitled "The Russian Provinces in the Context of Culture and History," with subjects ranging from Fashion and Tourism to issues of regional identity.

Sapelkin's own remarks on the festival affirm the view that his city's comparison to Paris constitutes a step away from Moscow and toward recovering Russia's national traditions and pride: "We decided," Sapelkin states, "to set provincial Russia [*gubernskuiu Rossiiu*] in opposition to the capital." His next statement exudes nationalist sentiments: "At the heart of this Russia's fashion aspirations lies the 'ethnic style.' Ethnic style means the use of folklore and folk elements in the design of modern clothing. After all, we didn't spring from a void: we have a rich historical and cultural heritage. Traditional folk wear won't be resurrected overnight. But little by little we are preparing the ground, including [with] the performances we organize, which showcase Voronezh folk costumes."[77] All of this, Sapelkin concludes, establishes "Voronezh as a center of fashion and tourism."

The ideas of "center" and "capital" figure prominently in all accounts of the event. An online Voronezh newspaper reports: "Thanks to 'Guberniia Style,' Voronezh region [*oblast'*] began to be regarded in the circles of professional designers as a fashion and tourism center of European Russia; and the city of Voronezh as the true capital of provincial fashion [*podlinnaia stolitsa gubernskoi mody*]."[78] In an online interview in 2012, Sapelkin reiterates that "'Guberniia Style' is one of the few fashion initiatives in the country enjoying the extensive participation of designers from small towns. Thanks to the festival, Voronezh has become the fashion capital of noncapital Russia [*stolitsei mody nestolichnoi Rossii*]."[79]

Hosting events is a common and effective city branding technique, allowing municipal governments to highlight the most appealing aspects of their cities or propose new ideas.[80] The "Guberniia Style" festival organizers focus on creating a "fashion capital." In order to justify their ambition, they need to reimagine a symbolic space in which Voronezh can claim this status. The *Guberniia Style* journalist reporting on the 2010 festival, attended by the dean of a Beijing design school, attempts to do just that. She expresses pride in the winners' international achievements as those, too, of Russian provincial culture, which "is moving toward success and flourishing at a steady pace; and [having] its own style lends its movement a particular gracefulness."[81] She concludes the report, entitled "Guberniia Style, from Beijing to Paris," with a bit of symbolic geography by linking the fashion capitals of the West and Far East with a line drawn not between them, but rather through Voronezh: "And this is how 'The Guberniia Style' develops: from Beijing to Paris, with its center in Voronezh. And while the distance between Voronezh and Paris is only three thousand kilometers, whereas it is twelve thousand to Beijing—these cities are equally close to Voronezh and its residents."[82]

The festival has undoubtedly been of genuine help and interest to aspiring local designers. However, the organizers' rhetoric functions on a global and decidedly abstract level, thereby eliciting questions as to: the effects of positioning a real city as the capital of the mythical realm of noncapital Russia; whether ceasing to measure the provincial city against the capital frees the provinces from the confines of the capital-provinces binary, allowing them to define their own identity; and why this new identity might recreate the same binary opposition, albeit with different cities. Apparently, the regional tradition remains as undeveloped in contemporary Russia as it was in Gogol's day, and the provinces remain a cultural myth that, as Roland Barthes has claimed, is an empty form that can be filled with any content. The world map on which one sees the line "from Beijing to Paris with its center in Voronezh" is more than symbolic: it is fantastic. No statistics, ratings, indexes, or public opinions polls hold sway over the realm of the myth. The purveyor of the provinces (to use Catherine Evtuhov's term) is not obliged to make good on his claims.[83]

And that gives him the extraordinary freedom to create. If, as branding theory suggests, places may be "constituted through a plethora of images and representations"—that is, if stories take on a reality of their own—then Sapelkin, in a bold postmodern act of inventing reality, turns Voronezh into Paris simply by renaming its residents. At the 2013 festival's roundtable discussion, Sapelkin introduced his Voronezh—Identification project. He discussed the kinds of advertisements displayed on the city streets and the state of its illumination and lawns, and then he proposed changing the demonym for its residents from the customary *voronezhets*, to *voronezhanin*. By adopting the same suffix as that in *parizhanin*, denoting a "Parisian," he dubs a resident of Voronezh a "Voronezhian." He also suggests the city's colors be red and white, its taste—salty, and its fragrance—meadowy.[84] Sapelkin's suggestions do sound arbitrary. The issue, however, is not whether Voronezh residents care about being referred to as Voronezhians, but the fact that an identity-formation project, especially in a region having few historical markers of self-identity, is neither supported nor bound by geographical, economic, or cultural reality. Rather, it is an exercise in myth-making, unconstrained by (or ignoring) existing regional traditions, identities, and even realities.

The Voronezh World Tour (*Voronezhskaia krugosvetka*) adds another dimension to this vision. Its organizers sense no conflict between the outward, worldly, even cosmopolitan pose of the Paris of the Russian provinces and this journey within the administrative borders of Voronezh Oblast. While the linear logic of Paris-Voronezh-Beijing propels Voronezh into the world beyond the Russian border, the *krugosvetka*, with "circle" embedded in its very title, visually draws a line around the Voronezh region, locking it in.

As we know, stories of journeys often tell of self-discovery. Russian travelers returning from Europe are known for turning to Russia's heartland in search of their own roots and identity.[85] In the 2010 interview, Sapelkin claims that those traveling around Russia can't help but become patriots, whereas the traveler within the encircled Voronezh region is not searching for patriotic values; already a patriot, he expresses and propagates them: "The project is implemented in order to contribute to the patriotic and moral education of citizens, establish the Voronezh region as a tourist attraction, draw attention to the problem of preserving historical and architectural monuments, gather information about the lifestyle of the region's population, and promote healthy lifestyles and traditional Russian cultural values."[86] Even the patent, businesslike tone of "tourist attraction" cannot obscure the statement's nationalist bent.

What does this blend of branding techniques and nationalist and anti-Moscow rhetoric tell us? It tells us that the authority denied to Moscow has not been transferred to the provincial city and that the emphasis on the provinces as the repository of true Russianness keeps the provincial discourse and provincial identity tied firmly to the speculative discourses of nationalism and cultural mythology.

Scholars around the world have been divided with regard to the efficacy of city/territory/nation branding. Simon Anholt, an authority in branding studies, insists that it is only possible to use the "B-word" as a metaphor. Places, he points out, may have brands—"in the sense that they have reputations"—but the idea that one can brand a city in the same way that corporations brand their products is, in his opinion, "both vain and foolish." In reference to nation branding, he further claims that in his fifteen years of study, he has seen no evidence of a "correlation between changing a national image and expenditure on 'nation building campaigns.'"[87] Addressing the Russian branding practices, Abalmasova and Pain assert that "the Russian practice of regional and urban policy at present demonstrates the extremely scant experience in implementing integral symbolic programs. And even in cases when such programs have been carried out, they have rarely earned the elites [the] sociopolitical 'profit,' valuable for the intrapolitical goals of a region."[88] Some scholars link the failure of regional branding projects in Russia to the ideology and economic policies of the Putin era: "The quests for regional identities and brands that record local uniqueness do not fit into the new discourse, now gaining strength in the mass media: the discourse of self-isolation, Byzantinism, Eurasianism, and national unity on the basis of Orthodoxy."[89]

The above observations do indeed explain why the provincial elites rarely succeed in articulating positive, unique, and provable city and regional brands and identities. The Russian provincial city faces additional challenges in this process: while regional identities remain subsumed by national identity, itself still being articulated and disputed, the provincial space remains the ill-defined noncapital void within the realm of cultural myth. Myth has little to do with reality; branding has been defined as "a reality with delay,"[90] and the postmodern view of reality blurs the boundary between what exists and what exists only as a story, to the extent that one engages in producing reality armed with nothing but a set of names and concepts. The life-creation efforts of Nikolai Sapelkin and others may constitute the first step toward formulating, and imparting, meaning to their city's identity. For the time being, however, we are left with the incongruous image of a "Voronezhian" in ethnic-style attire, taking a world tour within the borders of the Voronezh oblast.

The reevaluation of the provinces–capital binary began in the early 1990s and continued throughout the following decades with little change in substance. The provincial cultural elite initiated the process with enthusiastic assertions of the provinces' parity with, even superiority to, the capital; soon thereafter, politicians and business people discovered the usefulness of the provincial myth's rhetoric in serving their own purposes. Appropriating the rhetoric of national identity allows the provincial elite to claim a different kind of relationship to the capital within a symbolic geography that they restructure according to their needs. Retaining the essential elements of the ternary structure the provinces–Moscow–the West, they envision different hierarchies and, where previously defined by dependence and inadequacy, they now claim autonomy and superiority.

Within the hermetic model of national self-identification, the relationship between the provinces and Moscow has developed in a manner similar to that between Russia and the West—as a combination of attraction and resentment. Creating a positive image of Russia, with the West as its Other, has clearly become unfeasible. The provincial Other, envisioned as a more acceptable alternative, has appropriated, and exploits, the themes and lexicon of the provincial myth to its own end. Nevertheless, this hermetic "us versus us" model allows for an alternative, much less conflict-driven vision of the nation than that of "Russia versus the West." Perpetuating the myth benefits both parties in the relationship: the center gets its locale of true Russianness, and the provinces exact their "revenge." Even as the provincial mythmakers feel confident enough to envision a binary relationship with the West, bypassing Russia's capital, the ternary structure of the provinces–Moscow–the West does not dissolve into its component binaries. These three cornerstones of Russian symbolic geography remain firm, and amid their various reconfigurations, the Russian national identity is still waiting to be articulated.

2

Literature
In the Provincial State of Mind

Paris—is it far from us? Three thousand miles? My God, how provincial!

M. Kharitonov, 1992

Russian writers who live and work in the provinces frequently address questions regarding the center–periphery dynamic when they speak of not having access to prestigious publishing houses, being ignored by literary prize committees, and of being cut off from the literary scene. However, while these writers' acute awareness of their provincial status is repeatedly articulated in interviews, it is not always explicit in their literary works. And why should the authors' place of birth and residence influence their choice of subject, themes, and characters? The literary setting of a provincial town does not necessarily comprise a statement on the nature of provincial life, or the relationship between the provinces and the center. Not all literary characters who walk the streets of Russian towns, fish off their riverbanks and picnic on the clearings in their woods, are explicitly marked as provincials. My interest, however, lies in those cases when the setting is indeed endowed with meaning—namely, that of the provinces as the "true" Russia, distinct from, and often opposed to, the Russian capital. In emphasizing the symbolic geography of a given work, and characterizing the setting, the protagonists, and the implied author as being either of the provinces or the center, the author articulates a certain perspective on what it means to live in Russia's heartland or capital. In the texts examined in this chapter, the provincial topos is an important theme as well as an element of characterization and a means for contemplating Russia's identity. The cultural myth of the provinces serves as a shortcut to the themes of Russia's national idea and symbolic geography. Regardless of the authors' capacity, or willingness, to offer viable definitions of Russianness, their works explore the problems intrinsic to Russian national identity in terms of the relationship between the capital and the provinces.

The Provinces as Philosophy

Mark Kharitonov's trilogy *Provincial Philosophy* includes the novellas *Prokhor Menshutin* (1971, published 1988) and *Provincial Philosophy* (1977, published 1993). The last work in the trilogy, the novel *Lines of Fate, or Milashevich's Trunk* (1980–85), was awarded the first Russian Booker Prize upon its publication in 1992. Though its writing predates my specified period of analysis, the work is nevertheless indispensable to this study. It develops the provincial topos in the manner typical to late-Soviet culture: as a nonideological and ahistorical locale, similar in function to the concept of the private sphere. By the same token, it prefigures the heightened importance of the post-Soviet provincial trope in the discourse of national identity. As such, it serves as a literary counterpart to the journalistic discovery of the provinces' unique role in preserving Russian cultural riches and national character, which I discussed in the previous chapter.

Critics have been divided in their evaluations of the novel: some have predicted its future significance to Russian culture as comparable to the impact of Umberto Eco's *The Name of the Rose* on Western culture, while others have found it to be contrived and painfully slow-paced.[1] In the introduction to her 1996 translation of the work, Helena Goscilo calls it "Russia's *Doctor Zhivago* for the 1980s," while *The New York Times* review of her translation finds the novel's philosophical premises unoriginal and Kharitonov's "fondness for superfluous details, baffling digressions and enigmatic fragments" tiring.[2] Naum Leiderman and Mark Lipovetsky praise its "complex, multilayered and multivoiced double-edged dialogue between the World and the Text," while Andrei Nemzer suggests parallels to Gogol and Rozanov.[3] Be they sympathetic or exasperated, critics focus on the novel's form: its postmodern, metafictional, and metahistorical nature; its complex structure; and its explicitly philosophical stance. While I believe that *Lines of Fate* poses Russia's eternal questions in a truly original and hauntingly complex way, my primary interest is in its setting, the highly charged locale of the Russian provinces. My inquiry into Kharitonov's novel focuses on two particular aspects: first, on the ways in which it participates in, and anticipates, the shifts in the discourse of the provinces, and second, on the growing interest in the provincial topos at the time of its publication.

Like much Russian literature of the post-perestroika period, *Lines of Fate* is metafictional and metahistorical; it depicts a "contemporary" writer and literary scholar who painstakingly reconstructs the texts of a literary "precursor," searching for autobiographical clues in his writings and the historical documents of his time. Anton Antonovich Lizavin, a literature instructor at a provincial university in the 1970s, becomes interested, to the point of obsession, in Simeon Milashevich—a little-known local writer in the 1910s and 1920s. By chance Lizavin comes across a trunk full of Milashevich's disjointed notes, most of which consist of a mere phrase or two written on bits of candy wrappers (*fantiki*) from the local candy factory. Hence, the *fantichny*, a typically postmodern style of text comprising a puzzle-like collection of pieces that do not neatly fit together, are subject to constant rearranging and reinterpretation, with the resulting text never a certainty, but rather only one of many possibilities.

The fragmented nature of Milashevich's text directs the reader toward Vasili Rozanov's similarly fragmented texts of the 1910s—namely, *Fallen Leaves* (1912–13) and *Embryos* (1918). In a seemingly haphazard manner, Rozanov's notes combine short sketches and even shorter statements on life, death, and the fate of the writer. Like a series of snapshots, together they capture the author's life and his times. Lizavin's task is more difficult than that of Rozanov's reader: there is as much order to Milashevich's trunk of notes as in a bushel of leaves. It is Lizavin's task to create order out of these notes, thereby imposing meaning upon them. Thus, he is much more deeply committed to these texts than the reader or interpreter since, in effect, he becomes Milashevich's coauthor. As the novel progresses, Lizavin becomes ever more engrossed in Milashevich's fate while his own comfortable existence and career gradually slip away. Essentially, he retreats from the normative and collective into a world where the boundaries between text and life are obscure and priorities shift to the extent that, as Nemzer suggests, "the question of whom to marry becomes the problem of saving the world soul."[4]

Lines of Fate opens with a quotation from one of Milashevich's stories—the first of several partially autobiographical texts that guide Lizavin though the process of untangling and reconstructing Milashevich's life story, in which the latter's wife appears to be at the center of a domestic idyll. In several stories, the woman's presence "is felt not so much directly as in the various pieces of needlework, napkins, chair pillows, the jam making, Shrovetide pancakes, and the other joys of a provincial existence Milashevich so lovingly incorporates into his descriptions."[5] These details—needlework, napkins and, most persistently, tea and raspberry jam—form the basis of what Lizavin calls Milashevich's provincial philosophy, one that is "completely alien to any system and requires no proof. Its truth lies in the ability to guarantee inner harmony and vouchsafe a feeling of happiness independent of life's outer structure. It has no pretensions to grandeur; indeed, its strength lies in its general accessibility."[6] Milashevich's philosophy is a hymn to provincial life where the home is a refuge from the outside world and the place where one can withstand the pull of history. The tea and raspberry jam assume a symbolic meaning that far exceeds their traditional role as markers of domesticity and a proper family life.[7]

Tea drinking also serves as an additional intertextual reference to Rozanov's *Embryos*, in which tea and jam are the answer to one of Russian culture's eternal questions: "—What is to be done?—asked the restless youth from Petersburg.—How do you mean, what is to be done? If this is *summer*—washing berries and making jam; if it's *winter*—drinking tea with the jam." Milashevich's *fantiki* and Rozanov's small form are genres ideally suited to the times, which are equally disjointed and incomprehensible; moreover, they endow these age-old questions with new relevance. "Chernyshevsky's question," Rozanov continues, "raised in the [very] title of his novel, is an essentially lyrical question, untimely; the answer can only be mundane: one must do what was being done yesterday."[8] Whether this focus on tea drinking is a conscious intertextual device or a nod to the special place the custom occupies in Russian literature—from Chernyshevsky to Tolstoy, Dostoevsky, and Isaak Babel—this simple domestic activity acquires symbolic meaning, evoking stability and continuity.[9]

Significantly, though Milashevich wrote his early stories in St. Petersburg, he situates his idyll in a small provincial town; thus, the "in absentia" provincial dimension is essential to Milashevich's philosophy. It is clear to Lizavin from the outset that Milashevich's provinces are "not a geographical notion but a spiritual one, a way of existence; it has its roots in the human soul independent of the place where he lives."[10] Lizavin performs the role of interpreter, here and throughout the novel (to the extent that, Nemzer laments, the critic's job in reviewing the work has been done in the work itself), to lay bare the dichotomy underlying Milashevich's philosophy: the provinces are both real and symbolic. What is a recognizable provincial town is also a state of mind. The spiritual aspect comfortably incorporates the everyday, even elevating it to the status of the "poetry of unpretentious philistine coziness, the warmth of the stove, the summer dust, the spring dirt, the evening foot washing, the tea drinking in the garden under the small apple tree."[11]

The almost exaggerated positing of a quiet provincial existence as a philosophical stance conflicts with the traditional Russian literary representation of the provincial town. The towns of Nechaisk and Stolbenets, depicted in the novel, have their origins, as do most provincial towns in Russian literature, in the dreadful provincial backwater that is Gogol's town of N. The infusion of the idyllic element alludes to another tradition—the Rousseauistic representation of the provinces as an uncontaminated realm, the stronghold of morality and national tradition. This view implies spatial and temporal distancing: the provinces are situated far from the center and in the past, in an inevitably idealized place and time.

One of the "truisms" of the contemporary discourse of the provinces credits their slow rhythm of life with keeping the national tradition intact: "The provinces are often perceived as a kind of foundation, a conservative structure, the bulwark of traditionalism"; "the contemporary provinces represent a composite community, with a common integrity, determinacy, and stability of boundaries."[12] Also familiar is the list of dichotomies characterizing the provinces–capital opposition, including nature/culture, static/dynamic, structured/chaotic, passive/active. At times of political and ideological shifts, these elements are reconsidered alongside the main issues of the day, and reevaluated accordingly. Kharitonov's novel, written in the 1980s, summarizes the experience of the Soviet intelligentsia, for whom the escape into the private sphere became a worthy alternative to political opposition. "In the 1970s," Svetlana Boym writes, "after the Soviet tanks had driven into Prague, the intelligentsia retreated into the private domain and reexamined its own 'kitchen communities' of the 1960s."[13] O. V. Konfederat discusses a number of periods throughout the course of the twentieth century during which intellectuals leaned toward "provincial forms" of art, "intentionally reducing the pathos of Art to the level of the daily grind," turning to "the native, ancestral, Orthodox-religious roots of existence" as a source of "alternative identification," in reaction to the official orientation toward Western models of politics, ideology, and culture. During the 1930s, 1960s, and the late 1990s, works of art exhibited the tendency toward "rehabilitating the sphere of [private] existence as a cultural value, and a tangible form of cultural existence." Typically, the characters of these times stroll along the "'provincially' sleepy streets of small towns, the roads of the Russian heartland," and they inhabit and celebrate "the quiet world" of the everyday.[14]

The heightened awareness of the importance of the private sphere as a form of opposition to official ideology is typical of the last decades of Soviet rule: "The peculiarity of the Soviet cultural space consisted in the total division into the public and the personal. The borders of the empire ran externally [relative to] the person, between the person and the system.... What proves emblematic of this cultural practice is not the oratorical podium, but the kitchen table and the campfire, around which everyone is equal and significant."[15] Boym defines "the private" by means of the same imagery: "The private in the post-Stalinist decades, while not delimited by personal or property rights, is reconstituted... by means of poetic escapes, obsessive scribbling, and a few unofficial guitar songs shared with friends in the crowded kitchen."[16]

Kharitonov traces the line between the state and the individual in the same space: his provinces–capital dichotomy is synonymous with the opposition between the individual and the state. His characters experience the traumas of history—the state sphere—through the destabilization of their private sphere. The value they put on distance and protection from the demands on life imposed by official ideology—on one's right to a quiet cup of tea with raspberry jam—becomes symbolic of the forms of social protest characterizing the last two decades of the Soviet period, during which the intelligentsia retreated into private spaces. Kharitonov's characters escape ideology by means of spatial and temporal retreat: Milashevich returns from St. Petersburg to his native provincial town, creates (or imagines) the quiet domestic idyll, and justifies it in his disjointed notes on candy wrappers. Lizavin, a fellow provincial, "travels through time" to enter into dialogue with Milashevich, appropriates Milashevich's views as his own and, in his turn, attempts to live according to his provincial philosophy.

Milashevich's philosophy consists of multiple and interconnected layers: it posits the individual's right to a private world and possesses wider existential appeal as a tribute to ordinary life, a stance transforming "everyday life into Being" (*byt* into *bytie*).[17] It can be read as a utopian philosophy, as brittle and fated to self-destruct as its more famous kin, the Communist utopia.[18] Milashevich, as is revealed, fails in the practical application of his philosophy—that is, in his attempt to assert the individual's right to a private existence, by creating a hermetically sealed private idyll around a beloved wife. It turns out the idyll never existed, except in Milashevich's mind: the two were separated during the revolutionary years, after which an illness left her virtually comatose for years. Her suspended state of being neither dead nor truly alive is symbolic of the contradiction inherent in Milashevich's attempt to capture an ordinary moment and elevate it to an object of philosophical contemplation. Moreover, Milashevich's own awareness of his undertaking causes its failure: "Here is where the contradiction lies: happy tranquility doesn't let you sense anything, pain reminds you of feeling."[19]

Milashevich's story ends with his going mad. His philosophy of the ordinary turned out to be a dream and the survival technique of one extraordinary man: "The sick woman lay behind the partition, in the musty air of the cramped dwelling, while he surrounded her with something resembling the flowery paradise, jotting down words on the backs of the *fantiki*, where on the front, a fair-haired beautiful woman embroidered, watered flowerbeds, poured tea from a decorated teapot, the feminine symbol of the Stolbenets or Nechaisk coat of arms. Now one can see behind all this a mad, doomed attempt to save, to protect his beloved from a universal human fate; till the very end he refused to recognize not defeat, but a collapse, and maybe not only because of pride he insisted that he was happy, that he experienced happiness in all its unbearable fullness."[20] Lizavin's experience also foregrounds the fatal paradox of Milashevich's philosophy: people who are capable of reflecting on the allure of the ordinary cannot be satisfied with it. While attempting to live out his mentor's ideas, Lizavin slips into a truly philistine existence, a life on a couch with a science fiction novel, into which he escapes. To a great extent this is a pronouncement on the Soviet intelligentsia of the 1970s and 1980s: its escape into the private space of kitchen tables and campfires had been a technique of survival, an attempt to imagine their escape into the private as an active social position. Lizavin is well aware of the significant leap from escaping ideology to opposing it: "if he had to be perfectly honest, he somehow wasn't drawn in that direction—into a world of political passions and intrigues, part struggles, epochal flourishes, programs, sacrifices, wars, and shocks. He is of our blood, is Anton Antonovich, the peaceful blood of the provincial... Are we really so eager and impatient to venture forth under the cold skies into the tragic arena of history? In the sincerest depths of our being, don't we prefer material that is more in proportion?—that is, is it really true that the provinces have no power at all over our souls?"[21] The provinces are thus truly a state of mind: it has little to do with the geographical remoteness from the capital, and everything to do with the human need for shelter from the "cold skies of history."

At the end of *Lines of Fate* the news of the suicide of another enigmatic character, a civil rights activist, shakes Lizavin out of his semi-comatose existence. This socially engaged hero, a common heroic type in Russian literature, is a direct refutation of Milashevich's philosophy of "happiness independent of life's outer structure." His story and suicide offer no decisive alternative, but they force Lizavin to face the fact that the escapist pathos of tea with raspberry jam cannot satisfy a person of conscience and intelligence. He reenters the world in which one must create for oneself both life and its meaning. The novel concludes on a cautiously hopeful note: "There is still hope. There is hope while someone tries to revive it. And there is no one except you to do it. There is no meaning besides that which you yourself can create. We're doomed to hope; we have to live in such a way as if it depends on us to start from the beginning."[22]

Kharitonov's *Lines of Fate* reflects on the relationship between the individual and the state, between man and history, and in many ways it summarizes the experience of the Soviet intelligentsia. Had it gone to press upon its completion in the mid-1980s, it would have been thus perceived: as an early perestroika text about Russian history, addressing the traditional questions of social engagement and moral responsibility. Having been published in 1992, however, with Soviet ideology no longer in the role of the great adversary, it was received within a radically different (non-)ideological context. Natalia Ivanova observes that, "To take a look at the domestic literature of the nineties, its distinguishing feature would be the liberation from ideology.... The romantic period of conflating literature and ideology, of saturating literature with ideological problems and idea-driven values is over.... Only now, in retrospect, the first Booker jury's *provocation* in awarding the prize to Mark Kharitonov's novel, *Lines of Fate*, or Milashevich's *Trunk*, being far from ideological, is becoming more fathomable and explicable."[23]

I would add to Ivanova's conclusion that Kharitonov's novel was awarded the Booker because it was also interpreted within the context of a different, more recent ideological discourse—that concerning the quest for a national idea. Though unable to sustain its creator, Milashevich's provincial philosophy substantiates the significance of the provinces in the discourse of nationalism. From this perspective, Milashevich's provincial philosophy both embodies and comments on the fundamentals comprising the contemporary cultural myth of the provinces. Provincial Russia stands in contrast to the westernized, degenerate centers as the habitat of purity and nature and the stronghold of national tradition. All of these features of the provincial myth are reflected in recent works of literature, film, and the popular media. Taken as a whole, they reflect the atmosphere of nostalgia characterizing post-Soviet culture. The provinces, too, have become an object of nostalgia in that they represent a "longing for the slower rhythms of the past, for continuity, social cohesion, and tradition."[24] Milashevich reflects on the tendency of the provinces to overcompensate for their peripherality by taking the ideas they receive from the center to a fantastic extreme, turning the fantasy into reality and, more importantly, by giving that reality back to the world as a force capable of real change:

> [The] provincial soul is nourishing for utopia—Milashevich already knew that. We produce dreamers who come with eyes irritated to the point of redness, with pupils fixed in the distance; it's our visions that roam over the country and the world, like troubled dreams. Others aren't in the mood for that; they are always busy with matters at hand.... But the main thing is that we, as distinct from others, don't stop at powerless visions, but rush to incarnate them without delay. And if people say to us that to do that we need to change human nature itself—well, so what—someone in our midst is even ready to think of that. New people will appear earlier among us—one has to look around more attentively.... We, we have the shoots of all of future civilization breaking through the eggshell.[25]

One cannot help but notice the echo in Milashevich's musings of the "Russia-as-savior" discourse. Best articulated in Dostoevsky's *Pushkin Speech*, but familiar long before, the image of Russia as an outsider who will save the world, and the accompanying transformation—through the logic of ressentiment—of backwardness into advantage surfaces with particular insistence during periods of revolutionary transformation. It is highly relevant to the present-day rhetoric of patriotism. In

Lines of Fate, as in a number of contemporary works, the Russia versus the provinces opposition replaces that of Russia versus the West but follows the same logic: Russia, rather than Europe, is in need of the savior, and this role is assigned to the provinces. In this cultural context it is easy to see how a novel that explores Russian history through the prism of the provincial topos might have appealed to the participants in the discourse concerning Russia's national identity and its position in relation to the West.

Lines of Fate is both a precursor to this discourse and an independent exploration of its central issues. Read against the background of the recent transformations of the provincial topos, the novel provides a mutually illuminating approach to both: it introduces, explores, and essentially deconstructs all issues central to the recent privileging of the provinces in Russian cultural discourse. Kharitonov posits the provincial topos as an object of serious reflection, even without directly commenting on the ideological issues that made the provinces so important in the post-Soviet Russian quest for economic independence as well as for a distinct cultural identity and new, noncombative expressions of patriotism. The novel not only carefully develops these topics but also exposes them as at best ideologically charged and at worst tools of self-deception.

It takes a voice from the center—that of a Moscow literary scholar—to provide a historical reading of Milashevich's antihistorical provincial philosophy: "Milashevich took into account," the scholar says approvingly, "that the truth of great minds should not be applied to all humanity." However, this provincial philosophy, which is, "incidentally, the dream and guiding idea of any revolution,"[26] may well serve to gratify the great majority. The post-Soviet celebration of the provinces, in which *Lines of Fate* is an inadvertent participant, is driven by the impulse behind all ideological constructs: to justify changing historical realities by packaging them in forms that appeal to the majority's need for comfort and stability. Just as Milashevich attempts, and fails, to create reality out of its idealized conceptions, the provincial discourse serves as a tool in the creation of a post-Soviet Russian national idea out of those elements of the myth that most appeal to the general public. Healthy as the desire may be to recover and rediscover national tradition, Kharitonov's novel exposes the other function of the provincial discourse—as a self-deceptive survival technique on a national scale.

The stable attributes of the provinces in Russian cultural discourse—remoteness, unhurriedness, backwardness; the lack of sophistication and economic and cultural resources; and the tendency to locate meaning outside itself—are reevaluated in recent sociological discourse concerning Russian national identity. The scholarly discourse of the 2000s abounds in reflections on the subject that could be characterized as an apology for the provinces and summarized as follows: "the provinces do not need an apology." Predictably, most of these materials can be found in collections of articles and conference proceedings published by provincial universities. Scholars from Nizhniy Novgorod, Penza, Ulyanovsk, and Tver sound conspicuously uniform in recognizing the change in provincial (self-)perception. Their rhetoric is both nonacademically poetic and authoritative:

> In short, the provinces invariably end up being more rational and calmer than the capital, and this characteristic is often mistaken for their passivity. Of course, the provinces are not the "hearth" of culture, brimming, like the capital, with fire and cinders [ash], so that it's either blazing, or choking on its own fallout. The provinces distinguish themselves with the purity and composure of a mirror that keeps illuminating and even gives off a little heat. But the point isn't only, or so much, in the intensity of this reflected fire. This fire is the reflection of two celestial bodies, two suns—the indigenously archaic (of the forest) and inherited antiquity (of the capital), as not the most ancient, but the most dominant. The capital absorbs the forest, incinerating it in its furnace. The provinces warm themselves at one fire, at another fire, or at both together, which is why it isn't hot there, but warm, not blinding, but bright.[27]

Kharitonov's novel contains analogous statements that are similarly subjective and emotional, but more appropriately so, as in the following instance: "In the provinces, everyday life [*byt*] becomes existence [*bytie*]. Precisely because they're unstructured and essentially dreadful, it's very possible they engender the hope of a momentary, blinding flash that will transform everything, and light everyone's way."[28] These statements base their pathos on the notion of the provinces as the birthplace of Russia's future, its source of sustenance, and the place where backwardness becomes a guarantee of greatness that will "light the way." Kharitonov makes this pathos an object of reflection and analysis, an element of the cultural myth of the provinces he deconstructs. Contemporary scholars present the reconfiguration of the provincial myth as a *fait accompli* within the broader discourse of Russian nationalism.

Because they emphasize the notion of the provinces as the custodian of the national tradition, their apology for the provinces enters into the discourse of national identity.

Tea Drinking in a House Built on Sand

Sergei Yakovlev's *Letter from Soligalich to Oxford* (1995, in *Novy Mir*) participates in the discourse of the provinces as a method of national self-identification in a style that seems to amalgamate literature and journalism in an emotional statement. Yakovlev operates within the ternary model of the provinces–the capital–the West. By adding the element of the Russian provinces to the traditional binary opposition that pits Russia against the West, he addresses both paradigms: he situates the Russian provinces in the role of the stronghold of national character and Russia in that of a provincial in relation to other European cultures. Yakovlev's novel unequivocally proposes turning away from the West (while utilizing some aspects of the "European experience") and looking for a solution to the nation's problems in its unique national resources. His protagonist finds these resources far from the capitals, and farther still from the European cultural centers, in the ancient provincial town of Soligalich: "Paris and London, not to mention some Copenhagen, are boring provincial towns. The true capital is Chukhloma.[29] Or perhaps Soligalich—where I'm going now?"[30] These lines echo one of Milashevich's *fantiks*: "Paris—is it far from us? Three thousand miles? My God, how provincial [*kakaia provintsiia!*]."[31] In both instances, moreover, the reversal of hierarchies, both provocative and humorous in its defensiveness, signals the narrator's intent to undermine the traditional perceptions of "center" and "backwater."

Having spent two months as a visiting professor in Oxford, the protagonist returns to Moscow in the midst of the economic and ideological crisis of the 1990s. He leaves the capital temporarily and settles in Soligalich, where his aunt has left him a house. There he attempts to rebuild, literally and metaphorically, the house that is Russia: "I didn't need just any old roof over my head in Soligalich; to tell you the truth, I didn't need a roof at all (I couldn't imagine what I'd do with myself in this backwoods of a town—I didn't consider living and working outside the capitals permanently). I needed to construct something sublime, a sort of temple, in order to prove to myself and others that this country still serves a purpose of some sort. And why not here, seeing as that's the straw I've drawn?"[32] Far from accepting everything in England as the ideal, he is nevertheless inspired by European traditionalism, which he perceives as a form of healthy self-respect and respect for the past, which he initially dreams of transplanting to his native Russian soil: "I wanted to introduce all of this (not only [what comes] from England, but basically the best of everything that was etched on my memory by then) into the world of Soligalich, where the Russian fatalism peered out at me from behind every corner."[33] In time, he realizes that the foreign remains alien, and the resources are to be found not in his European experiences but right here, in Russia's own history: "I realized that everything I stumbled upon in Soligalich was also culture: the centuries-old philistine ways, many of which are simply essential for survival in a place like this, and appealing in their own way. I began to suspect that the cowshed or granary distinct to Soligalich, living out its days somehow or other, didn't yield in its youth, for the sake of practicality and beauty, to your stone *barns* with thickly armored oaken doors."[34] Yakovlev consistently employs architectural metaphors that allow him to combine the literal rebuilding and metaphorical reconstruction, on the one hand, with the spatial-temporal dynamic of provincial discourse, on the other. The decrepit house in Soligalich and the well-preserved houses in Oxford, while testifying to the differing economic situations governing their respective locations, also serve as visible and persistent markers of both nations' attitudes toward the past. In his moments of weakness, during which he is haunted by the futility of his endeavors, they too take the same metaphorically architectural turn: "It's just that we Russians are a people who've built our house on sand. And are thus at once impetuous and fearful (one doesn't contradict the other). How can you seriously rely on something when you live with stoves like these for instance? Surely our mystical perception of life, the sense of its impermanence, has to do with this. Why bother to peel old wallpaper off, paint doors and fences, build a convenient, sturdy staircase to the attic, if the rivers will flood, the winds will gust, and a fire will break out anyway? Why dress up and lighten the load of a life that could turn to ash at any second? This habitual and completely justified anticipation of misfortune may be one of the most pivotal of our distinctions from the West, which has built its house on rock."[35]

Nevertheless, the protagonist persists. Restoring the house becomes a symbolic act, an attempt to prove that Russia possesses a rich heritage of its own. This symbolism alone explains the otherwise incongruous remarks on Russia's unique and central position in the European hierarchy expressed in a "letter" detailing the harsh conditions of post-Soviet reality. Russia, he insists, remains the true center, and Europe, at least for the Russians, is the provincial backwater—as dull as it is comfortable: "Western Europe, along with Britain, suddenly appeared before me as a not very big province, where people simply die of boredom."[36] The only true link, and similarity, between England and Russia is their people's fondness, if not reverence, for tea: "Tea... I'd like to dedicate a separate section to it. It may be that everything I'm writing to you will ultimately end up being a lengthy panegyric to tea. After all, one of the foreigners said that tea, in particular, would save the stomachs and brains of the Russians."[37] Among the items the protagonist brings back from Oxford is Twinings tea, bought with the money he had saved by strict economizing. One of the first things he does in the Soligalich house is make tea, properly, by putting the leaves in a warm, dry teapot. Somehow, he fails in this simple endeavor but remains "certain of succeeding in future."[38] In the novel, tea creates an atmosphere of comfort and coziness and designates the home as a private space.

In Kharitonov, tea with raspberry jam serves the same function. Also like Kharitonov's hero, Yakovlev's protagonist fails in creating his provincial idyll: just when he manages to make the house comfortable and, most importantly, in a European style on the inside, the rotted-out roof he neglected to repair caves in, making the house almost uninhabitable. After a futile trip back to Moscow, where he finds no viable future, the now seriously ill protagonist returns to Soligalich, where it appears he expects to die. Already somewhat forced as his story begins, the rhetoric whereby "Russia is the center of the universe" yields toward the end to bitter musings about Russia as "the house built on sand."

Neither Kharitonov nor Yakovlev leaves much room for interpretation, albeit for different reasons. While *Lines of Fate* is a genuine work of literature, Yakovlev's *Letter from Soligalich* is not. Despite its generic characterization as a "novel," it is a journalistic piece—an essay addressing the most pressing matters of its day, which in this case (as always) comprise the questions of Russian national identity and Russia's position vis-à-vis the West. Yakovlev thus directly contributes to the contemporary debate of these issues and, like others, operates with the ternary structure of the provinces–the capital–the West. The fact that his protagonist "writes" from Soligalich might suggest that he places Oxford and Soligalich in an opposition that brackets off Moscow. However, the Russia–West dichotomy has its own stable discourse, in which the Russian capital is firmly embedded. Adding the Russian provinces as a third element allows Yakovlev to bring into focus the point where these major binaries of Russian identity interact: Russia's concern with its provincial, peripheral status in the world.

Never the *Three* Shall Meet

By the 2000s, this ternary structure had become a fixture in Russian cultural discourse. The popular writer Aleksei Ivanov is well aware of this configuration: in a 2006 interview, he suggests precisely this shift in point of view from "Russia versus the West" to "the provinces versus Moscow versus the West":

— In the provinces, no matter what you do, you are still a second-rate person. On the basis of geography.
— Perhaps everything in Russia today is second-rate?
— It all depends on your point of reference. If Paris is first-rate, then Moscow is second, and the provinces third. But if Moscow is first, then the provinces are second.[39]

Bracketing off the West allows the provinces to gain the prestige usually attributed to the capital and makes of Moscow the ultimate and ideal center. Thus, unlike the fixed Russia–West opposition, the relationship between the capital and the provinces seems mutually rewarding, allowing for shifts in hierarchies.

Aleksei Ivanov is a writer whose popularity depends largely on the reader's awareness that like the characters that made his novels famous, he lives in Perm. His first successful novels, the historical epics *Heart of the Uplands* and *The Rebellion's Gold*, are situated in the Ural region, whose history, while part of the history of the Russian empire, is also emphatically localized. The setting, characters, events, and even the language of the novel could be from no other area. Ivanov thereby participates in the newly emerging trend of regionalism, with its view of history as both global and local, though emphasizing the latter. Il'ia Kukulin locates the temporal source of Ivanov's approach to historical events in the late 1990s, at which point the history of Russia, as a comprehensive discourse, was being divided into multiple local stories: "Two processes—the mass recognition of history as catastrophe and the discovery, peculiar to the intelligentsia outside the capitals, of history as a regional event that reflected global patterns (historical 'glocalization')—enabled the shaping of a new view of history in Ivanov's novels."[40]

Ivanov is passionate about his cultural project and its focus on Ural regional identity. He believes that regional identities can and should be acknowledged, developed, and even celebrated, whereby they assimilate into the global culture. In an interview entitled "Russia: A Mode of Existence. Where Do We Look For National Identity And How Do We Live With It?" Ivanov confidently posits the history of Perm and its contemporary culture as valuable components of both Russian and world culture: "Perm has a set of brands that are of global significance. The Permian period, the Perm Animal Style, the Perm wood-carvings. And these ought to be in the spotlight. . . . What with the internet and the open borders, the world has long since become global. And in a global world, what's valued is the unique."[41] In his view, the different regional identities across Russia are equally valid and thus pose no threat to the Russian identity as a whole: they are "like facets of a diamond. The facets can be different, but it's one diamond." Of his own historical novels set in the Urals, he says: "I didn't set out to tackle contemporary issues as such. I tried to write the something that would address regional identity. What the Ural is in particular and the provinces as a whole; what the peculiarities of life are in Ural; how the character of the district, that is the terrain, is linked to the regional mentality. That is what I was writing about. Maybe the novel ended up being topical because these things were represented accurately. I'm not drawing any parallels between the past and the present; they crop up on their own."[42]

Critics have recognized and accepted Ivanov as a Perm writer in the sense that he actively participates in creating and promoting Perm's regional identity: "Naturally, literature in and about Perm existed before Ivanov and continues to exist independently of Ivanov, but it is under his pen that Perm coalesces into a unified image, acquires a mystical (virtual) body and soul, becomes steeped in art history, mythology and legends, and a phenomenon of national proportions."[43] Ivanov is a proud bearer of a particular regional identity; as a non-Moscow writer, however, he also bears the identity of a provincial. In addressing the provincial label, like all provincial authors, he comments on the stigma associated with it: "The provinces really oppress—not because they themselves are so shabby and uninteresting, but because they're trying to do everything like the capital does. Whereas you shouldn't do what the capital does! You're better off just going to the capital, then. If you want to be yourself, then live according to principles that are essential to you." "What do you mean by 'oppress'?" "Driving home their inherent sense of inferiority. In the provinces, no matter what you do, you're still a second-rate person. On the basis of geography."[44] Ivanov proposes celebrating regional identity as a remedy for this "inferiority complex" and a way of supplanting the vague and unflattering term "provincial." Stressing the necessity of rethinking the center-provinces dynamic, he says:

> This kind of reassessment ought to work both ways. The capital should admit that provincial Russia isn't an acutely deteriorated version of Moscow, but rather [a series of] other worlds, where they also happen to speak Russian. And the provinces should determine who they are: what kind of "country" they are, what constitutes their exclusivity. That is, decide on their identity. In a global world, only the unique is valued. When this uniqueness is acknowledged as such by both society and the state, the situation will change as well.[45]

One of the challenges for Ivanov and other authors interested in maintaining their regional specificity is that also faced by the developers of regional and city brands: both must work out a unique story to promote a city that, in the minds of most readers, is far from unique and is, in fact, barely distinguishable from other provincial locales. Ivanov's publicly shared views on the provinces-Moscow opposition only emphasize precisely how commonplace the subject of the provinces has become, and to what extent all provincial places seem interchangeable. The very repetitiveness of Ivanov's replies reveals the fixed set of elements and value hierarchies comprising the familiar center-provinces discourse in which the journalists and the author participate. Ivanov's insistence on the value of the local as a constitutive element of the global is a common means of rehabilitating the provinces and reimagining them as distinct places of importance and vitality.

Ivanov's novels, too, reveal the growing engagement with the cultural myth of the provinces. In *The Geographer Drank Away the Globus* (1995), for instance, the word "provinces" and its derivatives appear only rarely; this early 1990s novel portrays provincial life without overt mention of the provinces-center dynamic (since this discourse had not yet fully developed). Composed at the height of the crisis informing all spheres of Russian life—ideological, economical, and cultural—the novel situates its protagonist at the height of his own multiple personal crises, ultimately permitting their resolution, however tenuous. The novel is a school story, a bildungsroman, and a hymn to the natural wonders of the Perm region. This "pedagogic-adventure-erotic novel about a geographer"[46] tells of a young teacher—a drinking, womanizing, and infantile man—who is unqualified to teach any discipline and less suited still to the moral education of his high school students. Yet Viktor Sluzhkin finds himself on a quest: to remain a good person (because he is, at heart) and teach his students what it means to be "a good person." His symbolic quest includes an actual journey, when he takes his class of seniors on a boating expedition down a wild, Ural river. The river raises their individual moral awareness to a level that should qualify the quest as successful:

> And I remember our entire excursion—all the way from the Perm II railway station to the village of Mezhen'.... We sailed along these rivers—from Semichelovechia to Rassokha—as [though] through the history/destiny/fate of this land/this earth—from the ancient pagan temples to the concentration camps.... And I sensed I was more than just the native son of this land. I am a small, but exact likeness of it. I imitate its significance with all the turns of my own destiny, my love, my soul. I thought I'd arranged this journey out of my love for Masha. But it turned out I'd arranged it simply out of love. And perhaps love is what I wanted to teach the seniors? Although, I hadn't wanted to teach anything. Love of the land, because it's easy to love a holiday resort, whereas a wild flood, snowfalls in May, and river storms downing trees are hard to love. Love of people, because it's easy to love literature, whereas those you meet on either shore of the river are hard to love.... I don't know what happened to me. In any case, I tried as best I could so my seniors would become stronger and kinder, without demeaning themselves, or others.[47]

In *The Geographer*, Ivanov neither juxtaposes Perm with Moscow nor makes pronouncements on the nature of provincial existence or regional identity (or any other notion of identity, for that matter).[48] He traces the hero's path through difficult times and his experience traversing the land of the Urals as he sets out to discover his own inner strength and his individual self through a set of universal values. These values—love for one's land, spiritual strength, and self-respect—are not specifically associated in the novel with Perm or Moscow, the provinces or the capital.

By contrast, in *Center for Supplementary Fornication* (*Bluda i Mudo*,

2007), Ivanov makes explicit statements on the nature of provincial life. The protagonist, the provincial artist Boris Morzhov, who devotes his creative energy to seducing women out of sheer boredom, saves the town's Center for Supplementary Recreation from being shut down. In the process, he philosophizes about the crisis facing the traditional way of life, including such seemingly basic concepts as love and family ties. As one critic summarizes the novel, Ivanov "provides a detailed account of the tragedy that has befallen us over the past 20 years. Obsessed with the spirit of individualism and success, Ivanov's protagonists reject not only the national myth, but affinities in general: with family, friends— of any kind. They try to exist in this world autonomously."[49] The novel also directly addresses the "provinces versus Moscow" dichotomy, the nature of patriotism, and the role of the provinces in determining Russia's identity and future; the word "provinces" and its derivatives are used freely. The critic Lev Danilkin, who has followed Ivanov's work since his first publications, also emphasizes the novel's setting: "Provincial Koviazin brings to mind all provincial towns at once; it is zoned variously, and densely stocked with typical inhabitants—bureaucrats, criminals, traffic cops, teachers, prostitutes, migrant workers and alcoholics."[50] The protagonist reflects on his life as a provincial artist and chooses to resolve his sense of ressentiment by rejecting the superiority of the center and adopting a different set of values: he refuses to measure the value of his town in comparison to Moscow and looks for sources of pride and status not in the past, but in the future:

> In Moscow they regarded Morzhov with respect, though one tinged with sympathy and amazement. My God, they said, people lived in a hellhole like that! Whereas Morzhov didn't consider the city of Koviazin a hellhole. He even took pride in the city of Koviazin. . . . But he took pride not in the . . . Koviazin of the past, but of the future. No, the city's municipal administration wasn't preparing to build a new cosmodrome on the Talka, the president wasn't planning to turn Koviazin into an offshore [tax haven], they hadn't found a diamond deposit under the city fire hall yet, either, and archeologists doubted that Koviazin was the birthplace of humankind, on the basis of which you could've set up the biggest Disneyland in Eurasia. But Morzhov knew in his gut that the city of Koviazin was the future personified. The time would come, and all cities would be like Koviazin, because right now, Koviazin was the first on the planet. That made for remarkable bragging rights.[51]

Morzhov thus situates the sources of Russia's future greatness in his unremarkable provincial town. However, the ironic tongue-in-cheek tone of the passage suggests that the statement on the provincial Koviazin as "the first on the planet" is a nod toward a fashionable topic and included of necessity, as though a provincial setting obligates the author to reflect on the provinces–capital dichotomy. In fact, such reflections are unessential to the plot and even less important to the primary themes of individualism and the disintegration of human ties.

All the more interesting, then, is Ivanov's recent duology, comprising *The Dog-Headed* (*Psoglavtsy*, 2011) and *Community* (*Kom'iuniti*, 2012), whose focus on the provinces–Moscow dichotomy is overt: the first depicts the horrors of life in the Russian heartland through the eyes of Muscovites, whereas the second condemns Moscow as diseased and duplicitous from the perspective of a provincial, who acts as the author's mouthpiece. Setting aside his familiar Ural region and identity as a local studies enthusiast (*kraeved*), Ivanov turns to a different genre, adopts a different narrative voice, and, in the case of *The Dog-Headed*, even assumes a penname. The novels are formulaic in every sense, from their combination of mysticism and sociology to their simplistic divisions of Russia into zones with fixed boundaries, the most forbidding of which is the line between Moscow and the Russian heartland.

In *The Dog-Headed*, three young Muscovites arrive in a central Russian village to remove from the wall of a dilapidated church a valuable fresco of St. Christopher—a man with the head of a dog. Thus the novel incorporates legends about both the saint and the packs of mystical dog-headed beings who kill anyone trying to leave the village limits. Layered over this mystical plane is a portrait of the degraded Russian village as perceived by those who have never truly experienced the world outside of Moscow:

> The first time Kirill saw a Russian village up close he was in school, in the seventh grade. He was just outside of Maloiaroslaviets with a friend, who was visiting his grandmother. And Kirill even liked being in the village. Everybody knows each other, clean little houses with carved lattices, acacias enclosed in picket fences, so the goats don't nibble at them. The men there drove kids around in the back of pickup trucks. The women, even the elderly ones, rode to the store on frameless bicycles. Roosters crowed in the morning. There were strawberries growing in the gardens. They even played

"Potato" and "Moscow Umbrella"—by lifting up the girls' skirts. They swam in a stream they called The Puddle.

Kalitino was similar, but not the same at all. As though it were cursed. Kirill walked along the squishy road toward the intersection with the well. Tree branches with their wilted foliage hung over the fences. The slate roofs, checkered with patching, shone dully. The blue glow of television sets danced in the windows. The tall, wooden telegraph poles jutted out as though they'd been driven into the ground hastily, like a spear into a hunted animal, without any kind of telegraphic altruism. The sidewalks were long since overgrown with shaggy grass, and Kirill walked along the road. It was dark, smoky and hot all around. Kirill loved summer nights, but it turned out he loved the southern darkness—starry and deep. Whereas this darkness was oppressive, impenetrable, dangerous. You couldn't see through it, which is why the entire village seemed like a stage set.[52]

The village of Kalitino is indeed a stage set, a background that allows the outsiders' imaginations and phobias to run wild. Kirill feels apprehensive and endlessly analyzes the source of his fears: "So, the problem isn't the objective demise of the village of Kalitino. The problem is degradation. What is degradation? Catastrophic oversimplification."[53] The simplicity usually associated with the positive notion of "the simple life" becomes synonymous here with degradation and otherness. As Ivanova notes: "It's not at all the simplicity that so delighted the Russian intellectuals, from the Slavophiles to the Village Prose writers of the twentieth-century."[54] The cultural paradigm shaping Kirill's perspective of the village and its inhabitants differs immensely from what inspired the multitude of intellectuals from the center to look to the Russian village for the mystical origins of the Russian national spirit. Yet, it is based on the same premise of otherness, of fundamental differences between the educated elite and "the people"; it merely switches positive values to negative and turns veneration into fear. Thus: "Kirill realized he was afraid of this village, just like a clever, trained setter, living in a lord's mansion, is afraid of the viper in the roadside puddle. And all of his boogeymen were just the objectification of his fear."[55]

An internet forum that for Kirill is a much more familiar form of social organization than Kalitino offers further explanation and advice on how to maintain the distance between Moscow and the people of the village:

>   MISSIA: The demise of the Russian village—that's Belov, Rasputin, Astaf'iev.
>   DISKOBOL: I agree completely.
>   VALERV1985: My point too, ladies and gents. The world of the Russian village is no more. What still exists has deteriorated. And my experience tells me, the culture of these residual communities isn't the culture of village communes, but the culture of the tribes. They must be studied not according to Propp, but according to Lévi-Strauss.[56]

Thus, "the village" should be regarded as alien to the rest of the country—as an exotic tribal community, barely civilized and ruled by its own savage laws. The anthropological (Lévi-Strauss) approach to mythology is immediately explored: "We've known for ages that the best horror novels are created from mass phobias. Europe was afraid of the legacy of its Middle Ages, and the gothic novel was born with Dracula. The America of megalopolises is afraid of little towns, where God only knows what goes on, and Stephen King becomes king. The Russian provinces are afraid of deranged Moscow, and the ravings of the provincials generate the vampirish Moscow of *Night Watch*."[57] This comment on the cultural mythology that produces fear and imagined monsters applies equally to both of Ivanov's novels. Endlessly analyzed and mythologized by post-Soviet politicians and intellectuals, the great divide between Moscow and the rest of the country results in the Muscovite Kirill's mortal fear of "the unknown" beyond the capital. By the same token, *Community* depicts the "deranged Moscow" and thus the flip side of this myth. In the words of one reviewer, "If *The Dogheaded* exploited the big-city slickers' deep-seated fear of the provinces, then the current, second book of the duology is entirely and exaggeratedly 'Moscow-based.' Chthonian evil here crawls out of the very core of 'the heart of my Motherland.'"[58]

The protagonist Gleb Tiazhenko, the provincial who made it in Moscow, is as biased against the capital as Kirill is against the village. Gleb's Moscow, the city of foreign brands, forced conviviality, and rampant consumerism is as much of a cultural construct as the village of Kalitino. Instead of the dog-headed monsters, Moscow is besieged by an epidemic that originates in the virtual world of an internet community but breaks out into the physical world. This transparent metaphor for the plague establishes Moscow as "a feast in time of plague" and highlights the theme of blurred lines—between the real and the virtual, the authentic and the simulated.

In moving to Moscow from the small northern town of Apatity, Gleb does not just look for a better job and income, he makes a philosophical and existential choice. He consciously integrates himself into the consumer society and enjoys its artifice: "In Russia you've got two dirty puddles in place of Moscow and Petersburg, a few stars as the regional cities, a selvage for the Black Sea shoreline, and the Transsiberian ice ridge. That's it. And all around—enormous spaces that are unlit, and unpopulated. Only the lit zones are inhabitable. They won't inundate you here with gloomy truths you've known for ages anyway. They won't ruin your mood here. It's a consumer society. The real world is driven out of these zones. As it is, there's no escaping it anywhere—you need at least somewhere to catch your breath."[59] Gleb likes the shallow and glittery Moscow life for the respite it provides from the problems of the real world, which he imagines as the provinces. It is rather surprising, therefore, that the very artifice that attracted Gleb in the first place becomes his source of irritation with Moscow as the novel progresses: "I've worked my ass off, torn myself to pieces—all for the sake of living here. I fucking won! I'm here!" Gleb lowered the little window and tossed out his butt. "Everything's better here: I agree with that, otherwise I wouldn't have hauled ass to get here! I consume this very best! But fu-u-uck . . . I don't want the best to be like this!"[60]

The plot of the novel revolves not around fighting the plague, but around Gleb fighting his own private disease, his infatuation with the place from which he expected far too much: "All in all, Moscow's an existential city,—Gleb thought, turning off of Michurinsky Prospect onto Lobachevsky Street.—In and of itself, it's an impossibility: Russia's enormous, yet, as we know, there's nowhere to retreat to. If you live way out in Shitsville and *apatity has worn you down*, you've still got the hope of breaking away to Moscow, where everything will work out. But if it hasn't worked out for you in Moscow either, then there's no hope left, and your life is over."[61] As soon as he comprehends his fundamental misestimation, leaving him nowhere else to go, Gleb passively accepts death.

The vision of a Russia divided into disparate zones, among which those situated beyond the center are invisible and therefore unknowable, shares the public sphere with the opposing view of the provinces as a sacral place, a convergence point of different layers of existence. Where Gleb of *Community* sees a dark void, and Kirill of *The Dog-Headed*—a home of hostile forces, others see a more ambiguously defined mystical place. Thus the philosopher Stanislav Gurin suggests the provinces are linked to the sacral worlds of a past mystical knowledge inaccessible to the capital: "The provinces express the immanent presence of the sacred in the world, divine incarnation.... The provinces hold treasures (material and spiritual), preserve eternal values, and impart indisputable meanings.... The provinces safekeep deep-seated memory, the memory of beginnings, of values, of meanings."[62]

The Perm author Natalia Zemskova incorporates and cites Gurin's ideas and a number of other recent writings on the "provinces versus the capital" dichotomy in *The City on the Styx* (2013). Zemskova's novel addresses all the familiar issues: the regionalism trend, the provinces-as-savior theme, and the collapse of the formerly independent dichotomies into the ternary structure of Moscow–the provinces–the West. The work is subtitled "an art mystery about the provincial intelligentsia," and true to the eclecticism thus announced, it comprises a genre mix, combining elements of women's fiction, urban folklore, detective fiction, and mystery novels. The theme of "the provinces as the soul of Russia" is manifest in a great number of statements; in order to incorporate them into a story intended for mass readership, the narrator-protagonist adds a layer of mysticism into the mix, weaving the power and potential of the provinces into a story about the mysterious murders of the City's best artists.

The female protagonist from St. Petersburg arrives in the City (understood as Perm). Gripped by a mysterious power it wields over her, she extends her stay. Ultimately she leaves the City—not to return to the center, but to marry a Russian businessman who resides in Germany. A group of artists who call themselves the "White Knights" are five geniuses who were born in the City and, despite the pull of the world capitals, decided to stay and make their names there. A dancer, a theater director, a musician, a painter, and an illusionist, they die one by one, under seemingly mundane circumstances, as soon as they decide to leave the City for the major centers of culture (some of them foreign locations). The narrator concludes that the White Knights are victims of the City's powerful and vengeful matrix. The subterranean River Styx emerges there, at a certain "symbolic place, marking the invisible boundary between life and death, between our world and the next, and this contiguity of worlds can exist only at this symbolic place. Only not in the capital, but in the provinces."[63] Having tapped into the powerful and mysterious source as City-boys, the genius artists ultimately fall victim to its wrath because "the knights were more valuable to the City as myths than flesh and blood."[64]

In *City on the Styx*, the philosophy of the provinces as a sacral place serves the modest purpose of adding intrigue, and a veneer of intellectuality, to the rather simple plot. The heroine's reflections on these themes—"the provinces, the center, the 'genii loci' and the victim of villainy, abolishing the 'rule of Moscow'"[65]—come across as borrowed from scholarly and journalist articles, which means the provincial topos is a recognizable topic, worthy of popular and "serious" literature alike. Not surprisingly, the novel was awarded first prize in the regional "We Are the City" competition, sponsored by the Perm municipal administration; moreover, its publication was supported by a grant from the Ministry of Culture, Youth Policy, and Mass Communication of Perm Krai. Thus, the Perm administration has supported the novel that contributes to the Perm brand, as the "territory of culture." In addition to works by other Perm authors, most notably Aleksei Ivanov, Zemskova's novel presents Perm as a text, a city that is local in detail and global in spirit.

Kharitonov's and Yakovlev's novels are dense, thought-provoking reflections on Russian history; in contrast, these recent novels are intended for mass readership. Their incorporation of the provincial myth and the center–provinces divide serves as a reminder that the subjects have long since entered the mainstream. Their authors are as comfortable citing scholarly works on the provinces, Lévi-Strauss's anthropological theories, and village-prose writers as they are referring to the popular writers Sergei Lukianenko and Stephen King. The cultural myth of the provinces, having been belabored in multiple discourses, has lost its complexity; in exchange, it has gained recognition as a hyperlink to the themes of Russia's national idea and symbolic geography.

Zakhar Prilepin develops this congruence of the provincial topos and the national idea in his writings and as a public persona. He too is a well-known provincial author who, like Ivanov, accepts the "provincial" label, preferring to live in his native Nizhniy Novgorod, with the occasional trip to Moscow, which serves as "a kind of office." Having been nominated for, and awarded, an impressive number of literary prizes, Prilepin has been named, and even nominates himself, Russia's most promising young writer. He is very vocal about his conservative, nationalist political views in the press and social media, but he also considers himself a truer European than any of his liberal critics: "All told, I'm a consummate provincial. Along with that, I figure I'm a greater European, democrat and liberal, than all of those people who claim they are. . . . In essence, Russia is the provinces. It's just that one part of the provinces regularly perceives itself as such, whereas the other puts on airs and pretends it is Europe."[66]

Prilepin is very clear about belonging to those who are conscious of, and cherish, their provinciality. In his "Letter from The Provinces to the Best People," addressing Moscow's liberal intellectual circles, he posits his provincial status as essential to his identity as a true Russian and, paradoxically, a true European. Rather than elaborate on this point, Prilepin merely emphasizes the breadth of his foreign travels and popularity across borders and varied political camps. "Ultimately," he concludes, "I'm a Russian, which will never happen to you."[67] As understood from Prilepin's journalistic work, being a true Russian and a patriot is contingent on being a provincial.

One would expect Prilepin's literary works to comprise the same unapologetic, right-wing nationalist rhetoric and anti-Moscow/pro-provinces stance. Though generally set in the provinces and the village, however, Prilepin's novels betray no particular interest in maintaining any clear-cut boundaries between the country's "zones." Rather, in Prilepin, the village, the provinces, and Moscow are all diseased, each in its own way. Perhaps this is a testament to his talent and literary intuition: handling the provincial myth is easy in interviews and provocative essays, but it does not readily lend itself to realistic representation.

As his literary precursors, Prilepin lists the Village Prose Writers of the 1970s and 1980s, who mythologized the Russian village as the Russian Golden Age. In the important short essay "I Came from Russia" (2003), he writes: "Every Russian writer is at least a little bit of a village [prose] writer, if he's Russian. The whole of Russia is a village, and the slightest scattering of provincial cities, and the solitary St. Petersburg. And Moscow, populated with non-Russians. And then more villages. How can you not become a village writer here, if more people in Russia [still] live in [those eternal Russian] huts than in three European countries."[68] Yet the poetic view of the village, even with melancholic overtones, is nowhere to be found in Prilepin's literary works. Sankya, the hero of the eponymous 2006 novel, arguably Prilepin's best, does not feel at home anywhere: he is depressed in the dying village; angered by the provincial city's combination of deterioration and luxury, MacDonalds, and the city officials' foreign cars; and unimpressed with a Moscow that is wholly alien to both the village and the provinces. The young man, like many others around him, needs an "idea" worth living for, and his quest leads him to a party that organizes youth for protests and violence, without offering any positive program.

Sankya regularly travels between the village where his grandparents live, the provincial city where he lives with his mother, and the party headquarters in Moscow, which is home to his new family of brothers-in-arms. The village is the site of death, where Sankya's grandparents lost their three sons, including Sankya's father, to drink. The grandfather is on his deathbed, and the grandmother cannot find solace in her grandson or see in him the continuation of his father. Sankya doesn't blame her for her detachment; he, too, feels no true connection to his grandparents, or his childhood home: "Sasha did not experience any revitalization from returning to the place where he had grown up. For a long time it was difficult for him to feel any kind of joy upon returning to the village—the very sight of it was bleak and sickening."[69] A native of the village, he sees its degradation much as Ivanov's Kirill does: "The village was disappearing, dying out—one could feel it in everything. Like a pockmarked, hardened, dark ice floe, it had separated from the shore and was drifting away quietly."[70] Sankya's hatred for the provincial city runs so deep that he refuses to bury his father there: "They could not bury father in this repulsive town, a place that Sasha always loathed."[71] Finally, Moscow is empty, artificial, and easily intimidated: "The city turned out to be weak, toy-like—breaking it open was as meaningless as breaking open a toy: there was nothing inside, only a plastic emptiness."[72]

The party headquarters, the bunker, belongs to neither of these locales and is the only place where Sankya feels good: "The bunker was always rowdy and fun, like a boarding school for young delinquents, a mad artist's studio, and the military headquarters of barbarians who decided to go to war God knows where."[73] Yet, for all the comradery, the bunker is not a home, but a temporary refuge—a place to plot the course for Sankya's true destination: the Russia he is unable to describe, situated "God knows where." Sankya feels as though his country has been taken from him, and he is "trying to bring her back."[74] Neither he nor the reader have a sense of where or what this Russia is. Rather, Sankya conceives of this lost Russia as an ideal place, situated either in the past or in the future, but inaccessible to the disenfranchised post-Soviet youth. M. V. Selemeneva summarizes Sankya's, indeed his generation's, sense of homelessness: "Not having cut out a place for himself either in the village, his provincial home town, or the capital, Sasha Tishin finds himself in the same global space as Russia . . . In Prilepin there is no future in either the waning village, the sleepy provinces, or 'plastic' Moscow; there is only a future in Russia, which the 'party member' tries to retrieve at the risk of his life. The idealism behind the current privileging of space testifies to the fact that the 'hero of our time' in twenty-first-century literature finds himself in search of new geocultural coordinates."[75]

These new geocultural coordinates, however, can only be found on the old map—that is, within the Russian geography comprising the capital, the provinces/village, and the West. Russian culture has not introduced any new coordinates to define its symbolic geography. Prilepin's angry young men do not realize it, but the author as essayist does; he allows himself to dream of rearranging this map to accommodate his ideal Russia, with no division into center and periphery and with a rotating capital: "today it's on the Volga, tomorrow on the Yenisey, the day after that on the Don, the Ob', the Dnieper."[76] At the very least, he dreams of parity, within and across the nation: "I'd like Russia to have forty thousand centers for development, each with the right to vote and the right to life. I dream of a time when an artist paints on Sakhalin Island and in so doing is known throughout the country, when musicians don't pull up stakes in Ekaterinburg and head for the capital chasing success, and when the inhabitants of Perm and Salekhard have just as much money as Muscovites."[77]

Prilepin reserved this dream of doing away with boundaries and binaries for one of his short, witty essays. To work these scenarios into literary plots, Prilepin the realist would have to become a different kind of writer.

The Logical Conclusion: The Monsters of "Mozharovo"

Dmitri Bykov is indeed a different kind of writer and no stranger to fantastic plots. Bykov is Prilepin's polar opposite, from his hometown (Moscow), to his liberal politics, to his view of the provinces. A journalist, writer, literary scholar and school teacher, he was awarded the "Big Book" and "National Bestseller" prizes for his biography of Boris Pasternak, and he also received numerous literary prizes for his novels. Like Prilepin, Bykov is very vocal about his political and ideological stance on all the pressing topical issues, including the provinces. Bykov's skepticism about the provincial myth and its manipulation confirms that he is well aware that the provinces have become a feature of the nationalist discourse. "Frankly, I'm not a supporter of this apology for the provinces," he states, and he goes on to denounce all of the clichés that typically accompany such an apology: "In the provinces there's less love for the motherland, less patriotism, much less source-like purity. I regard the Russian provinces unenthusiastically because . . . We had a 'cult of provincialism' for the longest time; they said, 'Genuine source-like purity, roots, Turgenevian women exist only there.' Of course, the contemporary capital is much more spiritual, much less concerned with the prosaic problems of survival. That's how things worked out. I'm not saying it's good. But the provinces are awfully resentful. They've got a great many pent-up complexes: 'We're the poorest, that's why we're the best.'"[78]

Bykov's short story "Mozharovo" (2007) could be the literary counterpart of this publicly stated opinion. It is a part of a cycle of short stories, all of which take place on a train, written for the railway on-board magazine "*Sakvoiazh-SV*." "Mozharovo" features the journalist Vasiliev, on assignment and traveling on a train carrying humanitarian assistance through the dangerous zones between Moscow and the Urals, in the aftermath of a national project that has taken the capital–provinces divide to the extreme. The country now comprises seven enormous cities, while the vast Russian lands beyond and between them have become the land of the truly unknown. The project made "the seven megalopolises priority development zones, leaving pretty much wild, untended countryside between them, we don't need all that land. Everyone who could made their way into the cities, as for what happened to those left behind in the vast expanses of Russia, Vasiliev had only the vaguest of ideas."[79] Now that the provinces have deteriorated into "gray uninhabited little villages" and the dilapidated remains of factories, the new "national project for the support for the Russian provinces"[80] is in place.

The premise of the short story is clear: it is both a parody and a cautionary tale. The object of the parody is the view of the Russian provinces as distinctly different from the capital—as the land of origins, of the "genuine source-like purity, roots, and Turgenevian women" Bykov mentions in the interview. His protagonist sees the provinces according to the same premise, as "nature reserves and wildlife" inhabited by old women with "kind haggard faces."[81] Bitov also parodies the typical Muscovite, "self-distancing" from the provincials, mostly out of distrust and condescension, but sometimes from outright fear and hostility. The cautionary element of the story is that fears are justified: the inhabitants of Mozharovo, as a result of their complete isolation in the "reserve," have become bloodthirsty monsters. These monsters take on human form to deceive the passengers on the passing trains, though they appear, and appeal, differently to everyone. To Vasiliev they resemble images from children's songs and Christmas cards, guaranteed to inspire compassion and encourage him to open the window in his compartment. The well-trained agents of the Ministry of Agriculture accompanying Vasiliev manage to prevent him from doing it, but in another carriage the siren call is effective, and this is what results: "Half of the windows had been smashed out, the doors to the compartments broken off, the walls crumpled, as if some relentless, terribly strong giant had been scampering around, getting his fill. The roof of the carriage bent slightly up, as if it had been inflated from the inside. The surviving panes of glass were covered in blood, scraps of clothing were scattered all over the corridor, and you could see a gnawed shinbone in the nearest compartment. There was a strange smell in the carriage, tinged with the disgusting smell of blood—putrid, ancient, like the smell in an empty hut where the greasy rugs have long since been rotting, and the mice are running the show."[82] Like Ivanov's dog-headed monsters, these provincials differ not only from ordinary humans. They also differ from what the visitor from the capital, passing through on the train, or stopping off for a few days, expects to see: that is, the simple people of the provincial cultural myth, who are attached to the traditional way of life and have preserved the Russian national spirit. Once the provincial has been designated as the Other, and imagined solely in contrast to the inhabitants of the capital, the process of "othering" spins out of control, until the Other becomes as different, and frightening, as the aliens in the most gruesome of science fiction horror films.

Like Ivanov in *The Dog-Headed* and *Community*, Bykov does not attempt to demonize either the provincials or the people of the capital; rather, both authors comment on the mechanics of "othering," taking the provincial myth to an extreme but logical conclusion. In relying on the images of Others, nationalist rhetoric promotes an essentialist approach to differences, widens the cultural divides, and generates multiple "monsters." The "us versus them" split functions similarly in all cases, positing the differences as fundamental and dangerous; by means of the same logic, the journalist Maxim Shevchenko, quoted earlier, asserts that Europeans belong not to the same species as the Russian people, but rather to "differing humanoid species, outwardly similar, but fundamentally different on the inside."[83]

The texts I have presented approach the provincial myth as crucial to reflecting on Russian identity but do not align their visions with either the demonization or idealization of the provinces. Rather, they proffer both extremes as objects of analysis and contemplation. They do not depict the Russian provinces as the reader might experience them in everyday life; Kharitonov's Nechaisk, Yakovlev's Soligalich, Ivanov's Kalitino, Prilepin's nameless village, Bykov's Mozharovo, and everyone's Moscow are merely coordinates on a symbolic map, drawn in the hope of accommodating the whole of Russia. Russian identity, however, remains undetermined because its parts do not merge into a meaningful whole. This vision is much less optimistic than the one offered by the provincial journalists, politicians, and businessmen who herald the provinces as the reservoir of national tradition and strength. These writers of different generations and political views are skeptical about the hermetic national model's potential to bring forth a positive definition of a Russian identity. They present the country's capital and its heartland as distinct zones with unbridgeable boundaries; moreover, both the capital and the provinces can be defined only apophatically, in relation and contrast to one another. Like Prilepin's hero's ideal Russia, the Russian national idea is lost amidst the multiple visions of what it is not.

3

Film and TV
"My Country—My Moscow!"

> My country—my Moscow,
> You are the most beloved!
> V. Lebedev-Kumach, 1937

Because TV and cinema rely on governmental financial support as much as on popular approbation, they provide a major arena for constructing and reflecting upon national cultural discourses. Films set in the provinces and the more numerous films and TV serials featuring provincials attempting "to make it" in Moscow reveal the current hierarchical shift in the meaning of the noncapital space. Arthouse cinema reflects on the moral crisis of Russian life—the breakdown of family ties, human loneliness, and the inability to adjust to the new post-Soviet reality. Meanwhile, mainstream cinema and TV appeal to the myth of the provinces as the locale of authenticity, moral values, and tradition. In both cases, Moscow's role is limited to that of the provinces' counterpart in the long-established binary opposition.

Film and media scholars have produced an impressive range of studies of contemporary Russian cinema from a variety of viewpoints. Nancy Condee explores the problems of empire and nationhood in her analysis of works by Russia's leading contemporary filmmakers.[1]

David MacFadyen, Stephen Hutchings, Yana Hashamova, Natalia Rulyova, and Birgit Beumers explore the role of official ideology and control in the rewriting and reconstruction of Russian history and Russian identity, both in post-Soviet film and TV programming.[2] Beumers also examines the role of the TV serial in reconciling audiences with the realities of the post-Soviet situation, by promoting stability and the apparent continuity of life.[3] In addition, a number of recent studies trace the turbulent history of the industry, its financial and ideological problems, and its artistic failings and achievements.[4] Dominant myths of Russian culture (and especially the nationalist discourse) comprise the focus of many of these inquiries.

The Russian film industry is concentrated in the capital; hence, it represents the center in both the geographical and the ideological sense. In other words, cultural production by these means belongs to the cultural elites, who make use of the provincial myth in the process of reformulating the major binaries of Russian culture. Two developments shaping this cultural production are the recent surge of *ressentiment* toward the West and the demand for a positive image of Russia. The bleak realism of art-house films depict the provinces as the "true" Russia, thereby providing an ideological counterpoint to the officially sanctioned positive image of commercial cinema. The radically differing portrayals of the provinces in these cinematic texts suggest that the provinces become a symbolic locale for alternative political and artistic discourses about contemporary Russia and its identity. The following films, despite their alignment with different cultural discourses, work within the same imaginative space of the cultural myth of the Russian provinces. Within this space, two distinct but tightly contiguous traditions of provincial representation, as the Gogolian distorting-mirror-like reserve of nightmares on the one hand, and the idealized custodian of the Russian national code on the other, often form interesting, if not always aesthetically fruitful, hybrids.

Yuryev Day and the Logic of *Ressentiment*

In Kirill Serebrennikov's *Yuryev Day* (*Iur'ev Den'*, 2008, screenplay by Yuri Arabov), both views of the provinces are represented in their pure form and on an equal footing. An opera singer named Liubov (Ksenia Rappoport) arrives in her native city of Yuryev-Polsky together with her son, Andrei, before her departure for Vienna. She has planned a day trip to show her son around Yuryev, which she herself hasn't visited for many years, before leaving the country, possibly for good. However, during a tour of the decrepit museum at the old monastery, Andrei disappears, and for the duration of the film, having forgotten all about the Viennese Opera, Liubov searches for him, gradually losing hope but refusing to return to Moscow. Little by little she loses the trappings of her identity as a resident of the capital: her foreign car becomes buried under a snowdrift, and she trades in her expensive shoes and clothing for a pair of felt boots and a quilted cotton jacket. She readily accepts a series of surrogates for Andrei: a lay brother at the monastery and then a hooligan who is found dead. When Liubov loses her voice and even her name (after she is addressed as Lusya), her despair appears complete, until she becomes a mother figure to a gang of consumptive young convicts in the prison hospital where she takes a job as a janitor.

The film provides sufficient material for its interpretation, variously, as the "Russian embodiment of surrealism," a "patriotic tragicomedy," a critique of an intelligentsia that has forgotten its roots, and an anthem of Russian spirituality. However, critics agree on one thing: the film both puts forward and undermines all of these interpretations, one by one, by conveying their very premises ironically, or by means of "obvious overkill."[5] Quite possibly, the filmmakers were striving for precisely this effect: their position is consistently ambiguous, making all of the interpretations possible. Indeed, the problem, or perhaps the value, of *Yuryev Day* lies in its development, on equal terms, of incompatible ideas: the film is poised at the junction between opposing views regarding spirituality and the role and responsibility of the intelligentsia in determining Russia's fate.[6]

However, it also depicts the transformation, through pain and suffering, of an opera diva, neglectful mother, and volitional outsider (the Other) into a "mother-protectress" who willingly accepts responsibility for the suffering of *all* of Russia's sons. This being the case, *Yuryev Day* is modeled after the logic of *ressentiment*: be it out of destitution, filth, or pain, its heroine is afforded the opportunity to rise to unprecedented spiritual heights. If this is an ironic and detached deconstruction of the provincial myth, then *Yuryev Day* is a cautionary tale for the authors of this myth—namely, the intelligentsia who are looking to the provinces in search of self-affirmation on both personal and national levels.

Liubov's arrival in Yuryev constitutes a very literary gesture, whereas her elation (unconvincing to the viewer and even her son) over the "date" with her birthplace is the quintessence of the provincial myth. Several strata of literary clichés lie between Liubov and the realistic experience of an actual Russian provincial city; not only does she recall a poem by Blok, but her every utterance could be a quotation from a work of Russian literature. Andrei doesn't make the literary connection, but he understands the mechanism behind the play of cultural clichés: "you need boots for the Russian 'look' [*dlia russkogo* look'*a nado sapogi*]," he says, to which Liubov adds, "and a Solzhenitsyn-style quilted jacket [*i solzhenitsynskii vatnik*]." This glance from the capital at the charm of desolation, while turning a blind eye to the *actual* desolation and exaltation of a city some "200 kilometers from Moscow" (factors that force the heroine to "retrogress 20 years"), exemplifies the obvious clichés of the imperial gaze at the periphery from the center.[7]

The actual town of Yuryev is not charming—it is dreadful. When Liubov remains, in order to search for her missing son, she passes through all the circles of provincial hell, amid the destruction, neglect, and drunkenness of *byt* (everyday life) and the triumph of the violence and hopelessness of *bytie* (existence). Thus the authors of the film appear to expose the illusoriness and contrivance of the provincial myth. And yet, this is the very world in which Liubov acquires her new essence, rising to spiritual heights so great that the ordinary criteria of happiness, morality, and freedom no longer apply. According to ordinary criteria, Liubov has lost everything, but according to those offered up in the film, in which the spiritual is valued over all baser concerns, she attains something incomparably more precious. If neither the viewers nor the critics can accept any single possible interpretation, it is because the film does not commit entirely to one.

Until the end of the sixteenth century, it was on "Yuryev Day" that Russian serfs could leave their masters in search of another. Echoing this transitional status of the serf, as the shift from old to new, the film exists in a fluid conceptual space, wherein the traditional binary oppositions dovetail, thereby forming the ternary structure of the West–the Russian capital–the provinces. Depicted "with deliberate overkill," the setting of *Yuryev Day* provides an extreme contrast to the image of the West personified implicitly at the beginning of the narrative by the heroine, who returns to Yuryev only because she is leaving Russia *for* the West. Her affluence, European car and mode of dress, her gaze from afar and on high, her anticipatory nostalgia, and even the Italian arias she performs denote her status as a glaring Other, removed not only from Yuryev, but also from Moscow. Thus, by remaining in Yuryev and donning a *genuine* (and not the playfully quoted "Solzhenitsyn-style") quilted cotton jacket, Liubov makes a choice—not between the provinces and the capital, but between Russia and the West. At the very moment she is to cross the border, at once real and symbolic, she stops short of leaving the country, a move that could have meant the loss of her true Russianness.

The meaning of the "day of freedom" in the title is as ambiguous as the rest of the film: after all, the peasants moved from one situation of nonfreedom to another. Any audience bearing this in mind has another reason to doubt the value of what Liubov acquires in her new life in Yuryev. Mark Lipovetsky argues that the title "suggests the 'spiritual' interpretation of the film as a story of the liberation of Liuba's spirit from pride and individualism, a story of finding peace through tragedy and through her newly acquired sense of belonging to the collective 'people's' body,"[8] and this is certainly one of the valid interpretations supported by the film. In the battle for Liubov, Russia proves more powerful than the West. The question is, whether it manages to reclaim the heroine by degrading her soul or elevating it. The authors of the film offer no unambiguous answer. In the final scene, Liubov is shown singing in the church choir (another quotation from Blok, but on a narrative, rather than verbal level now), no longer as a soloist, however, but as an ordinary member of the chorus, the color of her dyed hair, "intimate red-ochre" (*intimnyi surik*), identical to everyone else's. Cheap and available in only the one shade, the dye is used by all the women in town, as if red hair were the universal stamp of poverty. Yet this very color can be interpreted much more positively: in the circus tradition, the red-haired (*ryzhii*) clown, who makes fun of his quiet, intellectual, white-haired counterpart and boxes his ears, is a symbol of optimism. Like Russia, he may be perceived as ridiculous by adversaries, but he does ultimately triumph. Thus, the semantics of the film's details remain ambivalent: as either a harsh indictment of Russian life or a celebration of its spiritual power. Liubov's story might be seen as that of finding one's roots and strength in the native soil, or as a sequence of terrible losses. The filmmakers invite the audience, alternately optimistic and terrified, to choose their own interpretation.

The paradox of the ternary West–Moscow–Provinces model lies in the fact that Moscow is incapable of representing Russia metonymically from any perspective because of its status as the Other in relation to both the West and "noncapital space." In today's process of creating a new national identity, Moscow's role is insignificant, whereas that of the provinces proves to be disproportionately significant. It follows, then, that the obvious contrast between a practical knowledge of provincial life and its idealization by virtue of a passéist mindset is altogether characteristic of the post-Soviet period. This collective passéism imposes on the provinces their role as the repository of national character. It is precisely in this role that the provinces stand in opposition to Moscow, thereby providing a different framework within which to situate the national discourse. No less than that between Russia and the West, the relationship between periphery and center becomes the venue wherein the drama of *ressentiment* unfolds, value priorities are established, and the conception of Russianness is elaborated.

Moscow as Occidental City

In the topography of *Yuryev Day*, the Provinces–Capital–West alignment is offset when the heroine, having temporarily returned to the provinces, ends up trapped in a vicious circle within which a typically Russian tragedy of actual losses and symbolic gains unfolds. The topography in Andrei Konchalovsky's film *Gloss* (*Glianets*, 2007) is equally symbolic but more typical of contemporary cinema. The film begins with a schematic representation of the provinces and follows its heroine, Galia, to a no less schematically represented Moscow, where the seamstress from Rostov-on-Don hopes to make it as a model in the world of glamour magazines and colorful TV commercials.

Both the provinces and the capital are depicted parodically in *Gloss*, one no less than the other. Like the "signs of *chernukha* [from the word *black*] and spirituality"[9] in *Yuryev Day*, the blend of "gloss and *chernukha*"[10] informing *Gloss* does not aspire to a realistic portrayal;[11] rather, it draws attention to the long-standing perceptions, or cultural myths, manipulated by the film. Both the redheaded women in *Yuryev Day* and the symbolic transformation in *Gloss* of the brunette from Rostov-on-the-Don into a Hollywood blonde[12] are semiotic markers of the territory, wherein the provinces, the capital, and the West form a symbolic sequence of recriminatory *ressentiment*—a chain of apophatic, negative self-determinations, incapable of offering a stable, positive image of Russian reality.[13]

In the process of locating, or imagining, true Russianness outside of Moscow, the capital acquires the important negative characteristic traditionally assigned to the Other as the West: prosperity based on Western market practices and a parasitical relationship with the periphery. As such, Moscow becomes an object of *ressentiment* and acquires the reviled features of the Occidental City. Here I refer to the concept of Occidentalism as it relates to postcolonial discourse, and I employ the term as a discursive feature of *ressentiment*. Konchalovsky's depiction in *Gloss* of the capital by means of a deliberate, "crude reductionism"[14] conforms to an Occidentalist view of Moscow as a city where "one can purportedly become rich and famous, albeit at great moral cost; the modeling business is akin to prostitution; everything can be bought or sold; and rich people are unhappy."[15] In the case of post-Soviet, postimperial Russia, within the hermetic national model of the provinces versus the capital, the notion of Occidentalism underscores the persistence of the discourse of alterity, *ressentiment*, and the need for an Other as a condition of self-representation.

As defined by Ian Buruma and Avishai Margalit, Occidentalism is "the dehumanizing picture of the West painted by its enemies."[16] In this sense, it is as reductive in its approach as Orientalism, whereby non-European cultures, when viewed through the lens of European cultural and religious and societal values, are reduced to objects of fascination or hostility. Occidentalism simply "turns the Orientalist views upside down."[17] That is, Occidentalism "reverses the gaze" by focusing on the West from without and stereotyping it negatively.

Couze Venn defines Occidentalism as discourse originating in this process and as a reaction to European modernity. The view "from without" "directs attention to the becoming-modern of the world, and to the becoming-West of Europe, such that Western modernity gradually becomes established as the privileged, if not hegemonic, form of society, tied to universalizing and totalizing ambition."[18] Today, Occidentalism shares its discursive space with other non-Western narratives of modernity, including that of postcolonial critique; it helps to illustrate the "mutually constitutive nature of Western and non-Western identities."[19]

In encompassing the entire spectrum of ways in which Europeans "could locate themselves"[20] in relation to the Other of Third World, this approach may seem too broad; and in categorizing all visions of the West from without as negative, it is too limiting. However, Occidentalism is a useful critical category in analyzing the cultural discourses of Russian nationalism, precisely because it helps to address the unresolved issue of whether Russia belongs to the West—that is, whether it is the subject or object of the Western objectifying gaze. In other words, is Russia Western and modern, or does it scorn these concepts and regard the West as an outsider to be subjected to negative stereotypes?

The Occidentalist perspective is not limited to non-Western societies. Those who feel marginalized by modernity or alienated within their own society could conceptualize the center as corrupted and soulless; similarly, the urban intelligentsia, feeling displaced in the world of rationality and commerce, might turn to the idealized spiritual past of their nation. Russian urban intellectuals often imagine the national spirit in the distant heartland and adopt its constructed point of view to critique the corrupted modern center as an Occidental city. As characterized by Buruma and Margalit, the Occidental city represents "hubris, empire building, secularism, individualism, and the power and attraction of money."[21] It is a place of trade and commerce; as such, the marketplace is one of its symbolic locales, and the prostitute—one of its most representative figures—serves as an object of trade and lust. The films of the late 1990s, most notably Aleksei Balabanov's *Brother* (*Brat*, 1997) and *Brother 2* (*Brat 2*, 2000),[22] explicitly portray urban settings, especially the American city, as the realm of corruption, greed, and lust.[23] While more recent films and TV serials refrain from the unrestrained representation of crime and prostitution, the vast number of films depicting women from the provinces who come to Moscow in search of a wealthy "beau" does suggest that the principle of transaction continues to apply.

Since the early 2000s, Moscow has most often been perceived in terms of "interregional inequality," or profiting from the resources of the rest of the country while growing increasingly alienated from it.[24] Vladimir Kagansky, in *Cultural Landscape and Soviet Inhabited Space*, sums up this transformation as a severing of ties between the country and its center—a symptom of "radical transformation, instability, and the loss of certainty."[25] The country and the capital, he writes, "live in increasingly differing epochs and regimes, see and experience reality in different ways. Moscow ignores most of Russia, for which it has become an external and distant element."[26] Buruma and Margalit note that Occidentalism is not a "dogma favored by downtrodden peasants." Rather, it reflects "the fear and prejudices of urban intellectuals."[27] Public opinion polls reveal that the young and educated inhabitants of Russian cities, capable of reflecting on the economic and cultural divide between center and periphery, are those who see Moscow as a monstrous, soulless metropolis that lives off the resources provided by the rest of the country.[28] This view of Moscow as a city-colonizer is similar to the perception of the West (mostly America) as the cultural and economic colonizer of Russia.

However, the primary distinction here is that Moscow *has recently become* (while the West *has always been*) the Other for the rest of the country. Thus, the contemporary dissatisfaction with Moscow develops not only along the lines of Occidentalist resentment of the city as greedy, arrogant, and ultimately non-Russian (because it is ruled by the Western values of individualism and consumerism). The discontent also superimposes this negative image over a nostalgic vision of the true Moscow, capable of symbolically representing the best of Russia. This ambiguity precludes the complete demonization of Moscow and keeps the Occidentalist impulse in check. Moscow is both the Occidental city *and* the center of an imagined symbolic past of the nation—a city that needs to be revived and employed in creating a non-Western discourse of modernity. While today's Moscow is endowed with truly Occidental features (its role as the country's epicenter of commerce, lust, individualism, secularity, and materialism), the Moscow of the past, including the very recent past, is readily available for nostalgic reflection.[29] In many respects, Moscow remained a place of dreams and the heart of the motherland until perestroika, at which point the myth of Moscow finally underwent reconstruction, alongside the other grand metanarratives of Soviet ideology.

Thus, the Moscow of Occidentalist discourse is not sufficiently removed from the Moscow of nostalgia, in either the geographical or temporal sense, to serve as an object of unqualified hostility. Moscow's dual nature, as both the heart of Russia and its enemy, mirrors a complex attitude toward the West that combines admiration and *ressentiment*. For this reason, the paradigm of Moscow versus the provinces dominates recent cultural production: it redirects nationalist discourse away from the West and positions the most pressing concerns of the nation-building process within the new national borders. The interaction of provincials with the inhabitants of the capital provides the framework for the discussion of what it means to be Russian, and whether this meaning is compatible with Western values. While the Russia versus the West opposition remains irresoluble, Russia and Moscow can be reconciled. The ways in which popular cinema actualizes the reconciliatory potential of this shift in focus and attitude are examined below.

The TV serial *Lines of Fate* (*Linii sud'by*, 2003), the first successful domestic noncrime serial,[30] revolves around the fates of several provincials trying to make it in Moscow. Most of them rent rooms in the same big apartment and/or meet at their workplace, the market. These are the two settings featured in the serial. The apartment constitutes a post-Soviet twist on the trope of the *kommunalka* (communal apartment) microcosm—the space of forced cohabitation, and the setting for so many plots of Soviet literature. Yuri Slezkine employs the communal apartment as a metaphor for the relationships between different nationalities and ethnicities under Soviet rule.[31] Similarly, the apartment in *Lines of Fate* is a metaphor for the relationship between people of the center and the provinces. Most important is that these people from different walks of life are above all provincials who are drawn to Moscow by its myriad attractions and dangers. Most came to Moscow in pursuit of a utopian vision of the capital as a fairytale place where dreams come true and, significantly, where the "provincial Cinderella" finds her Prince Charming.

The principal characters are an aspiring singer and his girlfriend, a professional accountant; a ballerina who dreams of performing at the Bolshoi Theater; a film director with an idea for a damaging exposé; an unlicensed medical doctor, who now tells fortunes; a businessman from the Caucasus with a shoe stall at the nearby market; and a disabled Chechen war veteran with his family. They become entangled in a complex web of personal and business relationships. With the exception of the ballerina and the fortune teller, each of these protagonists is directly connected to the market where the accountant, the singer, and the war veteran are employed and the film director conducts his research.

The fact that most of the characters are renting rooms in a communal apartment brings to the fore the motif of homelessness: they are perpetually on its brink and acutely aware of being outsiders looking in. The market, where they reluctantly embark on their road to success, is another microcosm of contemporary society. It immediately acquires a symbolic dimension as well, best expressed by the frustrated singer (played by Konstantin Khabensky), who asks, "Why won't Moscow let us in beyond the market!?" By the end of the serial, most of the provincials have achieved their respective goals. However, their achievements are tainted by compromise: the singer's fame is crudely manufactured, the director's exposé quickly forgotten, and the provincial Cinderella's prince is old and blind. Moreover, their sense of accomplishment is muted, at best, by the cost of their success: a break-up, an abortion, a turn to prostitution, and even death. Ultimately, then, Moscow does let them in beyond the marketplace, but the riches they find on the inside are not the stuff of dreams.

Still, the authors of the serial, producer-director Valeri Todorovsky and the award-winning film director Dmitri Meskhiev, do not demonize Moscow. Rather, they deconstruct the utopian and fairytale aspects of its myth in Soviet cinema: the closing scenes take place on New Year's Eve, a time when TV fare typically features miracles, but the success stories of the provincials are emphatically not of the fairytale variety. The image of Moscow remains ambiguous: it is both the home and marketplace, alternately desirable and cruel, seductive and soullessly mercantile. Like most serials of the 2000s about provincials in Moscow, *Lines of Fate* ultimately endorses the capital: having found a place in the center, the provincial imparts his or her strength and authenticity to the capital, thereby removing the stigmas associated with it and reconciling its contradictions.

Birgit Beumers analyzes *Lines of Fate* in terms of the shift from the crime serials of the 1990s to those serials portraying contemporary life in the 2000s—a shift that indicates the audience's growing complacency "with the status quo in the illusion of social development on the blue screen that ultimately replaces life."[32] As a genre, the serial establishes and maintains the status quo and a sense of normalcy. The dark realism of literature and film in the post-perestroika period gives way under Putin to a cultural production that responds to both the official and popular demand for nationally distinct productions capable of constructing a positive image of Russia. Within the Russia versus the West paradigm, this task is impossible, as clearly illustrated by the recent surge of *ressentiment* and anti-American rhetoric. However, this goal can be achieved internally, so to speak, within the paradigm of the Russian capital versus the Russian provinces, which employs the familiar mechanism of *ressentiment* but affords the potential for reconciliation and mutual improvement. In employing the provincial topos, authors are, in effect, asking Russian viewers to imagine their country as a self-contained entity. To some authors, this country is healthy and capable of resolving its differences; to others, it is in crisis, divided by unbridgeable differences. These authors do not address other conflicts, especially ethnic tensions, coupled with the increasing animosity in Russian cities toward migrant workers—the subject of numerous films in recent decades. The provincial topos confines participants in the national idea discourse to only the internal Other and the conflict of "us versus us."

The Provincial Cinderella as the Missing Link

Since *Lines of Fate*, numerous films have featured the plot of a provincial, most often a girl, on a quest to conquer Moscow. A character's journey to the city in search of success is a classical bildungsroman plot: the journey might not always lead to a fortune, but it always paves the way to moral and psychological growth. Similar journeys with the provinces–capital trajectory are familiar to the Russian viewer: from Stalinist musicals to the late- and post-Soviet films about provincials arriving in Moscow, the trope of movement from the periphery to the center has served as a synonym for the ideological growth and social ascent of the characters.[33] Thus, both film types participate in the ideological scheme of bolstering the status quo, and the journey to Moscow in both is undertaken predominantly by a woman,[34] typically cast as a Cinderella figure; the Cinderella plot was a staple of Soviet cinema.

Naturally, the cultural constructs underlying the respective texts differ. The Stalinist musical was created within the rigid ideological framework of Stalinist utopia, in whose topography Moscow is the center, and the very arrival there of the provincials signifies their success. Richard Taylor discerned the fairytale as a constitutive element of utopia, as depicted by means of the Stalinist musical, wherein a Cinderella figure, be she a domestic servant, a mail carrier, or a swineherdess, is given the opportunity to attain professional *and* personal fulfillment in Moscow—"the fairyland at the heart of the Stalinist utopia" and the place where the fairytale completes its transformation into reality.[35] Thus, Stalinist Moscow is the destination on the heroine's path to self-realization.

Conversely, the post-Soviet provincial Cinderella's arrival in a decidedly unidyllic Moscow marks only the start of her journey, in consonance with the evolving, and still unstable, cultural-ideological discourse of nationalism within which contemporary serials were conceived. However, the fundamental distinction between the two models of cultural texts lies elsewhere. Both the Stalinist musicals and such early successors as Vladimir Menshov's *Moscow Doesn't Believe in Tears* (1980) permitted their heroines to follow potentially diverse paths to self-realization; even while emphasizing the protagonists' careers, these texts illustrated the importance, too, of personal happiness. In her overview of literary and cinematic images of Moscow from WWII through the subsequent decades, Olga Bogoslavskaya notes, for instance, that:

Moscow is the city where dreams come true. If the characters have gone there to pursue noble goals, Moscow puts them through a series of tests (*A Girl Without an Address, A Man Is Born, Moscow Doesn't Believe in Tears*), and sometimes demands some kind of sacrifice (*Come Tomorrow*), but in the end always rewards these characters with the utmost in happiness and success, or at least the unambiguous promise of their attainment.[36]

To the frustration of critics and the chagrin of many a (female) viewer, the provincial Cinderella of contemporary popular cinema is much more limited in her quest for success: she arrives in Moscow in search of either a prince *or* professional fulfillment. Either way, the plot invariably obliges the provincial girl to first accept a menial job in the service of a wealthy man, typically as a domestic servant to a Moscow oligarch or, less frequently, as a salesclerk, cook, seamstress, or hairdresser (or in at least one case, as a surrogate mother). Since, as Svetlana Stepanova observes, "in new Russian cinema there doesn't seem to be a single film about a woman who has succeeded in obtaining a career," and "[a] mere comparison of the number of provincial girls to the number of Moscow millionaires makes you realize that there aren't enough princes to go around,"[37] the odds are against her. Thus, there is no unambiguous promise of her success. The one certainty is that whatever her original dream and aspirations, the girl's ability or failure to capture the wealthy man's heart becomes the measure of her success, and the focus of the plot. Unlike her Stalinist precursor, then, the post-Soviet provincial Cinderella comes to Moscow not to conquer it, but rather to find her conqueror there.

Clearly, then, the post-Soviet Cinderella is defined and stymied by her quest for success. In contrast, the much rarer male provincial protagonist almost invariably finds himself embroiled in a criminal adventure along the road to success. The genre definitions of the films featuring male versus female provincials reflect these differences. Consider, for example, this pair of TV serials: Arminak Nazikian's *The Provincial* (*Provintsial*, 2013), regarded as a "crime thriller," and Artem Nasybulin's *The Provincial Girl* (*Provintsialka*, 2008-9), usually classified as either a "crime melodrama" or simply a "melodrama." Like its lighter-hearted cousin, the romantic comedy, the genre of melodrama involves a female protagonist and revolves around domestic and family concerns.[38] In both serials, the provincials move to St. Petersburg or Moscow in order to investigate a murder and find the perpetrator. But while the hero of

The Provincial seeks only revenge, his female counterpart in *The Provincial Girl* is also looking for love. According to one synopsis of the latter, "as befits a true Cinderella, in the end, [the heroine] wins the grand prize: the triumph of justice, and the love of a 'Prince Charming,' [in the] wealthy heir, Mark."[39]

This gender determinacy informing the female provincial's move to Moscow stems from the way in which the provincial myth governs the interpretation of the classic story. That is, the post-Soviet context demands that she bridge the divide in Russian symbolic geography before she can transgress the boundaries of class and wealth. "The female transgressor," Kathleen Rowe observes, "can rarely define herself except as a romantic heroine."[40] Only as such can a female character succeed in transgressing real and symbolic borders. For a transgressor of such magnitude, however, the provincial Cinderella is strikingly passive. A virtual tabula rasa, she is characterized only by what she is not—namely, a Muscovite. By tracing this Cinderella's journey from naiveté to knowledge of herself and the world of which she longs to be a part, the viewer is offered an image not of the provinces, but of Moscow.

Films featuring a provincial Cinderella fall roughly into two categories: art-house cinema and commercial films. In the first, the girl's journey ends in trauma, or even death. Depicted either as artists, such as the bitterly disappointed composer-heroine of *Listening to Silence* (Aleksandr Kasatkin, 2007), or beings not entirely of this world, as in *Mermaid* (Anna Melikian, 2007) and *The Blessed* (*Blazhennaia*, directed by Sergei Strausovsky, 2008), these girls are either crushed by the soulless metropolis or forced to flee it in order to preserve their essence, having been disillusioned by Moscow and its inhabitants.

The second category, comprising such commercial films as *Cinderella .ru* (Aleksandr Zamiatin, 2007) and *Love without Rules* (Dmitri Svetozarov, 2010), and innumerable serials about provincial women in Moscow, including *Beauty Salon* (2000), *Leading Roles* (2002), *Tatiana's Day* (2007-8), *One Day There Will Be Love* (2009), *The Capital of Sin* (2010), *Housekeeper* (2012), and *The Top Model* (2104), add very little to the familiar Cinderella model. The provinces as depicted in these films and serials are taken to connote and (surprisingly) combine two seemingly incompatible views: as both the repository of naiveté and innocence embodied by the girls, who bring these virtues ("the ideal non-Moscow,"[41] so to speak) to the capital, *and* the spiritual and economical desolation they are escaping. As *Yuryev Day* has illustrated, however, these attitudes can only be reconciled within a fundamentally different system of values, in which economic destitution is magically transformed into moral wealth. Such complex constructions are extraneous to the "provincial Cinderella" serials, which merely demonstrate, time and again, the workings of the device of defamiliarization: by showing Moscow through Cinderella's eyes, they deconstruct and, at the same time, standardize its image.

By the time the "Russia" TV channel commissioned the making of *The Milkmaid from Khatsapetovka* (*Doiarka iz Khatsapetovki*, Anna Gres, 2006), the "provincial Cinderella" trope had become a cliché. Any film on the subject entailed a lyrical storyline, stock characters, and a predictable (if not entirely formulaic) plot. The viewers' enjoyment lay in identifying the various melodramatic formulas, evaluating the quality of their realization, and appreciating the ironic treatment of familiar elements. Like all genre films (and texts), the melodrama strives not for originality, but rather for the flawless execution of generic conventions. To employ Lidia Ginzburg's characterization of romantic elegiac poetry to the genre film, its poetics are the poetics of recognition.

In taking on *Milkmaid*, Gres was well aware that she was making a film "about a Cinderella from the provinces,"[42] and she adhered closely to the familiar formula: the provincial girl, Katia, comes to Moscow to pursue her dream of professional fulfillment as a famous chef. Predictably, her path to realizing this dream involves marrying a wealthy man; thus, when she lacks the money to enroll in the Culinary Institute and finds herself on the street, penniless, she has no choice but to accept the proposition of Dima, a young man who must get married within a month or lose a sizeable inheritance from his grandfather. After the wedding and the lavish reception, Katia can now afford to study at the Culinary Institute, and Dima resumes his playboy lifestyle; the marriage is a sham. Over the next few months, however, Dima falls in love with the wonderful Katia, who manages to reform the former playboy. Ultimately Dima enters the family business and treats his wife with respect; the film ends with a modest but "real" wedding.

However, the filmmakers do modify the formula through the extreme exaggeration of its components: the provincial Cinderella is a great deal more provincial than could be considered realistic, while the prince is less prince-like than most of the wealthy Moscow men depicted in similar films. Katia hails from Khatsapetovka—a tiny village somewhere in the south of Russia that isn't even on the map. Although this is an actual place, it belongs to a list of real and fictional places such as Uriupinsk

Title card for the serial *The Milkmaid from Khatsapetovka* (*Doiarka iz Khatsapetovki*, dir. Anna Gres, 2007).

and Mukhosransk, whose names both signify and ridicule provincial backwaters. Life in Khatsapetovka is emphatically nonmodern: in the film's opening scene, Katia is milking a cow, and when a neighbor takes her to the train station, their mode of transportation is a horse-drawn cart. Her shapeless floral print dress, her little braids tied with red ribbons, and especially her sheepskin coat hark back to 1930s musicals and exaggerate her provinciality to the extent that the cliché becomes a quotation. The heroine thus embodies a world apart from modernity and life in the capital. The stylized drawings used for the opening credits suggest a simplified, *lubok* version of an important theme and emphasize the formulaic plot and the absence of any pretense of a realistic representation.

Katia's naiveté challenges common sense: she intends to complain "to the Kremlin" on discovering that her expectations of a free education, with a dorm room and a stipend, are less than realistic. Her speech exhibits typically southern mispronunciations; her table manners are abominable: she insists on drinking her tea from the saucer, slurping loudly, and would rather eat in the kitchen than learn dining etiquette. Naturally, her mother-in-law is horrified: "She is a wild creature," she says, and asks, "What if she's contagious?"

This reaction is typically Orientalist: as the object of a gaze that spans the geographical and cultural divide and originates from a representative of an ostensibly superior civilization, Katia is perceived as a

From *The Milkmaid from Khatsapetovka*, episode 2.

savage—an alien object of study. However, her "wildness" proves advantageous: Dima's father spins it to benefit his political campaign when he styles himself as the candidate whose daughter-in-law "comes from the people." The media reports that focus on Dima and his father "visiting his new relatives in the far-away Russian provinces" are not mistaken. When Katia leaves, they both follow her back to Khatsapetovka, where Dima and the audience discover a different Katia. While the first half of the film emphasizes Katia's uncivilized nature, there is a sharp shift at this point toward the opposite extreme in depicting provincials as morally superior. This dynamic is also typical of the Orientalist gaze: the lack of civilization is an advantage when construed as a lack of corruption. This image of the provinces is also devoid of any pretense at realist representation; it presents a set of clichés typical of the Orientalist's image of the noble savage.

In Katia's room, for instance, Dima reads her favorite poetry, by Sergei Esenin, and an unattributed piece (perhaps Katia's own) on the value of respect; quoting the Bible, it starts with "In the beginning there was the word," and proceeds thus: "and the word was respect. Respect is valor, labor, and honor. It is giving each person the right to the kind of life he strives to achieve." Next, Katia's elderly aunt enters the room, wearing a distinctly folkloric-looking dress and holding an embroidered towel. To Dima's comment, "So many books," she replies: "There are more in the attic. Our TV reception is bad, so Katia read a great deal.

She read and dreamed." We also learn that Katia had to walk six miles to school but that did not stop her from attending and even receiving a gold medal—the highest of honors. One is faced, at this point, with the dilemma of how to reconcile the wild creature slurping tea from the saucer with the well-read gold medalist with a dream, and the determination to fulfill it. However, the two conflicting extremes are precisely those elements required of the provincial Cinderella construct: she must at once embody the material poverty and the moral wealth of the provinces she strives to escape.

The "wild creature" remark and the superior attitude of the Muscovites are consistent with the logic of Orientalism, whose discourse defines the other by means of negation: the savage is contemptible because she lacks the positive attributes of true civilization; but the savage is also desirable because she is free of the faults (especially corruption and hypocrisy) of that same civilization. The Orientalist gaze thus uses the only categories and values available to it in imagining the "noble savage," pure, poetic, and in tune with the natural world. Gres's film illustrates how the gaze allows the subject to define itself in opposition to the Other it creates. Just as the Romantics fashioned the literary Caucuses as the Russian Orient, the filmmakers of the Putin era look to the provinces in search of an appropriate site for their exotic Other.

Occidentalism, as the reversal of the Orientalist gaze, shares with its counterpart the same reductionism and penchant for apophatic (by negation) definitions. Seemingly at cross-purposes, the films portraying the relationship between the Russian capital and its provincial Other construct both perspectives at once: the Orientalist view of the provinces as the repository of moral traditions and cultural riches, and the Occidentalist view of Moscow as corrupted by Western values. However, the intended effect is to moderate the extremes intrinsic to both assumptions and, ultimately, to eliminate their mutual opposition altogether. Thus, in *The Milkmaid from Khatsapetovka* and numerous other similar films, the center both studies and civilizes its object of interest, while the "wild" girl brings "true" civilization to the center by bestowing upon it some of her purity and moral strength.

The few minutes spent in Katia's world provide the impetus that propels Dima along his own path of becoming the man worthy of Katia's love. Diametrically opposed at the start of the film, their respective worlds are happily reconciled by the end. Katia learns to dress, sound, and eat like a Muscovite, and Dima learns to be a responsible adult and a better human being. Unlike the other of the West, the other of provincial discourse is both more familiar and more manageable, and these oppositions are easily reconciled.

The center–provinces binary opposition is further complicated in the film's sequel. A different director, with a different cast, continues Katia's story and, most significantly, complicates the center–periphery topography. In the sequel, Katia's husband throws her out on the street, pregnant and penniless. Rather than return to Khatsapetovka, however, she goes to Paris under a new identity. Ironically and inexplicably, the symbolic border between Moscow and Paris proves easier to cross than that between Khatsapetovka and Moscow. Twenty years later, Katia and Dima reunite to rebuild Khatsapetovka together, and the three geographical locations coexist conflict-free. The stylized illustration in the sequel's title card represents Katia's ascent from the rather abstract Khatsapetovka to Moscow in the first season and then to Paris in the second season. In this image, the hackneyed symbols of both capitals, a Stalinist building and the Eiffel Tower, appear on either side of a representation of the Russian heartland in the form of a country house surrounded by trees and meadows. The casual simplification of these symbols testifies to the fact that the ternary structure of the West–the provinces–Moscow has become as familiar, if not cliché, as the binary paradigms it incorporates. The title card's elimination of the borders demarcating the provinces, the West, and the capital reflects the symbolic geography of the cultural myths that informs the identity discourse in post-Soviet Russia. These three elements signify not the real geographical destinations, but the abstract notions of this discourse: neither Paris, nor Moscow, nor a real Khatsapetovka, but the concept of the West, the symbolic center, and the provincial heartland. Their relationship involves little animosity, their differences are easily reconciled, and in fact, they stand next to each other as equals. By eschewing the notions of hierarchy, the film offers a version of positive Russian identity as one who is at home in Moscow and in Paris but cherishes his or her roots in the Russian heartland. This identity is based not on conflict but on reconciliation with the Other.

That the rigid binary constructions yield to ternary models can be regarded in a positive light. This is precisely what Yuri Lotman suggests, albeit with guarded optimism, in *Culture and Explosion* (1996). He interprets the "switch from a binary system to a ternary one," which he expected in the post-Soviet epoch, as the transition to "evolutionary consciousness," to liberation from the polarity and maximalism inherent

Film and TV

Title card for *The Milkmaid from Khatsapetovka 2: Challenging Fate* (*Doiarka iz Khatsapetovki 2: Vyzov sud'be*, dir. Pavel Snisarenko, 2009).

in Russian culture. Lotman observes nevertheless that this very transition is understood in traditional binary terms because "ethical maximalism has become so deeply enrooted in the very foundations of Russian culture."[43]

Building on Lotman's foundation, and with a similarly guarded optimism, I propose, first, that while the ternary structure of the provinces-the capital-the West does not annul these deep-seated oppositions, it reflects the evolution of Russian nationalist discourse at the dawn of the twenty-first century. Second, the transition from the rigid binary pattern to the more inclusive and flexible ternary model may well constitute a step toward the creation of a noncontentious national model, based more on the pursuit and affirmation of the positive within its Self than on the negative in the Other.

"Away from Moscow!"

Thus far, this analysis has illustrated that in the symbolic geography of contemporary culture, Moscow has acquired the features of the Occidental city of sin. In popular film and TV, however, this negative representation is cancelled out when a pure provincial girl is integrated into life in the capital. In more complex films, such as in *Yuryev Day*, the provinces are posed as a microcosm of Russia, an alternative to Moscow.

Julian Graffy observes that a number of films of mid-2000s possess "a recurrent trope of leaving the big city in search of a meaning the metropolis has been unable to provide." He notes, however, the schematic representation of that undefined place outside the capital that "gains its significance by means of not being Moscow or St. Petersburg, and through its consequent ability to provide a moral lesson of some kind to the lost and misguided inhabitants of the capitals."[44] Thus, the various authors' inability to show those places outside Moscow independently of the capital-provinces binary comes as no surprise: the provinces after which these protagonists quest are not real locales, but abodes of enduring meanings and values—that is, the provinces of myth. Attempts by filmmakers to represent them realistically inevitably reduce the provinces to one of two opposing clichés, either emphasizing the "sweet and sentimental" or exaggerating the "dark and naturalistic."

The TV series *Broad Is the River* (*Shiroka reka*, 2008), illustrates the former: its provinces exist only in opposition to Moscow and, moreover, as a positive alternative to it. The serial is also noteworthy (if not for its quality) for the way it has capitalized on the interest in the subject over the past decade and followed the logic of Occidentalism only to lay bare its mechanisms and limits in a contemporary Russian context. Its plot, setting, and even its title and theme song provide a snapshot of the peculiarities of Russia's internal Occidentalism.

At the beginning of the first episode, a train makes a three-minute stop at a faraway station, and two young men step down onto the platform. One, a Moscow doctor, looks around and declares: "Well, this is *not* Rio de Janeiro!" The other, a local man returning from having fought in Chechnya, replies: "This *is* Russia! I'll bet you couldn't even see it from Moscow." Before this opening dialogue, while the eponymous song accompanies the opening credits, the Russian heartland is metonymically sketched: a broad river, soaring birds, fields, and a train cutting through the mighty forests—in other words, the forests, fields, and rivers of the song "Broad is the Motherland": "Broad is my motherland / many are her forests, fields, and rivers." Subsequently the first episode proceeds to list every element of the myth of the pure and uncorrupted provinces.

The small town (*posielok*) of Staro Tugolukovo is a place where a Rousseauian image of the countryside struggles to prevail over that of the dreadful provincial town depicted by Gogol and Chekhov. This shift toward a positive view of the provinces necessarily entails a vision both schematic and hackneyed: the provinces figure as a cultural myth rather than any real place in the Russian heartlands. Similar to the Orientalist view of the East, the gaze from the capital creates the little town and imagines life there as a reversal, and negation, of life in the capital.

A mixture of cinematic and literary clichés paints a picture of the purity of life in the small town: simple womenfolk are busy in their gardens; a young girl refuses to consider moving anywhere, least of all to Moscow, because she was born and belongs here; Frol Fedotych, a town doctor with a Chekhovian beard and glasses, displays curiously old-fashioned (and literary) speech and manners. The fairytale peeks through as well: the same young girl takes one look at the Moscow doctor and says, only half joking, "Take a look at the prince from beyond the sea I've been waiting for." The authors thus check off every feature of the myth of the provinces as the "authentic" Russia. Having done that, they abandon the subject altogether, shift the action to Moscow, and continue in the much more familiar vein of a Mexican or Brazilian prime time soap opera. In other words, having paid homage to the socially important theme and authentic Russian setting, they indeed abandon Staro Tugolukovo for Rio de Janeiro.

The love triangle set up in the first episodes between the Moscow surgeon, the Russian beauty, and the local fisherman reproduces the triangular structure described by Etkind as a constitutive element of the internal colonization plot. The woman is the object of desire of both men—the Man of Power and Culture and the Man of the People—and a mediator in their conflict.[45] Mark Lipovetsky has applied this model to post-Soviet cinema, where the woman's role as a mediator is reduced to the extent that mediation as such is impossible; the distance between the two men either collapses or becomes unbridgeable.[46] In *Broad Is the River*, this structure suggests nothing of the complexities in the relationship between power and the people, and it breaks down under the sheer weight of the endless melodramatic plot collisions.

Overwhelmingly consistent, the audience's reaction to this has been conveyed as a sense of having been cheated (*kak budto menia obokrali*): on multiple opinion boards the viewers admit to having started watching because of the small-town setting and then being disappointed when the action shifted to Moscow: "Watched the first episode with pleasure . . . The classical plot of a love triangle, but in a Russian manner—against the background of our nature and the emotions of our Russian soul... the strength of character of our Russian woman and the gallant struggle of our men."⁴⁷ "Disappointed by the film! Began to watch because of the locale: the taiga, rugged Russian houses, local color. But in the end the action moved to Moscow, as usual." "The film started out so interestingly, I even thought that finally, they'd put out something worthwhile, unusual, and not like all of those little serials. Now I realize I was mistaken." "Nonsense. The primary means of attracting the audience's attention is a clumsy provocation, a useless attempt to graft the image and morality of the capital's bohemia (more in keeping with the authors) onto the image of the Russian periphery. As a result we have a faceless town outside Moscow, where summer cottagers from the capital perform the roles of the 'locals.'"⁴⁸

The last post is most insightful; its author in fact describes the very mechanism of Orientalism: the cultural elite of the center imposes its idea of the exotic onto the Russian periphery. The view from the center can realize itself in no other form than as an agglomeration of cultural clichés because it is itself a cultural reaction to the nationalist discourse of the last few decades. If Moscow has become the West, authentic Russianness must be located elsewhere. However, while Moscow filmmakers and TV producers recognize the appeal of Occidentalist discourse for the majority of viewers, they cannot fully participate in perpetuating it. Moreover, by its very nature, a popular TV serial is a genre that can only simulate social concerns; ultimately it resumes its major function—namely, of maintaining the status quo and the audience's contentment with the way things stand in present-day Russia.

The title song, "Broad is the River" ("Shiroka reka"), by the popular folk singer Natalia Kadysheva, similarly capitalizes on nationalist discourse but is incapable of balancing the social and the personal. The first line echoes the famous opening line of "Broad is the Motherland" ("Shiroka strana"), the song from the film *Circus* (1936) that served as an unofficial anthem of the USSR until 1943. The move from "broad is the motherland," with its ideologically consistent message of optimism and homogeneity, to "broad is the river" (that divides lovers) represents the shift away not only from ideology, but from all forms of social engagement. As such it participates in the shift, discussed by Birgit Beumers, away from the distressing images of post-perestroika films and TV crime serials and toward the illusion of social stability in the recent films and serials depicting private lives.

The combination of the song (with its layered composition of elements from folklore, Soviet nostalgia, and the theme of love) and the serial of the same title (with its confusing articulation of the Moscow versus the provinces opposition) makes for a puzzling picture. There is an unresolved tension between a westernized Moscow that cannot even see the true Russia and the true Russia itself—the provinces, which can only be portrayed as a composite of cultural clichés and hence remain largely invisible. This tension reflects the underlying problem of all nation-building, where the legitimizing myth of the past must be balanced against the notions of change and becoming. Homi K. Bhabha speaks of this tension as that "between signifying the people as an a priori historical presence, a pedagogical object; and the people constructed in the performance of narrative, its enunciatory 'present' marked in the repetition and pulsation of the national sign."[49] "It is through this process of splitting," he insists "that the conceptual ambivalence of modern society becomes the site of *writing the nation*."[50] The split between Moscow of the imperial past and Soviet utopia on the one hand, and Moscow the Occidental City on the other, clears a vast space for writing the Russian nation.

In this vast space, "the provincial" is constructed and employed in the performance of the nationalist narrative. Regardless of whether the provincial is the bearer of the Occidentalist view or the object of the Orientalist gaze, his or her interaction with the center proves the boundaries porous and the differences reconcilable. Moscow involves the Russian provinces in mutual fascination and *ressentiment* but ultimately disperses the hostility inherent in most "us versus them" paradigms. The internal dynamics of center versus periphery in the hermetic model are thus potentially more satisfying, psychologically, for the Russians than those rooted in *ressentiment* toward the West.

Russian official ideology is engaged in creating a new concept of Russianness, free of imperial pathos while nevertheless relying on the legitimizing myths of the imperial past. What remains unresolved in this notion of Russianness is the tension between internal Orientalism and internal Occidentalism. Herein lies one of the paradoxes of "writing the nation" in contemporary Russia: the Orientalist gaze of the center employs the Occidentalist rhetoric of the periphery in order to offer the public a psychologically satisfying nationalist model that omits the West altogether.

Katia Shagalova's *Once Upon a Time in the Provinces* (2008, the same year that gave us *Yuryev Day* and *Broad Is the River*) is an example of a film whose portrayal of the provinces goes to the other extreme, depicting the periphery as a terrible place devoid of meaning and hope. Other filmmakers whose works are characterized by viewers as uncompromising and harsh portrayals of contemporary reality also situate their characters in the provinces: Boris Khlebnikov's *Free Floating* (2006), Aleksei Balabanov's *Cargo-200* (2007), Vasili Sigarev's *Spinner* (2009) and *Live* (2012), and also Andrei Zvyagintsev's *The Return* (2003) and *Leviathan* (2014). The choice of a provincial setting is due, in part, to the fact that situating the action in Moscow would require addressing the familiar trope of Moscow as the Occidental city. At the same time, the reality of life in provincial towns better supports a dark portrayal than does the more affluent Moscow. The focus in these films on the darker side of life—poverty, violence, drunkenness, broken families, and the overarching sense of hopelessness—seems to revive the style of dark naturalism typical to the perestroika period.[51]

The nature of *chernukha* as a style or even genre has been amply discussed. Eliot Borenstein sums up definitions of late-Soviet and early post-Soviet *chernukha* as "the pessimistic, naturalistic depiction of and obsession with bodily functions, sexuality (usually separate from love), and often sadistic violence, all against a backdrop of poverty, broken families, and unrelenting cynicism."[52] Seth Graham offers an in-depth analysis of such *chernukha* aesthetics as "a terminal, invasive parody of the entire teleological trajectory of Soviet ideology and culture."[53] In another study, he explains the public's dissatisfaction with the dark naturalism of post-perestroika cinema as a desire for stability and contentment. Moreover, the Self presented by *chernukha* is not only the "Russo-Soviet self," unrepresented by official Soviet culture, but also a superimposition onto that self of "the primary Other, the rotten West." *Chernukha* has thus presented a threat to the ongoing construction of Russian nationhood by blurring the boundaries of the Russia versus West opposition, thereby challenging a major cultural myth.[54]

While resembling in many ways the *chernukha* of perestroika, the dark naturalism in the films of the mid-2000s functions in a different way and has little to do with the exposé impulse of early post-Soviet cinema. The films of the 1990s dealt with what was quickly becoming the past; and the audience had the right to expect that a new and better reality would bring new, and less disturbing, aesthetic styles. "It functioned like satire," Borenstein explains, "without necessarily being satirical—that is, it exposed flaws and inspired outrage among readers/viewers who presumably would want to live in a different world."[55]

By the mid-2000s, to create "depressing films ... about the moral crisis of the Russian man," as Daniil Dondurei described the works of the new generation of the filmmakers,[56] is to go beyond shocking the reader into a recognition of the darker sides of life "as it was" in the Soviet Union and to offer instead a bleak view of life "as it is now" in Russia, two decades after the dissolution of the Soviet Union. The earlier films operated with the implicit assumption that the political system bears full responsibility for the horrors they describe. The films of the 2000s deny the audiences the comfort of having a clear notion of who to blame, or whether the country's problems could even be solved. *Once Upon a Time in The Provinces* possesses the same shock value as other films of the decade. Moreover, it purports to present the provinces as a microcosm of the entire country, and as Russian reality proper, thus denying the viewer another kind of comfort: that of assuming that the events of the film could happen only in some remote provincial place. While TV films and series about provincials in Moscow both suggest the possibility of young people finding their place in the new reality and give this reality the status of the norm, *Once Upon a Time in the Provinces* offers neither hope nor illusions, thereby challenging the status quo endorsed by mass culture.

The film's heroine, Nastia, leaves Moscow to settle in the small town Uletovo, for reasons quite different from Liubov's reasons for remaining in Yuryev; however, Nastia's journey indicates a similar trajectory from high to low, from Moscow to the provinces, and from success to destitution. She could well be a character from *Lines of Fate*—a provincial girl who achieves success in Moscow but finds herself unable, or unwilling, to pay its price. She rises to short-lived fame as a TV actress but, for reasons left unclear, ends up with nowhere to go but her sister Vera's place in Uletovo. The details of life in Uletovo are depressing and the film ends tragically, but there is no indication that its authors either demonize or idealize the provinces, or even acknowledge the topos of the provinces as cultural myth. Yet the film's very title, *Once Upon a Time in the Provinces*, insists on emphasizing its locale, a dreary provincial dump.[57]

Like the town of Yuryev, Uletovo is dreadful.[58] The protagonists reside in barrack-like housing with communal kitchens and showers. In their rooms they drink; in the littered yards and stadiums they play soccer, fight, and then drink some more. The roads and pavement, covered in mud and fallen leaves, fix the autumnal setting as a marker of decay and doom. The characters are young and good-looking; nevertheless, as Gerald McCausland points out, they are profoundly damaged: Vera's husband, Kolia, suffers from a war injury to the brain and beats his wife; his army buddies are also scarred, both physically and symbolically. Both Nastia and Vera are ridden with guilt over the consequences of past betrayals. When Nastia falls in love with Kolia's friend, there are no expectations of a happy ending; on the contrary, Nastia is likely destined for the same life of domestic abuse as her unfortunate sister. However, her fate proves to be more terrible still: after she attacks Kolia with a knife for beating Vera, she is arrested. When her lover threatens the police with a hand grenade, she escapes detention, and the fugitive couple manages to flee. But only minutes later, their car careens off the bridge and plunges into the shallow gray river below, where their getaway ends on a cold, gloomy day.

McCausland suggests that "by making her characters likable and attractive not only physically but also morally, the director avoids one of the chief characteristics of perestroika-era *chernukha*: an all-encompassing sense of decay and hopelessness that permeates both society and environment."[59] Yet it seems the film is packed with more doom and hopelessness than any perestroika-era film, and the characters' youth and beauty serves to further emphasize this hopelessness. Twenty years after the dissolution of the Soviet Union, these young people seem to be stuck in the same place, holding meaningless jobs, or none at all, and spending their time drinking amid poverty, disorder, and violence. In his 2008 Festival Report, the critic Klaus Eder singled out the film and interpreted it thus: "You may come from whatever part of the world, you may be a good person or a bad person, says the film; it doesn't matter, because you'll inevitably be sucked into this moral morass. This is Shagalova's bitter message. It is what she has discovered, even if it may not be her opinion. She is, however, honest enough not to introduce any hope or optimism in this remote place, and where neither can exist."[60]

The question remains, however, as to Shagalova's choice of title: if the town of Uletovo, as a microcosm of Russia, provides the means whereby the film criticizes the state of the nation, why emphasize its provincial setting? Would the circumstances of the traumatized protagonists be any less grave if they lived in the capital? The title and setting of *Once Upon a Time in the Provinces* allows the director to do more than offer harsh criticism of contemporary Russian reality. She also, like Serebrennikov, provides a scathing commentary on the tendency of the provincial myth to either idealize or demonize such remote places. Moreover, the provincial distinction in the title catches complacent viewers or critics in the act of distancing themselves from its bleakness as existing somewhere far away, in a "remote" place (as Eder puts it).

Nevertheless, Uletovo is "the provinces" and therefore also Russia. A number of details support this view, such as the emphasis on the multiethnic makeup of the town, which although not overtly articulated, is evident throughout. The most intriguing detail, however, is the recurrent talk of feng-shui, the Chinese philosophy that places supreme importance on the environment and physical surroundings. The subject first crops up in a scene full of evocative details at the beginning of the film, when the two sisters meet the local policewoman, Lena; she is the only character who appears to have any control over her life and, to quote McCausland, "who seems to live responsibly, to provide for her family, and to maintain a sense of personal dignity." Lena's importance in the narrative is emphasized by her appearance in the opening scene. Moments later, by which point the other characters have only barely been introduced, she meets Nastia and Vera. They converse about art, compassion, feng-shui, and Lena's white, high-heeled boots, which, she proudly announces, as she walks along the muddy road, exemplify her feng-shui credo: "If you wear white, dirt will be afraid of you." When Vera suggests that she and Nastia also buy a pair, Nastia replies half-jokingly, "Maybe this is what it's all about." At odds with the environment to the point of absurdity, Lena's boots serve as an unlikely, but potent, symbol of not giving in to circumstances.[61] As the film progresses, however, it becomes clear that the filth of their surroundings is not so easily repelled.

Lena performs her official duties with resolve and without cynicism, and offers Vera sound advice. She also writes poetry and decorates her house in an oriental style, which, incongruous as it seems, distinguishes hers as the only attractive living space depicted in the film. These factors should affirm her belief that one's life can be organized in the same way as one's physical surroundings and that one can attain happiness and a sense of self-respect merely by possessing the proper tools—in Lena's case, white boots, poetry, and dignity. Yet the film opens with this attractive, organized woman arguing with her alcoholic, teenage daughter while trying to look after her crying grandson. Apparently, then, not everything can be controlled; indeed, despite Lena's best efforts, the lives of the young people around her spin expressly *out* of control. Thus, her ability to counteract her surroundings is limited, at best. Her efforts, like the physical beauty of the characters, make more poignant the hopelessness of their situation.

Significantly, however, these limitations invalidate neither her efforts (after all, should one stop trying?) nor the importance of feng-shui for the film's message. On the contrary, as a doctrine whereby a life of harmony and awareness is attained by exerting control over one's environment, the role of feng-shui in *Once Upon a Time in the Provinces* is affirmed in two respects: first, it serves as a vehicle for Shagalova's ironic commentary on the Marxist postulate that social being determines consciousness; and second, it acts as a reminder that blaming one's environment for the inadequacies of existence is as tempting, and pointless, as situating social problems in an unspecified, exceptionally terrible, but remote provincial place. To believe in the unqualified relevance of location and presume that life in any big city, including Moscow, is somehow automatically better is to unilaterally apply the principles of feng-shui to the whole country. The title thus simultaneously offers and denies the possibility of perceiving the events and settings in the film as an unfortunate exception; the utter lack of hope and optimism in Shagalova's provinces encompass the whole of contemporary Russia.

Class and Wealth, Geographically Speaking

By the end of the 2000s, the topic of the provinces was firmly established in the discourse of what defines Russia and Russianness. My analysis of the following cinematic texts addresses precisely the pervasiveness of the provincial topos and the ease with which it, like all cultural myths, can be exploited to address a variety of issues, such as in this case other social divides, including class and wealth.

In *About Love* (*Pro Liuboff*, 2010), Olga Subbotina uses the hackneyed provincial Cinderella trope as a structural device: she establishes the plot in accordance with the cliché of the provincial girl looking for love and success in Moscow, then shifts perspectives, midfilm, to deconstruct the cliché. The film features two provincial girls, each with her own storyline. In the first, Rita, the secondary character, succeeds in marrying a wealthy man, whereby she "conquers Moscow" and proceeds to "dig into" the benefits of her newfound status.

Meanwhile, the lead protagonist, Dasha, starts working as a speech therapist for a wealthy businessman who is entering politics. They begin an affair, which represents her chance to find love and enter into the world of the new rich, but the affair ends abruptly and the story begins anew—this time from the perspective of the businessman and his wife. The shift in point-of-view betrays the businessman's true nature, including the fact of Dasha's utter insignificance to him, except in the bedroom and as a useful pawn in his political PR campaign. Most importantly, the second half of the film underscores the formulaic premise of its first half, wherein, true to the provincial Cinderella cliché, Rita finds her wealthy prince. Dasha does not find hers but is unable to break free of this cliché: she allows her perceptions to be clouded by the expectations of the familiar storyline that would end with her capturing her millionaire's heart.

Significantly, while reiterating the extent of their financial destitution, the film does not emphasize the fact that Dasha and Rita are provincials. Still, every online database provides a synopsis that begins, more or less, with, "Dasha and Rita come from the provinces to conquer Moscow." Even though Dasha's poverty is more significant than her origins, the film's promoters, too, are unable to see beyond the provincial Cinderella cliché. Of particular interest, then, is the fact that the film reconfigures the familiar center-provinces opposition along class lines, as the opposition of rich versus poor; thus, the geographical and cultural divide has been equaled, and even supplanted, by the class divide. Irina Makoveeva notes that the successful pulp novel (Oksana Robsky, 2002) on which Subbotina based her film "hardly deviates from the stereotypes circulating in the collective unconscious that predictably privilege the poor as the heirs to true values and condemn the rich as cynical and immoral characters luxuriating in materialism."[62] In that the provincial Cinderella, too, is both firmly established in the collective unconscious as a bearer of true values and definitely poor, the above binaries dovetail.

Both "texts" provide a fresh variation on the cliché in that the poor provincial girl is not a domestic servant, but a speech therapist. To be sure, her employer's attitude suggests he barely distinguishes between the two positions; the cynical new rich situate themselves so high above the crowd that it makes no difference whether the poor are provincials or Muscovites, educated or ignorant, sincere or calculating. But the fact remains that the provincial girl tutors the future politician, possibly even the next ruler of Russia, in "proper speech," as characteristic of an intellectual. For instance, the novel *Red Coffin, or Eloquence Lessons in the Russian Provinces* (Roman Solntsev, 2002) depicts an aging, provincial literature teacher, cast in the same role as Dasha and meeting a similarly disastrous end. Here eloquence represents not just proper speech, but also a proper way of life. Unfortunately, the teacher's expertise and lifelong devotion to teaching and the spiritual value of literature do not appear to be in demand. Taken as a metaphor, Dasha's occupation in *About Love* symbolizes the superiority of the provincial as a bearer of culture and moral purity, neither of which, however, improves his or her chances for success in a world where neither is valued. It is thus especially ironic that this educated provincial girl cannot see past the cliché and instead remains an eager participant in what she perceives to be her own Cinderella story. She happily and unthinkingly surrenders to the rhythms of the fairy-tale plot because the sheer volume of its reproductions by mass culture has made it seem ordinary.

The protagonists in Avdotia Smirnova's *Kokoko* (2012) are also locked in a conflict that is only secondarily a "geographical mésalliance"[63]—this time, between the intelligentsia and the people, as represented by Lisa, a scientist at the Institute of Ethnography and History (Kunstkamera) in Petersburg, and Vika, a waitress from Ekaterinburg. The uneducated, the backward, and the vulgar in *Kokoko* are situated where they have always been in Russian classical literature—in the provinces. The self-professedly educated, progressive, and sensitive reside in the literary capital of St. Petersburg. This traditional symbolic geography, with St. Petersburg rather than Moscow as the center in the film, is appropriate in that it addresses the age-old problem so central to Russian culture of the relationship between the intelligentsia and the people. Moreover, the film neatly overlays the intelligentsia versus the people dichotomy onto the capital versus the provinces one, with the characters replaying the familiar roles of the capital looking at the people with a mix of attraction and apprehension, and the people looking to the capital for validation and (material) advancement.

In brief, Lisa and Vika meet in their shared compartment on an overnight train. The following morning, on realizing they've both been robbed, they file a report at a police station. Lisa offers to put Vika up for a few days, but when a friendship between them develops, she invites her to stay indefinitely. In contrast to Subbotina's Dasha—a typical post-Soviet Cinderella, even if not the oligarch's cleaning lady—Smirnova's Vika differs radically from the "pure" provincial girls with whom the audience is familiar: older, more cynical, and downright vulgar at times, she is far from helpless. She is not searching for a prince and seems, in fact, quite capable of looking after herself. While keenly

From *Kokoko* (dir. Avdotia Smirnova, 2012).

aware of Vika's status as a girl from a remote provincial place, Lisa and her crowd refer to Vika not as a provincial but (explicitly, and not without derision) as a "representative of the people." Smirnova thus employs the provincial metaphor to reimagine the intelligentsia–the people relationship in contemporary terms—namely, on the basis of class, education, and geography.

The friendship between these two very different women progresses through three clearly discernible stages, which, as indicated by the final scene, may well comprise a potentially self-perpetuating, unending cycle. In the first stage, Lisa tries Vika's flashy style of dress on for size and "test drives" her easy attitude toward life. She perks up her drab wardrobe with Vika's gift of a red mink jacket, "loses" the tidy bun on her head, and lets her hair down, literally and figuratively, as the two start going to parties and bars and drinking to excess. Out on the town, against the background of the grey Petersburg night, Lisa and Vika form two bright dots—virtual mirror images in their matching red jackets of fur and leather, respectively. The jackets function as one of several markers of harmony in the film, most notably the Siamese twin fetuses on display at the Kunstkamera Museum. Lena Doubivko notes that the shot of Vika and Lisa, framing the jar containing the embalmed Siamese fetuses, is "the most symbolically loaded . . . of the film," observing, further, that "the intelligentsia and the people, as the twin fetuses, [are not only] infinitely bound to each other, their problematic relationship is going to remain stale and unaltered like the formaldehyde solution in the stuffy museum."[64]

This variation of the fixed plot featuring "a provincial in the big city" affords Lisa the convenience of engaging in the intelligentsia's traditional quest of "going to the people" without having to leave her comfort zone: it brings the representative of the people to her own home. That she perceives her friendship with Vika in terms of the populist quest, however, is clear: toward the end of the first stage of the relationship, Lisa defends Vika before her ex-husband, Kirill. "How terribly unfair we are toward our people," she says, in a speech worthy of a third-rate nineteenth-century populist novel.

Doubivko justly characterizes Lisa's stance as colonialist.[65] The intelligentsia's attitude toward the people as the Other includes both the contempt for and a desire to elevate the people to their own (proper) level of culture; it is indeed colonialist and Orientalist. Time and again, Lisa and her colleagues display their condescension toward Vika even as they appreciate her sparkle, her cooking, and her talented renditions of folk songs. This patronizing attitude finds its fullest expression in Lisa's speech to Kirill, where she refers to Vika as a "touching creature" who is "lively and original, [and] far from stupid." "Yes," Lisa admits, "she has terrible taste and vulgar manners; yes, she dresses like a prostitute, but with all that, what vitality and strength she possesses!" Finally, Lisa proclaims, "we are to blame. Since childhood, we've read books, been taken to museums, our parents belonged to the intelligentsia . . . whereas what did *they* see?" Lisa's "speech" is a typical example of Orientalist discourse, characterized by apophatic definition: "the people" are defined by their lack of what constitutes the norm for those who observe them—namely, books, museums, and a certain style of dress and speech. Also in truly Orientalist manner, the savage is endowed with an exaggerated (albeit appealing) vitality.

Lisa enjoys her own self-righteousness, Vika's talents at keeping house (alas, the provincial woman has not escaped the pigeonhole of being the domestic help after all), and the "good life" of drinking and party-going, to the extent that she invites Vika to stay on permanently. It follows, then, that in the second stage of their friendship, Lisa begins the process of educating Vika so as to transform her into someone more on a par with those in her circles, or at least the average "Petersburgian." She begins with a lesson on the various styles of architecture in Petersburg, during which Vika mispronounces *rococo* as "*kokoko*," a mistake she comes to repeat (hence the film's title). Throughout the film and her course of education, however, Vika is not unaware of being an object of study herself. She sees the pleasure Lisa takes in her role as benefactor and teacher and happily plays along: when Lisa lectures, Vika agrees she "must be stupid," and asks to be educated further.

However, by the third stage of their friendship, both women have grown disenchanted with their arrangement. On discovering her ex-husband Kirill and Vika "together," the furious Lisa decides to take action and throw Vika out, at which point it becomes especially apparent that this woman of the people is not so easily manipulated. Rather, Vika turns the tables with a host of recriminations: "You lied to me!" she screams through her tears, "Why did you promise me so much? I am not to blame! I believed you!" In presenting herself thus, as a pathetic object of the intelligentsia's neglect, Vika clearly, if only intuitively, behaves as she is expected to from Lisa's Orientalist perspective. Vika delivers a brilliant final blow by concluding her defense with a literary quote—namely, "We are responsible for those we tame."

Unable to fully forgive Vika's betrayal, Lisa tries to smother her with a pillow, at which point the camera cuts abruptly to the police station, where not Lisa, but Vika is behind bars. Thus, their friendship seems to end where it began, at a police station. In the final scene, Lisa goes back to the police and withdraws her complaint against Vika, insisting it was only an argument between friends. This time, however, Vika screams, "Do not give me back to her! I want to go home!" to the accompaniment of "Valenki," one of the most famous folk songs, in a rendition by Lidia Ruslanova, an acclaimed actress of peasant origins. As such, Ruslanova both represents and performs authenticity, in much the same way that Lisa and Vika perform their roles, respectively, as the face of the intelligentsia's *noblesse oblige* and, to a lesser extent, the object of an Orientalist's construction.

Smirnova is careful not to take sides. While viewers clearly discern the harshness of the criticism directed at the intelligentsia, on the one hand, Vika elicits such a broad range of responses, on the other, that it is impossible to characterize her as either a predator or a victim. The film's success at the box office affirms that Smirnova succeeded in "an almost revolutionary experiment filling the void between fierce arthouse and blockbusters."[66] The success of *Kokoko*—pleasing to all sectors of the viewing public—is itself a compromise between the intelligentsia and the people. That the encounter between them occurs in St. Petersburg and, specifically, in Lisa's home, rather than a village or provincial town, is particularly significant, the implication being that the post-Soviet version of the provincial myth renders it no longer necessary for the people-loving intelligentsia (and ethnographers!) to leave the capital in search of their objects of study. Thus, the cultural myth of the provinces provides a fresh angle from which to contemplate the age-old divide between the intelligentsia and the people as well as the many other "eternal" Russian questions.

Both the "terrible" provinces of "serious" cinema and the "not terrible" provinces of popular cinema constitute the cultural myth that is developed and exploited within the framework of the discourse of nationalism. The heightened interest in the provinces is part of the process of reevaluating the fundamental binary oppositions in Russian culture. The hermetic national "us versus us" model functions jointly with the ternary structure of the provinces–the capital–the West to accord the Russian heartland greater importance in its opposition to the capital and the West. For those with a hopeful view of the provinces, this emphasis signifies the affirmation of the positive within the Self and places much less focus on the negative aspects of the Other. For the ideological opposition, to speak of the provinces is to voice grave concerns over the present-day state of affairs in Russia. That the best Russian films of the twenty-first century, thus far, situate their anxious and despondent heroes in the provinces is hardly a coincidence. Critics have dubbed such directors as Khlebnikov, Serebrennikov, Shagalova, Zvyagintsev, Balabanov, Aleksei German, and some others "the new quiet ones" because their works are not intended as loud political manifestos. Rather, they voice their ideological and political opposition to the regime of Putin's Russia discreetly. The "non-Moscow" locales in these films play a crucial role in this quiet opposition; they provide a stark point of contrast to the prevailing idealization of the provinces by mainstream cinematic texts as the domain of Russia's spiritual wealth. In depicting the moral, ideological, and political crises reigning over these places, the diagnosis of the Russian condition in these films becomes all the more damning. By contrast, those films and TV series that reconcile the center with the provinces, and suggest their mutual permeability, promote an optimistic view of Russia's present and future. Itself a repository of sorts, the myth of the provinces, like all cultural myths, can be filled with virtually any content, as the means to the desired ideological ends.

Conclusion
On Cultural Authenticity

In Alexei Ivanov's *Community*, the protagonist lashes out against brands that claim to fill reality with easily discernible meaning but turn out to be empty signifiers: "all the brands in this place are a sham. And I went and hauled ass to come here for the brands." To his interlocutor's remark, "your car's not a sham. And your coat's not a sham," he replies: "*Life* is a sham. I put on my coat, get in my car, and there's nowhere to go.... Who's the one hyping this fake reality? Who's pumping bullshit full of false value?"[1] Most readers could tell Gleb that a brand is no substitute for reality and does not pretend to be. It merely aspires to promote a product by packaging it in an appealing way. In post-Soviet times, the provinces is a cultural product packaged to be used in the discourse of national identity. Depending on the producer, it is presented as either appealing or hideous. Those who are not satisfied with the brand are free to reject both versions. They cannot, however, escape the capital-provinces binary within which both locales are always interpreted. Like Gleb, whose infatuation with Moscow's glamorous artifice ended in his dissatisfaction with the very same, those who bring to the provinces their biases and preconceptions are caught between two opposing conceptions: on the one hand, the upbeat conception of the provinces as the reserve of the national spirit, and on the other hand, the depressing vision of provincial Russia mired in grime and degradation.

By examining the development of this binary at the beginning of the twenty-first century, I sought to denaturalize both approaches by exposing their ideological roots. Though all cultural myths are rooted in ideology, those serving the narratives of nationalism are all the more so. How unique is Russian nationalism in its reliance on the story of an authentic national core situated far from the prosperous and unauthentic centers of power? Not the least bit. The quest for true nation-ness is a global phenomenon, from Africa and the Middle East, to Latin America and Eastern Europe, to Ireland and the United States. "The nation's very reason for being," Colin Graham writes of Ireland, "its logic of existence, is its claim to an undeniable authenticity as a pure expression of the 'real,' the obvious, the natural."[2] American scholars of regional and ethnic literatures, fields that now often intertwine, have assumed the notions of organicism and authenticity as major critical concepts and objects of study. Jeff Karem describes the early twentieth-century American regionalism as seeking "a new national voice in regional writers, valorizing them for their connection to life distant from the metropole." Lothar Honninghausen sees in regionalism "the spirit of a holistic-organicist and nationalistic worldview, seeking in the return to the region a simple, wholesome and authentic America."[3] Over the course of the century, regionalism evolved into the contemporary interest in ethnic literature and literature in general that gives voice to marginalized groups and regions. The perception of national and cultural authenticity as belonging to those groups and places located far from the physical and metaphorical centers of power remains a potent force in national discourses. Yet authenticity, like the visions of national origins it supports, remains elusive and resistant to definition; it is best understood as "a series of claims, a desire for validation."[4]

The editors of the volume *True West* examine the mythology of the American "Old West" only to find that "whether it be past ways of life, distant landscapes, untainted but always corruptible nature, or the promise of spiritual fulfillment or material wealth, the horizons of authenticity—that which limits and thereby enables the desire for it—are always somewhere else in space or time."[5] The "real" American South, Scott Romine explains, is "a territory associated, in my mind at least, with a white quasi nation always, already consigned to an irretrievable past—a place where a certain kind of I wishes that it were."[6] The American Indian, the nation's own true native, is also coopted into the educated elite's vision of authenticity. Drucilla Mims Wall looks at how "Europeans and Euro-Americans have of late intensified their long-established predilection for representing American Indians as the human embodiment of the sacred in 'Mother Earth.' This phenomenon is as old as first contact but is receiving increased contemporary currency through nature writing, eco-tourism, alternative religious pursuits, and environmentalism generally."[7] Scholars of Latin America note that "since the inception of Latin America as the 'New World,' what characterizes this discourse is the constant referent of Europe, whether to position Latin America as the same or different, authentic or Other."[8] And in the Middle East, as Christa Salamandra illustrates, the reinvention of traditions, however commodified, is a practice of self-definition, as for "Damascenes [who] are producing and reproducing—and marketing—a sense of Damasceneness: a rich 'authenticity' as they see it, a bogus elitism to the newcomers who share the city with them."[9] The power of the myth of origins to elicit strong national sentiment is not diminished by its commodification. Thus, for instance, Nicola Macleod points out the enormous effect of the film *Braveheart* (1995) on young Scots. This American film, starring and directed by Australian born Mel Gibson, produced a genuine "sense of identity" in young Scots and "reasserted [their] interest in Scottish nationalism."[10]

For the mythological imagination, real historical data and geography are of no value. The Russian provincial myth, like the myths of the authentic America, Scotland, Ireland, or Syria, consigns authenticity to the "irretrievable past." It stems from such visions as the Slavophiles' pre-Petrine utopia and the Village Prose writers' pre-revolutionary village, whereby it shapes conceptions of the true Russian spirit that, if it is to survive at all, must be situated far from the modern centers of power and culture. These places are both deep in the past and deep in the country's heartlands. Mikhail Bakhtin writes about the "historical inversion" typical to mythological forms—that is, the inversion of time that transforms a vision of the past into a model for the future: "A thing that could and in fact must only be realized exclusively in the future is here portrayed as something out of the past, a thing that is in no sense part of the past's reality, but a thing that is in its essence a purpose, an obligation."[11] The subject of myth, Bakhtin observes, exists far away and long ago: "One need only conceive of its once having existed in its 'natural state' in some Golden Age, or perhaps existing in the present but somewhere at the other end of the world, east of the sun and west of the moon, if not on earth then underground, if not underground then in heaven."[12] The cultural myth of the provinces is governed by the same chronotope. Slavophile thought operated within the dual structure of "distant in time and in space": the Slavophiles found the forms of social organization best suited for the Russian people in ancient Rus', and they viewed their mission as the "revelation of the ancient, deep, mighty, and mysterious essence of Russia, its true spirit."[13] The early twentieth-century interest in the provinces also conflated the temporal and spatial perspectives in treating the provinces as "the national conservancy area." The provinces were understood as places situated far in the depths of Russia, where one gained access to Russia's past. They were perceived as "not here and now . . . but there and then," as removed both in time and in space from the country's cultural and political center.[14]

Moreover, the provincial myth integrates the vertical axis (i.e., higher and lower) in its very vocabulary: the term *glubinka*, "in the depths," implies such a vertical relationship. When Berdyaev, in the quote with which I began, admonishes the intellectuals for their illusion-driven quest after "the essence of the spiritual and social life of the nation . . . somewhere out in the depths of Russia," he adheres to the same vertical vision, as he also does in the suggestion that "the true center is neither in the capital, nor the provinces, in neither the highest, nor lowest stratum, but in the depths of each individual."

In "thinking about national identity," Edith Clowes posits a recent paradigm shift, from the temporal focus in Soviet ideology—"Soviet dominance in the race to control history"—to the post-Soviet focus on space, on "imagined geographies," with their familiar, and important, dichotomies of east and west, center and periphery, and self and other.[15] The emphasis on space is indeed more apparent in the aftermath of the Soviet empire's collapse and Russia's newly contracted borders. However, the discourse of nationalism is always organized along both axes; it integrates the vision of its legitimizing past with the imagined geographies in which it situates its Others. The dynamic of "yesterday and there" continues to inform post-Soviet nationalist discourse, as evidenced by the recent flood of historical films and TV productions that reinterpret key events in Russian history and celebrate the nation's past, from the Times of Troubles to (especially) World War II.[16] The rhetoric of official speeches, echoed by the state media, also supports such a reliance on the mythical notions of the past and the depths of Russia. In his 2012 Address to the Federal Assembly, President Vladimir Putin suggests establishing an unbroken link to the past: "In order to revive

Conclusion

national consciousness, we need to link historical eras and get back to understanding the simple truth that Russia did not begin in 1917, or even in 1991, but rather, that we have a common, continuous history spanning over one thousand years, and we must rely on it to find inner strength and purpose in our national development." In the same speech he promises to raise the standards of living for the educated members of the middle class, which he locates in the provinces: "This will be particularly noticeable in the regions. We will support the revival of the provincial intelligentsia, which was once Russia's professional and moral backbone."[17] In today's Russia, state nationalism has penetrated all levels of the public sphere. The State produces the discourse, and the public sphere reacts to it in a situation of total reach by the media (from TV to social networks) and total inclusion in the discussion of all social groups. The "imaginary authenticity of the native," as Viatcheslav Morozov puts it, plays a central role in the Kremlin's "promotion of traditional values both as a 'spiritual bond' inside and as a soft power resource in foreign affairs."[18]

Like nationalism, authenticity is an intellectual product of modernity; its understanding is culturally constructed and accords with cultures' contemporary concerns. "Our search for authentic cultural experience," Richard Handler writes, "for the unspoiled, pristine, genuine, untouched and traditional—says more about us than about others [and] proves to be a working out of our own myths."[19] The way in which the provincial myth has been reconfigured in Russian culture makes it an integral component in the Russians' attempts to work out their national mythology. As Lounsbery has demonstrated, provinciality has always been key to Russia's vision of its position in the world: "In Russia, provincialism is deeply worrisome because the provinciality of the provinces can be seen to reflect the provinciality and perhaps even the 'inauthenticity' of the nation as a whole." Thus, the Russian provincial myth's claim of preserving genuine nation-ness is complicated by the traditional perception of the provinces as derivative and inauthentic.

Yet, as I have demonstrated, in the post-Soviet period, the provinces no longer denote inauthenticity; on the contrary, they stand for true Russianness, regardless of their portrayal as either positive or negative. In fact, the provinces claim a different kind of authenticity: the kind employed with equal gusto in politics, marketing, and the tourist industry the world over. They have rebranded themselves as "the real thing"—the original, whose value is undiminished by any number of reproductions. The change in the meaning of the provinces follows this shift in understanding authenticity: from an aesthetic and metaphysical category to a tool of ideology and marketing. This understanding is both modern and postmodern: it reflects the modernist anxiety over a world perceived as fragmented and the longing for organic wholeness; it also proceeds toward the postmodern celebration of fragmentation as pluralism and distrust in unequivocal definitions and cultural certainties. Authenticity is thus textually constructed, variously understood, and disseminated through the multiple texts that claim or define it. Thus, it remains open to manipulation and, like all cultural myths, can be filled with any content. The myth of the Russian provinces as the locale of authentic Russianness, despite the shifts in hierarchies and ideologies, continues to define the Russian national idea.

To be useful, a cultural myth must be articulated and transmitted through texts, ranging from literature and film to folk festivals and ethno-parks.[20] One might expect that continuous transmission would lead to transmutation: the more explicitly cultural figures ponder a cultural myth, the more they expose its constructed nature. By this logic, the more people presume the formulaic nature of a cowboy Western's plot, or cringe at Disney's take on native Americans or a professional folk troupe's version of a folk song, the weaker the cultural myth's appeal should become; yet this has not occurred. As long as the Russian national identity remains preoccupied with the symbolic geography configured by binary oppositions, the provincial myth will preserve its key importance. Most of the texts I have analyzed present a rather mechanical division of Russia into the capital and the noncapital; their portrayals of both align with long-established cultural clichés. Still, this does not mean the provincial myth has exhausted its text-generating potential, or that the provinces have ceased to be the focal point of Russian identity. On the contrary, its importance is assured for as long as the Russian national idea is determined by its Others and Russian symbolic geography is defined by the oppositions of Russia versus the West and the provinces versus the capital. The quest for the Russian idea is ongoing, as is the quest for suitable Others, and both are driven by *ressentiment*. I conclude by turning, once again, to Ivan Aksakov, arguably the one nineteenth-century nationalist thinker who believed in the provinces' potential to regenerate Russia, and whose words are as relevant to today's Russia as they were to the Russia of his day:

> As long as the Russian intelligentsia lived by full, imperturbable faith in the West, they could ignore and scorn the provinces in their

language. But as soon as this faith was breached, as soon as the source of the West's spiritual powers, on which we subsisted for so long, was depleted, drained out, and we discovered it was impossible to draw on any longer, without losing all spiritual and material self-sufficiency; as soon as our boils and ugly warts started to reveal themselves ever more glaringly, as did our powerlessness to treat them; as soon as literature really started to gather momentum and its word began to exert influence over the concerns of social life—the shallowness of life in the capitals became instantly apparent. No longer did the provinces gravitate toward the capital, as in the past, but rather the capital, now, started gravitating toward the provinces. . . . You can definitely say, this is the dawning of a new era, the era of the capital's gravitation toward the provinces.[21]

Notes

Introduction

1. Nikolai Berdiaev, "O vlasti prostranstva nad russkoi dushoi," in *Sud'ba Rossii: Opyty po psikhologii voiny i natsional'nosti* (Moscow: Filosofskoe ob-vo SSSR, 1990), 62–63.

2. Nikolai Berdiaev, "Tsentralizm i narodnaia zhizn'," in *Sud'ba Rossii*, 70. On Berdyaev and the center-provinces opposition, see G. V. D'iachenko, "Dekonstruktsiia antitezy tsentr-provintsiia N. A. Berdiaevym," in *Zhizn' provintsii kak fenomen dukhovnosti* (Nizhnii Novgorod, 2009), 214–16.

3. Roland Barthes, "Myth Today," in *Mythologies*, trans. Annette Lavers (New York: Hill and Wang, 1988), 110.

4. On myth and cultural memory, see Lyudmila Parts, *The Chekhovian Intertext: Dialogue with a Classic* (Columbus: Ohio State University Press, 2008).

5. For a succinct but comprehensive overview of the terms and trends of provincial studies, see Susan Smith-Peter, "Bringing the Provinces into Focus: Subnational Spaces in the Recent Historiography of Russia," *Kritika: Explorations in Russian and Eurasian History* 12, no. 4 (2011): 835–48. An invaluable resource is E. G. Miliugina, M. V. Stroganov, "Tekst prostranstva. Fragmenty slovaria 'Russkaia Provintsiia,'" *Labirint* 2 (2012) and 3 (2012): 33–74.

6. L. O. Zaionts, "Istoriia slova i poniatiia provintsiia v russkoi kul'ture," *Russian Literature* 53 (2003): 308.

7. Ibid., 314.

8. See, for instance, Marc Raeff, *The Origins of the Russian Intelligentsia* (New York: Harcourt Brace, World, 1966); Mary Cavender, *Nests of the Gentry: Family, Estate, and Local Loyalties in Provincial Russia* (Newark: University of Delaware Press, 2007); V. A. Domanskii, "Russkaia usad'ba v khudozhestvennoi literature XIX veka: kul'turologicheskie aspekty izucheniia poetiki," *Vestnik Tomskogo gos. universiteta* 291 (June 2006): 56–60; Bella Grigorian, "'Figura blednaia, neiasnaia': Obraz pomeshchika v romanakh Goncharova," *Novoe literaturnoe obozrenie* 106 (2010): 117–29.

9. Michael Hughes, "The Russian Nobility and the Russian Countryside: Ambivalences and Orientations," *Journal of European Studies* 36, no. 2 (2006): 115–37.

10. Ibid., 131.

11. Zaionts, "Istoriia slova i poniatiia provintsiia," 318.

12. In analyzing the cultural landscape of Russia, Vladimir Kagansky makes this distinction central: periphery is defined by the lack of self-sufficiency; hence, it is fully governed by the State-Center. By contrast, the provinces comprise a connected network of smaller centers, relatively self-sufficient and equally removed from the center and form the country's periphery. Vladimir Kaganskii, "Rossiia. Provintsiia. Landshaft," *Otechestvennye Zapiski* 5, no. 32 (2006): 244–315.

13. A. P. Evgen'eva, *Slovar' russkogo iazyka v 4-kh tomakh* (Moscow: Poligrafresursy, 1999).

14. This 1937 newspaper article is quoted in Zaionts, "Istoriia slova i poniatiia provintsiia."

15. T. V. Klubkova, P. A. Klubkov, "Russkii provintsial'nyi gorod i stereotipy provintsial'nosti," in *Russkaia provintsiia: Mif—tekst—real'nost'*, ed. A. F. Belousov and T. V. Tsiv'ian (Moscow, St. Petersburg: Tema, 2000), 29.

16. A. F. Belousov, "Simvolika zakholust'ia (oboznachenie rossiiskogo provintsial'nogo goroda)," in *Geopanorama russkoi kul'tury. Provintsiia i ee lokal'nye teksty*, ed. L. O. Zaionts (Moscow: Iazyki slavianskoi kul'tury, 2004), 457–80; also Daria Aslamova, "Uriupinsk—eto my!" in Daria Aslamova, *V liubvi kak na voine* (Moscow: Olma Press, 2005), 236–43.

17. Aleksei Iudin, "Kontsepty 'provintsiia' i 'region' v sovremennom russkom iazyke," *Otechestvennye Zapiski* 5, no. 31 (2006): 35. See also Ia. E. Akhapkina, "Provintsiia, periferiia—problemy nominatsii," in *Provintsiia kak real'nost' i ob"ekt osmysleniia*, ed. A. F. Belousov and M. V. Stroganov (Tver': Tverskoi gos. universitet, 2001), 6–11.

18. See especially Anne Lounsbery, "'No, this is not the provinces!' Provincialism, Authenticity, and Russianness in Gogol's Day," *Russian Review* 64 (April 2005): 259–80.

19. I. A. Razumova, E. V Kuleshov, "K fenomenologii provintsii," in *Provintsiia kak real'nost' i ob"ekt osmysleniia*, 15.

20. Otto Boele, review of *Perm' kak tekst*, by Aladimir Abashev, *Slavic Review* 60 (winter 2001): 691.

21. L. O. Zaionts, "Russkii provintsial'nyi 'mif' (k probleme kul'turnoi tipologii)," in *Geopanorama russkoi kul'tury*, 428.

22. Ibid.

23. Ibid., 429.

24. Ibid., 429-30.

25. Etkind observes that "Customary for postcolonial mother countries is a composite of such sentiments as regret for indulgences, the aspiration to lower oneself in status and compensate the deprived, disappointment with one's identity, aggression toward one's own culture. In the internal colonization variant, this composite of sentiments is directed at 'the common people,' as a cultural construct." Aleksandr Etkind, "Fuko i tezis vnutrennei kolonizatsii: Postkolonial'nyi vzgliad na sovetskoe proshloe," *Novoe literaturnoe obozrenie* 49 (2001): 72.

26. For further details, see Irina Shevelenko, "Reprezentatsiia imperii i natsii: Rossiia na Vsemirnoi vystavke 1900 v Parizhe," in *Tam vnutri: praktiki vnutrennei kolonizatsii v kul'turnoi istorii Rossii*, ed. A. Etkind, D. Uffelmann, and I. Kukulin (Moscow: Novoe literaturnoe obozrenie, 2012), 413-46.

27. See, for example, Vladimir Abashev's *Perm' kak tekst: Perm' v russkoi kul'ture i literature XX veka* (Perm': Izdatel'stvo Permskogo universiteta, 2000), which studies the city of Perm as a cultural construction—an amalgamation of texts about it.

28. Abashev et al., "Liricheskuiu repliku Vitaliia Kal'pidi 'Provintsiia kak fenomen kul'turnogo separatizma' obsuzhdaiut Vladimir Abashev, Viacheslav Rakov, Andrei Matveev, Dmitrii Kharitonov, Nikolai Koliada," *Ural'skaia Nov'* 1 (2000), http://magazines.russ.ru/urnov/2000/1/otklik.html.

29. M. L. Spivak, "'Provintsiia idet v regiony': O nekotorykh osobennostiakh sovremennogo upotrebleniia slova *provintsiia*," in *Geopanorama russkoi kul'tury*.

30. See, for example, *Nestolichnaia literatura: Poeziia i proza regionov Rossii*, ed. D. Kuzmin (Moscow: Novoe literaturnoe obozrenie, 2001).

31. E. Trofimova, "Zhenskaia literatura i knigoizdanie v sovremennoi Rossii," *Obshchestvennye nauki i sovremennost'* 5 (1998): 147-56; Benjamin Sutcliffe, *The Prose of Life: Russian Women Writers from Khrushchev to Putin* (Madison: University of Wisconsin Press, 2009), 177, n. 2.

32. O. Boele, "Boris Nemtsov—provintsial. K voprosu o politicheskom imidzhmeikerstve v postperestroechnoi Rossii," in *Russkaia provintsiia: Mif—tekst—real'nost'*. See also Boris Nemtsov's autobiographical works—namely, *Provintsial* (Moscow: Vagrius, 1997) and *Provintsial v Moskve* (Moscow: Vagrius, 1999).

33. A. A. Dyrdin, "Dukhovnaia zhizn' Rossii: provintsial'noe izmerenie," in *Dukhovnaia zhizn' provintsii. Obrazy, Simvoly, Kartina mira. Materialy Vserossiiskoi nauchnoi konferentsii. Ul'ianovsk, 19-20 iiunia 2003 goda* (Ul'ianovsk: Ul'ianovskii gos. universitet, 2003), 8 [my emphasis].

34. I. A. Kuptsova, "Russkaia provintsial'naia kul'tura i rossiiskaia tsivilizatsiia: sushchnost' i vzaimodeistvie," *Srednerusskii vestnik obshchestvennykh nauk* 4 (2008): 13-19.

35. V. A. Fortunatova, "K istolkovaniiu semantiki provintsial'nogo," in *Zhizn' provintsii kak fenomen dukhovnosti. Mezhdunarodnaia nauchnaia konferentsiia 18–19 aprelia 2005 g.* (Nizhnii Novgorod: Vektor TiS, 2006), 4–9.

36. Ernest Gellner, *Nations and Nationalism* (Ithaca: Cornell University Press, 2006), 55.

37. Benedict Anderson, *Imagined Communities: Reflections on the Origins and Spread of Nationalism* (London, New York: Verso, 2006), 36.

38. Homi K. Bhabha, "Narrating the Nation," in *Nation and Narration*, ed. Homi K. Bhabha (London, New York: Routledge, 1990), 2–3.

39. Ibid., 1.

40. Anthony D. Smith, *National Identity* (Reno, Las Vegas, London: University of Nevada Press: 1991), 19.

41. Ibid., vii.

42. Simon Dixon, "The Past in the Present: Contemporary Russian Nationalism in Historical Perspective," in *Russian Nationalism Past and Present*, ed. Geoffrey Hosking and Robert Service (New York: St. Martin Press, 1998), 149–77.

43. Geoffrey Hosking, *Russia: People and Empire, 1552–1917* (Cambridge: Harvard University Press, 1997); Vera Tolz, *Russia* (London, New York: Oxford University Press, 2001); David G. Rowley, "Imperial vs. National Discourse: The Case of Russia," *Nations and Nationalism* 6, no. 1 (2000): 23–42. Other scholars see a more complex relationship between the national and the imperial: see Alexei Miller, "The Empire and the Nation in the Imagination of Russian Nationalism," in *Imperial Rule*, ed. Alexei Miller and Alfred Rieber (Budapest, New York: Central European University Press, 2004), 9–26; Olga Maiorova argues that nineteenth-century writers and thinkers worked to distinguish between the Russian nation and the Empire, reimagining the nation through cultural mythology and thereby freeing it from "the shadow of the Empire." Olga Maiorova, *From the Shadow of Empire: Defining the Russian Nation through Cultural Mythology, 1855–1870* (Madison: University of Wisconsin Press, 2010).

44. Terri Martin, *The Affirmative Action Empire: Nations and Nationalism in the Soviet Union, 1923–1939* (Ithaca: Cornell University Press, 2001).

45. Katerina Clark, *Moscow, the Fourth Rome: Stalinism, Cosmopolitanism, and the Evolution of Soviet Culture, 1931–1941* (Cambridge: Harvard University Press, 2011); Hosking, *Russia: People and Empire*.

46. Maiorova, *From the Shadow of Empire*.

47. Richard Wartman, *Scenarios of Power: Myth and Ceremony in Russian Monarchy from Peter the Great to the Abdication of Nicholas II* (Princeton: Princeton University Press, 2006).

48. Steven Usitalo, *The Invention of Mikhail Lomonosov: A Russian National Myth* (Brighton: Academic Studies Press, 2013).

49. Maiorova, *From the Shadow of Empire*.

50. Judith Kornblatt, *The Cossack Hero in Russian Literature: A Study in Cultural Mythology* (Madison: University of Wisconsin Press, 1992), 17.

51. John McCannon, *Red Arctic: Polar Exploration and the Myth of the North in the Soviet Union, 1932–1939* (New York: Oxford University Press, 1998). See also *Between Heaven and Hell: The Myth of Siberia in Russian Culture*, ed. Galya Diment and Yuri Slezkine (New York: St. Martin Press, 1993); Slava Gerovitch, *Soviet Space Mythologies: Public Images, Private Memories, and the Making of a Cultural Identity* (Pittsburgh: University of Pittsburgh Press, 2015).

52. For a useful overview, see Anthony Cross, "'Them': Russians on Foreigners," in *National Identity in Russian Culture*, ed. Simon Franklin and Emma Widdis (Cambridge: Cambridge University Press, 2004), 74–92.

53. Lounsbery, "'No, this is not the provinces!'" 266.

54. Anne Lounsbery, "Dostoevsky's Geography: Center, Peripheries, and Networks in *Demons*," *Slavic Review* 66, no. 2 (2007): 213.

55. Irina Savkina, *Provintsialki russkoi literatury (zhenskaia proza 30-40-x godov XIX veka)* (Wilhelmshorst: Verlag F. K. Göpfert, 1998).

56. To quote Etkind at length, "In view of the self-referentiality of internal colonization, the opposition of the state and the people has effectively replaced the opposition of West and East. The representatives of the state and the representatives of the people are depicted in nineteenth-century literature as people of a fundamentally different nature—or, more precisely, culture. The collision of the two personae, the Man of Nature and the Bearer of Power and Culture, formed the metanarrative of numerous classical texts, which dramatized the scenario of internal colonization, abiding by the rules of the genre." Aleksandr Etkind, "Russkaia literatura, XIX vek: Roman vnutrennei kolonizatsii," *Novoe literaturnoe obozrenie* 59 (2003): 111.

57. Lounsbery, "'No, this is not the provinces!'" 259.

58. Ibid., 266.

59. Ibid.

60. Liah Greenfeld, *Nationalism: Five Roads to Modernity* (Cambridge: Harvard University Press, 1992), 227.

61. Ibid., 250.

62. Boris Groys, "Russia and the West: The Quest for Russian Self-Identity," *Studies in Soviet Thought* 43, no. 3 (1992): 185–98.

63. See, for example, the analysis of nationalistic pathos in the final pages of *Dead Souls*, in Mikhail Vaiskopf, *Siuzhet Gogolia. Morfologiia. Ideologiia. Kontekst* (Moscow: Radiks, 1993), 403–31.

64. Friedrich Nietzsche, *On the Genealogy of Morals*, trans., Walter Kaufmann (New York: Vintage Books, 1989), 36.

65. Bernard Meltzer, Gill Musolf, "Resentment and *Ressentiment*," *Social Inquiry* 72, no. 2 (2002): 440–55.

66. Henri Tajfel, John C. Turner, "An Integrative Theory of Intergroup Conflict," in *The Social Psychology of Intergroup Relations*, ed. William G. Austin and Stephen Worchel (Monterey, CA: Brooks/Cole, 1979), 33–47; Deborah Welch Larson, Alexei Shevchenko, "Shortcut to Greatness: The New Thinking

and the Revolution in Soviet Foreign Policy," *International Organization* 57 (2003): 77–109; Linda A. Jackson et al., "Achieving Positive Social Identity: Social Mobility, Social Creativity, and Permeability of Group Boundaries," *Journal of Personality and Social Psychology* 70, no. 2 (1996): 241–54.

67. Olga Malinova, "Obsession with Status and *Ressentiment*: Historical Backgrounds of the Russian Discursive Identity Construction," *Communist and Post-Communist Studies* 47 (2014): 302.

68. Sergei Karaganov, "Novaia ideologicheskaia bor'ba?" *Izvestiia*, April 21, 2016, http://izvestia.ru/news/610812#ixzz473KfUlBz.

69. For a discussion of the concept of "false Europe," see Viatcheslav Morozov, "In Search of Europe: Russian Political Discourse and the Outside World," *Eurozine*, February 23, 2004, http://www.eurozine.com/articles/2004-02-18-morozov-en.html.

70. L. Gudkov, "Otnoshenie k SShA v Rossii i problema antiamerikanizma," in *Negativnaia identichnost'. Stat'i 1997–2002* (Moscow: Novoe literaturnoe obozrenie VTSIOM-A, 2004), 512.

71. Gellner, *Nations and Nationalism*, 119.

72. Iver B. Neumann, *Uses of the Other: The "East" in European Identity Formation* (Minneapolis: University of Minnesota Press, 1998); Larry Wolf, *Inventing Eastern Europe: The Map of Civilization on the Mind of the Enlightenment* (Stanford: Stanford University Press, 1994).

73. Tsvetan Todorov, *On Human Diversity: Nationalism, Racism, and Exoticism in French Thought* (Cambridge: Harvard University Press, 1993), 264.

74. Greenfeld, *Nationalism*, 258.

75. Andrzej Walicki, *The Slavophile Controversy: History of a Conservative Utopia in Nineteenth-Century Russian Thought* (Oxford: Clarendon Press, 1975), 231.

76. Ibid., 267.

77. Konstantin Aksakov, "'No title,' *Molva* 9 (June 8) 1857," in Konstantin Aksakov, *Gosudarstvo i Narod* (Moscow: Institut russkoi tsivilizatsii, 2009), 206.

78. Susanna Rabow-Edling, *Slavophile Thought and the Politics of Cultural Nationalism* (Albany: State University of New York Press, 2006).

79. Etkind stresses the foreign sources of the interest in the people as the Other: "Russian followers of the German romantics discovered in the common people a folklore, community, and completeness they themselves lacked. Russian followers of the French socialists discovered in the common folk a loathing for property, equality for women, and something akin to a civil religion." Aleksandr Etkind, "Fuko i tezis vnutrennei kolonizatsii," 66.

80. Fyodor Dostoevsky, *Winter Notes on Summer Impressions*, trans. Richard Lee Renfield (New York: Criterion Books, 1955), 71, 49.

81. Ibid., 46. The majority of Dostoevsky's key arguments in this work are prefaced with disclaimers: "Don't imagine that . . . ," "I most certainly do not think that . . . ," "Do not think, my friends, that I intend to argue . . . ," etc. For

this statement, too, the disclaimer serves as a marker of one of Dostoevsky's main points.

82. V. Bogomiakov, "Mify stolitsy i mify provintsii," in E. G. Miliugina, M. V. Stroganov, "Tekst prostranstva," 62.

83. Ivan Aksakov, "Ob obshchestvennoi zhizni v gubernskikh gorodakh," in Ivan Aksakov, *U Rossii odna edinstvennaia stolitsa*, ed. G. Chagin (Moscow: Russskii mir, 2006), 174.

84. Jean Levesque, "Foremen in the Field: Collective Farm Chairmen and the Fate of Labour Discipline after Collectivization," in *Dream Deferred: New Studies in Russian and Soviet Labour History*, ed. Donald A. Filtzer (Berne: Peter Lang AG, 2008), 243–64.

85. Katerina Clark, *The Soviet Novel: History as Ritual* (Bloomington/Indianapolis: Indiana University Press, 2000).

86. Kathleen Parthé, *Russian Village Prose: The Radiant Past* (Princeton: Princeton University Press, 1992), 3.

87. Ibid., 50.

88. Thus Fortunatova admits that the provinces mean "history, tradition, customs, i.e., the concentrated strength, produced by the local people, [that is,] if we don't pay attention to the dying villages, where this 'strength' is embodied by the abandoned old women, but think rather of little towns, lively and generating life." V. A. Fortunatova, "K istolkovaniiu semantiki provintsial'nogo," 7.

89. Ivan Kolodiazhnyi, "Russkaia provintsiia kak Noev kovcheg," *Russkaia narodnaia liniia*, December 21, 2015, http://ruskline.ru/special_opinion/2015/12/russkaya_provinciya_kak_noev_kovcheg/.

90. Nancy Condee, "Tales Told by Nationalists," in *Soviet and Post-Soviet Identities*, ed. Mark Bassin and Catriona Kelly (Cambridge: Cambridge University Press, 2012), 43.

91. Ibid., 41.

92. Joanna Overing, "The Role of Myth: An Anthropological Perspective," in *Myths and Nationhood*, ed. Geoffrey Hosking and George Schopflin (New York: Routledge, 1997), 1–18.

93. Anthony Smith, "The Golden Age and National Revival," in *Myths and Nationhood*, 36.

94. Emil' Pain, *Mezhdu imperiei i natsiei. Modernistskii proekt i ego traditsionalistskaia alternativa v natsional'noi politike Rossii* (Moscow: Novoe izdatel'stvo, 2004), 106.

95. See, for example, G. Diligenskii, "Druzhit' s Amerikoi," in *Desiat' let sotsiologicheskikh nabliudenii*, ed. A. A. Cherniakov (Moscow: Institut Fonda Obshchestvennogo Mneniia, 2003), 430–31; and L. Gudkov, "Ideologema vraga," in Lev Gudkov, *Negativnaia identichnost'*, 552–649.

96. See, for example, Thomas Parland, *The Extreme Nationalist Threat in Russia: The Growing Influence of Western Rightist Ideas* (Abington: Routledge Curzon, 2005); Vyacheslav Likhachev, *Natsizm v Rossii* (Moscow: Panorama, 2002); and

A. Umland, "Tri raznovidnosti postsovetskogo fashizma. Kontseptual'nye i kontekstual'nye problemy interpretatsii sovremennogo russkogo ul'tranatsionalizma," in *Sovremennye interpretatsii russkogo natsionalizma*, ed. Marlen Lariuel' [Marlène Maruelle] (Stuttgart: Ibidem-Verlag, 2007), 129–70.

97. G. Zvereva, "Diskurs gosudarstvennoi natsii v sovremennoi Rossii," in *Sovremennye interpretatsii russkogo natsionalizma*, 21.

98. Ibid., 41.

99. V. Voronkov, O. Karpenko, "Patriotizm kak natsionalizm (post)sovetskogo cheloveka," in *Sovremennye interpretatsii russkogo natsionalizma*, 109. See also Vitaly Bezrogov, "'If the War Comes Tomorrow': Patriotic Education in the Soviet and Post-Soviet Primary School," in *Soviet and Post-Soviet Identities*, 113–28.

100. *Molodezh' Rossii*, ed. L. Gudkov, B. Dubin, and N. Zorkaia (Moscow: Moskovskaia Shkola Politicheskikh Issledovanii, 2011), 28.

101. O. Mikhalin, "Est' li v Rossii demokratiia?" *The Moscow Post*, September 15, 2009, http://www.moscow-post.com/politics/001252991497517/.

102. J. Zwejnert, "Conflicting Patterns of Thought in the Russian Debate on Transition: 2003–2007," *Europe-Asia Studies* 62, no. 4 (2010): 547–69. Analyzing articles and monographs by Russian economists, Zwejnert concludes that many Russian anti-Western economists base their preference for the "Russian economic model" on the certainty that "Russians cannot develop fully within the framework of a market economy," "cannot live without a super-objective," and "ought to subordinate their personal interests to the interests of the state."

103. Maksim Shevchenko, "My ne Evropa? I slava Bogu! Rossiia—odin iz poslednikh oplotov cheloveka i chelovechestva," *Moskovskii Komsomolets*, #26160, February 11, 2013, http://www.mk.ru/politics/2013/02/10/810258-myi-ne-evropa-i-slava-bogu.html.

104. Petr Akopov, "Russkie osoznaiut svoiu samostoiatel'nost'," *Vzgliad*, February 4, 2016, http://www.vz.ru/politics/2016/2/4/792395.html.

105. Natalia Ivanova, *Russkii krest. Literatura i chitatel' v nachale novogo veka* (Moscow: Vremia, 2011), 73.

106. Condee, "Tales Told by Nationalists," 39.

107. Edward. E. Said, *Orientalism* (New York: Vintage Books, 1979), 68.

108. Homi K. Bhabha, *The Location of Culture* (London, New York: Routledge, 1994), 96.

109. "Liricheskuiu repliku Vitaliia Kal'pidi 'Provintsiia kak fenomen kul'turnogo separatizma' obsuzhdaiut Vladimir Abashev, Viacheslav Rakov, Andrei Matveev, Dmitrii Kharitonov, Nikolai Koliada."

110. Ian Buruma, Avishai Margalit, *Occidentalism: The West in the Eyes of Its Enemies* (New York: Penguin Press 2004), 8; see also Couze Venn, *Occidentalism: Modernity and Subjectivity* (London, Thousand Oaks, New Delhi: SAGE Publications 2000).

111. Lev Gudkov, "Resursy 'putinskogo' konservatizma," *Polit.ru*, January 31, 2016, http://polit.ru/article/2016/01/31/conservatism/. See also Lev Gudkov in the article "Demokratii v Rossii nikto ne khotel": "The peripheries, the provinces, are very depressed, poor, for all these years they've been extremely conservative minded, dreaming of the restoration of the Soviet distribution system, guaranteeing free healthcare, housing allowances, employment, with some assurances of [maintaining] day-to-day existence, but not of any changes." http://www.levada.ru/2015/06/15/demokratii-v-rossii-nikto-ne-hotel-2/.

112. Gudkov, "Ideologema vraga"; V. D. Solovei, "Revoliutsiia russkoi identichnosti. Rossiia dlia russkikh?" *Monitoring obshchestvennogo mneniia* 4, no. 80 (2006): 51–67.

113. "Velichie vmesto demokratii: kak Rossiia dognala SShA v umakh svoikh zhitelei," http://www.levada.ru/2016/02/04/velichie-vmesto-demokratii-kak-rossiya-dognala-ssha-v-umah-svoih-zhitelej/.

114. N. P. Popov, "Poiski natsional'noi idei Rossii prodolzhaiutsia," VTSIOM, November 27, 2009, http://russkie.org/?module=fullitem&id=16991.

115. "Moskva i provintsiia," VTSIOM, September 4, 2012, 2016, http://wciom.ru/index.php?id=236&uid=113000.

116. O. Mozgovaia, "Moskva teper' provintsii po nravu. My ne razdrazhaem, nam ne zaviduiut," *Vecherniaia Moskva*, September 7, 2006; Aleksandra Maiantseva, "Provintsialy ne liubiat moskvichei," *Komsomol'skaia Pravda*, August 31, 2013, http://www.msk.kp.ru/daily/26126/3018983/.

117. A distinction should be made between the widely used terms "migrants" and "provincials": the former refers to people from the former republics of the Soviet Union, especially form Central Asian countries such as Uzbekistan and Tadzhikistan. The latter term refers to Russians from other Russian regions. Internet forum lovehate.ru: http://www.lovehate.ru/Muscovites/12.

118. Aleksandra Maiantseva, "Provintsialy ne liubiat moskvichei": "A fifth of Russians believe Muscovites to be proud and arrogant. Ten percent of respondents believe that the residents of the capital are greedy and covetous. Many respondents believe that uncultured and rude people live in Moscow."

119. "First and foremost is the provincial's 'alienness'—residents of the capital have described it variously, . . . most frequently as [possessing] 'small-minded or unsophisticated interests, a certain coarseness'; 'cheesiness, outmodedness and lack of taste in clothing, choice of reading material, music, and recreational activities,' 'poor education.'" Anatolii Stesin, "Moskvichi priznalis', za chto nenavidiat provintsialov," *Maxpark*, September 24, 2011, 2016, http://maxpark.com/community/Rodina_Russia/content/810369.

120. See the interview with Levada's analyst Aleksei Levinson, "Moskvichi ne tak uzh ugriumy," *Moslenta*, April 24, 2015, http://moslenta.ru/article/2015/04/24/moskvichi/.

Chapter 1. Journalism

1. See, for instance, Vera Tolz, "Forging the Nation: National Identity and Nation Building in Post-Communist Russia," *Europe-Asia Studies* 50, no. 6 (1998): 993–1022; Daniel R. Kempton, Terry D. Clark, *Unity or Separation: Center-Periphery Relations in the Former Soviet Union* (Westport: Praeger, 2002); *Russian Nationalism, Foreign Policy and Identity Debates in Putin's Russia: New Ideological Patterns after the Orange Revolution*, ed. Marlène Laruelle (Stuttgart: Ibidem-Verlag, 2014).

2. *Russkaia provintsiia: Literaturno-khudozhestvennyi i istoriko-publitsisticheskii zhurnal* (Novgorod, Pskov, Tver: Novgor. pisat. org. i dr., 1991–2002); *Rossiiskaia provintsiia* (Naberezhnye Chelny: Mnogoprofil. khoz. assots. Prikam'e, 1993–1999); *Gubernskii stil': russkii provintsial'nyi zhurnal literatury i publitsistiki* (Voronezh: Tsentral'no-Chernozyomnoe knizhnoe izd-vo, 2006–).

3. Ia. Akhapkina, "Provintsiia, periferiia—problemy nominatsii," in *Provintsiia kak real'nost' i ob"ekt osmysleniia*, ed. A. F. Belousov and M. V. Stroganov (Tver': Tverskoi gos. universitet, 2001), 11.

4. M. L. Spivak, "'Provintsiia idet v regiony': O nekotorykh osobennostiakh sovremennogo upotrebleniia slova provintsiia," in *Geopanorama russkoi kul'tury. Provintsiia i ee lokal'nye teksty*, ed. L. O. Zaionts (Moscow: Iazyki slavianskoi kul'tury, 2004), 503–15.

5. Otto Boele, "Boris Nemtsov—provintsial. K voprosu o politicheskom imidzhmeikerstve v postperestroechnoi Rossii," in *Russkaia provintsiia: Mif—tekst—real'nost'*, ed. A. F. Belousov and T. V. Tsiv'ian (Moscow, St. Petersburg, 2000), 118–28; see also E. G. Miliugina and M. V. Stroganov, "Tekst prostranstva. Fragmenty slovaria 'Russkaia provintsiia,'" entry Provintsial/-ka v stolitse, *Labirint. Zhurnal sotsial'no-gumanitarnykh issledovanii* 3 (2012): 35, http://journal-labirint.com/wp-content/uploads/2012/07/journal/milugina-stroganov.pdf.

6. *Rossiiskaia provintsiia* 1 (1993): 1.

7. Iurii Milovanov, "So stolitsei naravne. Zametki o perezhivaniiakh provintsial'noi intelligentsii," *Rossiiskaia provintsiia* 1 (1993): 47–50.

8. Ibid., 49.

9. Ibid., 50.

10. Ibid., 49.

11. Nikita Moiseev, "Ia printsipial'nyi opportunist," *Rossiiskaia provintsiia* 1 (1993): 81.

12. Aleksandr Panarin, "Rossiia mezhdu atlantizmom i evraziistvom," *Rossiiskaia provintsiia* 1 (1993): 144.

13. Valentin Rasputin, "Skazhite vsem, chto Rus' zhiva," *Rossiiskaia provintsiia* 1 (1996): 4.

14. Iurii Solomin, "Provintsiia khranit talant dobroty," *Rossiiskaia provintsiia* 1 (1996): 10.

15. Ibid., 12.

16. Svetlana Khumar'ian, "Sizif byl schastlivee, chem my dumaem," *Rossiiskaia provintsiia* 2 (1996): 38.

17. Sergei Popadiuk, "Sviiazhsk," *Rossiiskaia provintsiia* 5 (1995): 83.

18. *Russkaia provintsiia* 2 (2000): 3. Translation excerpted and adapted from I. V. Stalin, *On the Great Patriotic War of the Soviet Union* (Moscow, 1946), 200.

19. *Russkaia provintsiia* 2 (2000): 112.

20. These titles, *Russia's* [rossiiskaia] and *Russian* [russkaia] *provinces*, affirm the distinction in the meaning of these words in the Russian language, discussed by Geoffrey Hosking and others, where the former refers to the state and empire and the latter to ethnicity.

21. Vladimir Putin, in a recent speech at the influential Valdai Discussion Club, similarly overemphasized the word "Russian" when formulating Russia's identity and mission as encompassing all ethnicities and religions. As in the case of Stalin's toast, the effect was to privilege the Russian people above all others: "Russia, as philosopher Konstantin Leontyev vividly put it, has always evolved in 'blossoming complexity' as a state-civilization, reinforced by the Russian people, Russian language, Russian culture, Russian Orthodox Church and the country's other traditional religions. It is precisely the state-civilization model that has shaped our state polity." http://russialist.org/transcript-putin-at-meeting-of-the-valdai-international-discussion-club-partial-transcript/; Russian original: http://kremlin.ru/events/president/news/19243.

22. Eliot Borenstein, "The Russia We Can't Find," in *Plots Against Russia*, http://plotsagainstrussia.org/eb7nyuedu/2016/2/15/ln58th5tzh526di36f71crsr9intb6.

23. *Novaia provintsiia* (Murom) 1, October 7, 1995, 1.

24. "O provintsii i provintsialakh," ibid., 6.

25. *Provintsial'noe slovo* 1, October 30, 2002, 1.

26. *Provintsial'noe slovo* 3, November 13, 2002, 2.

27. http://www.tk.permkrai.ru.

28. *Permskii period* 9 (2010).

29. http://magisters.narod.ru/sasastat10.html.

30. http://vk.com/vrn24.

31. http://www.gazpromspartakiada.ru/index.php?id=693.

32. http://www.dimitrovgrad.ru/projects/index.html.

33. http://www.bbc.co.uk/russian/russia/2009/10/091023_capitals_russia.shtml.

34. http://lurkmore.to/%d0%a1%d1%82%d0%be%d0%bb%d0%b8%d1%86%d0%bo.

35. M. P. Krylov, *Regional'naia identichnost' v evropeiskoi Rossii* (Moscow: Novyi khronograf, 2010), 12.

36. Ibid., 13, original emphasis.

37. Ibid., original emphasis.

38. Ibid., 71.

39. Leonid Smirniagin, "Transformatsiia obshchestvennogo prostranstva Rossii," *Otechestvennye Zapiski (Anatomiia provintsii)* 5, no. 31 (2006): 115.

40. Nadezhda Zamiatina, "Avtoreprezentatsiia regionov (po ofitsial'nym saitam sub"ektov Rossiiskoi Federatsii)," *Otechestvennye Zapiski (Anatomiia provintsii)* 5, no. 31 (2006): 272–82.

41. Semyon Pavliuk, "Chuvstvo mesta i nizovoi regionalizm," *Otechestvennye Zapiski (Anatomiia provintsii)* 5, no. 31 (2006): 109.

42. Zamiatina, "Avtoreprezentatsiia regionov," 282.

43. *Provintsialka* (Sergiev Posad) 1, October 1995, 1.

44. *Provintsial'nye vedomosti: Zhurnal dlia vsekh* (Volgograd) 12 (1994): 3.

45. See, for instance, I. V. Sibiriakov, "Tsentr i provintsiia v Rossii: Traditsiia tragicheskogo neponimaniia," in *Tsentr—provintsiia: istoriko-psikhologicheskie problemy: Materialy Vserossiiskoi nauchnoi konferentsii*, ed. S. N. Poltorak (St. Petersburg: Nestor, 2001), 194–98; Smirniagin, "Transformatsiia obshchestvennogo prostranstva Rossii."

46. Alexander Etkind, *Internal Colonization: Russia's Imperial Experience* (Cambridge: Polity Press, 2011), 7.

47. Bill Ashcroft, Gareth Griffiths, and Helen Tiffin, *Post-Colonial Studies: The Key Concepts* (London, New York: Routledge, 2009), 30.

48. David Chioni Moore, "Is the Post- in Postcolonial the Post- in Post-Soviet? Toward a Global Postcolonial Critique," *PMLA* 116, no. 1 (2001): 112.

49. Viatcheslav Morozov, *Russia's Postcolonial Identity: A Subaltern Empire in a Eurocentric World* (Basingstoke: Palgrave Macmillan, 2015), 22.

50. *Voronezh. Russkii provintsial'nyi zhurnal* 2 (1996); *Riazan' City*, May (2008).

51. http://ethnomir.ru/.

52. A. Iu. Nelepov, "Prakticheskaia realizatsiia kontseptsii razvitiia regional'nykh brendov," *Sovremennaia ekonomika: Problemy i resheniia* 2, no. 2 (2010): 16.

53. Gary Warnaby, Dominic Medway, "Semiotics and Place Branding: The Influence of the Built and Natural Environment in City Logos," in *Toward Effective Place Brand Management: Branding European Cities and Regions*, ed. Gregory Ashworth and Mikhalis Kavaratzis (Cheltenham, UK: Edward Elgar, 2010), 205.

54. Keith Dinnie, "Introduction to the Theory of City Branding," in *City Branding: Theory and Cases*, ed. Keith Dinnie (Houndmills, UK, New York: Palgrave Macmillan, 2011), 3.

55. N. E. Abalmasova and E. A. Pain, "Symbolic Management in Creating Regional Identity," *Regional Research of Russia* 1, no. 3 (2011): 275.

56. Can-Seng Ooi, "Paradoxes of City Branding and Societal Changes," in Dinnie, *City Branding*, 57; M. Iu. Timofeev, "Goroda i regiony Rossii kak (post) industrial'nye brendy," *Labirint. Zhurnal sotsial'no-gumanitarnykh issledovanii* 5 (2013): 29–41.

57. Anne Lounsbery, "'No, this is not the provinces!' Provincialism, Authenticity, and Russianness in Gogol's Day," *Russian Review* 64 (2005): 272.

58. T. V. Klubkova and P. A. Klubkov, "Russkii provintsial'nyi gorod i stereotipy provintsial'nosti," in *Russkaia provintsiia: Mif—tekst—real'nost'*, ed. A. F. Belousov and T. V. Tsiv'ian (Moscow, St. Petersburg: Tema, 2000), 27.

59. Alison Rowley, *Open Letters: Russian Popular Culture and the Picture Postcard, 1880–1922* (Toronto: University of Toronto Press, 2013), 59.

60. Lounsbery, "'No, this is not the provinces!" 272.

61. Pavliuk, "Chuvstvo mesta," 109.

62. Ibid., 111.

63. See for instance the following sites: *Vikislovar'*, Bombit' Voronezh, https://ru.wiktionary.org/wiki/бомбить_Воронеж; "Pol'zovateli Interneta: 'Zachem bombit' Voronezh, kogda mozhno prosto zapretit' postavliat' tuda edu?'" *Bloknot*, October 7, 2014, http://bloknot-voronezh.ru/news/polzovateli-interneta-zachem-bombit-voronezh-kogda-mozhno-prosto-zapretit-postavlyat-tuda-edu.

64. http://blog.fontanka.ru/posts/148409/.

65. *Gubernskii stil'* 1 (September 2006): 1.

66. Ibid., 3.

67. Ibid., 11.

68. *The Day of Literature* started out as a literary supplement to the newspaper *Tomorrow* and is just as openly nationalist, anti-Western, and anti-Semitic.

69. Vladimir Bondarenko, "Russkii lik patriotizma," *Gubernskii stil'* 1 (September 2006): 19–20.

70. Email from Nikolai Sapelkin to the author, July 14, 2012.

71. Zamiatina, "Avtoreprezentatsiia regionov," 276.

72. Nikolai Sapelkin, "Chem Voronezh ne Parizh?" *Gubernskii stil'* 8–9 (spring–summer 2010): 51.

73. Martin W. Lewis, Karin E. Wigen, *The Myth of Continents: A Critique of Metageography* (Berkeley: University of California Press, 1997).

74. D. N. Zamiatin, "Geokul'turnyi brending territorii. Kontseptual'nye osnovy," *Labirint. Zhurnal sotsial'no-gumanitarnykh issledovanii* 5 (2013): 13.

75. http://www.citymayors.com/marketing/city-brands.html#Anchor-Results-49575.

76. Ooi, "Paradoxes of City Branding," 55.

77. http://citycelebrity.ru/citycelebrity/Post.aspx?PostId=3104&PageId=8e215ac8-c7f5-4c24-9c51-ae738319fb94.

78. http://slovosti.ru/events/39885/.

79. http://www.gumilev-center.ru/voronezh-predstavlyaet-gubernskijj-stil/.

80. Ooi, "Paradoxes of City Branding," 96.

81. Mariia Sokolovskaia, "Gubernskii stil' ot Pekina do Parizha," *Gubernskii stil'* 8–9 (spring–summer 2010): 47.

82. Ibid., 50.

83. Catherine Evtuhov, *Portrait of a Russian Province: Economy, Society, and Civilization in Nineteenth-Century Nizhnii Novgorod* (Pittsburgh: University of Pittsburgh Press, 2011).

84. N. Sapelkin, "Voronezh Identity" (paper presented at the conference "Russian Provinces in the Context of History and Culture," Voronezh, May 17, 2013).

85. See, for instance, Sara Dickinson, *Breaking Ground: Travel and National Culture in Russia from Peter I to the Era of Pushkin* (Amsterdam, New York: Rodopi, 2006).

86. http://communa.ru/index.php?ELEMENT_ID=3331.

87. Simon Anholt. *Places: Identity, Image and Reputation* (Basingstoke: Palgrave Macmillan, 2010), 2.

88. Abalmasova and Pain, "Symbolic Management," 279.

89. O. V. Ignatiev, O. V. Lysenko, "Kul'turnaia politika i strategiia konstruirovaniia imidzha territorii," *Labirint. Zhurnal sotsial'no-gumanitarnykh issledovanii*, 1 (2015): 7.

90. Anholt, *Places*, 31.

Chapter 2. Literature

1. Karen Stepanian, "Realizm kak zakliuchitel'naia stadiia postmodernizma," *Znamia* 9 (1992): 236.

2. Helena Goscilo, introduction to *Lines of Fate* by Mark Kharitonov, trans. Helena Goscilo (New York: The New Press, 1996), 2; Clare Cavanagh, "Idiotika," review of *Lines of Fate* by Mark Kharitonov, trans. Helena Goscilo, *New York Times*, August 11, 1996.

3. N. Leiderman, M. Lipovetskii, "Zhizn' posle smerti, ili novye svedeniia o realizme," *Novy Mir* 7 (1993): 247; Andrei Nemzer, "Rasseiannye pomety na poliakh. Mark Kharitonov, Linii sud'by ili sunduchok Milashevicha," in Andrei Nemzer, *Literaturnoe segodnia. O russkoi proze. 90-e* (Moscow: Novoe literaturnoe obozrenie, 1998), 385–89.

4. Nemzer, "Rasseiannye pomety na poliakh," 388.

5. Mark Kharitonov, *Lines of Fate*, trans. Helena Goscilo (New York: The New Press, 1996), 17.

6. Ibid., 19.

7. Consider, for instance, the jam-making scene in *Anna Karenina*, which Tolstoy considered central for the novel.

8. V. V. Rozanov, "Embriony," in *Russkaia filosofiia. Konets XIX—nachalo XX v*, ed. A. A. Ermichev, B. V. Emelianov (St. Petersburg: Izd-vo S.-Peterburgskogo universiteta, 1993), 166.

9. On the tea-drinking motif, see A. K. Zholkovskii, M. B. Iampol'skii, *Babel'/Babel* (Moscow: Carte Blanche, 1994), 330–34.

10. Kharitonov, *Lines of Fate*, 19.
11. Ibid.
12. V. A. Fortunatova, "K istolkovaniiu semantiki provintsial'nogo," in *Zhizn' provintsii kak fenomen dukhovnosti. Mezhdunarodnaia nauchnaia konferentsiia 18–19 aprelia 2005 g.* (Nizhnii Novgorod: Vektor TiS, 2006), 6.
13. Svetlana Boym, *Common Places* (Cambridge: Harvard University Press, 1994), 40.
14. O. V. Konfederat, "Identifikatsiia russkogo provintsiala v smeshannoi kul'ture," in *Chelovek v prostranstve kul'tury (tsentr—provintsiia, provintsiia—tsentr). Materialy mezhregional'noi nauchno-prakticheskoi konferentsii. 21 aprelia 2004 g.* (Cheliabinsk, 2006), 35.
15. Ibid., 37.
16. Boym, *Common Places*, 74.
17. Kharitonov, *Lines of Fate*, 153.
18. See Amy Isaac Obrist, "The Russian Metahistorical Imagination and Russian Fiction of Perestroika" (PhD diss. University of Southern California, 2005).
19. Kharitonov, *Lines of Fate*, 155.
20. Ibid., 310.
21. Ibid., 109.
22. Ibid., 331.
23. Natalia Ivanova, "Bandersha i sutener. Roman literatury s ideologiei: krizis zhanra." *Znamia* 5 (2000): 174–75.
24. Svetlana Boym, *The Future of Nostalgia* (New York: Basic Books, 2001), 16.
25. Kharitonov, *Lines of Fate*, 160–61.
26. Ibid., 172.
27. A. G. Kislov, I. V. Shapko, "Sotsial'no-topologicheskoe opravdanie provintsii," *SOTsIS* 8 (2000): 120.
28. Mark Kharitonov, *Izbrannaia proza* (Moscow: Moskovskii rabochii, 1994), 153. This excerpt is missing from Goscilo's translation; translation is mine.
29. While a real place, Chukhloma has been used as a generic derogatory name for a provincial backwater.
30. Sergei Iakovlev, "Pis'mo iz Soligalicha v Oksford," *Novy Mir* 5 (1995): 107.
31. Kharitonov, *Lines of Fate*, 161.
32. Iakovlev, *Pis'mo iz Soligalicha*, 112.
33. Ibid., 133.
34. Ibid.
35. Ibid., 135.
36. Ibid., 106.
37. Ibid., 57.
38. Ibid., 110.
39. Aleksei Ivanov, "Rossii nuzhny dvoinye standarty," *Profil'*, October 7, 2006, http://www.profile.ru/arkhiv/item/50930-items_19552.

40. Il'ia Kukulin, "The Heroization of Survival," *Russian Studies in Literature* 45, no. 2 (spring 2009): 61.

41. Aleksei Ivanov, "Rossiia: Sposob sushchestvovaniia. Gde iskat' natsional'nuiu identichnost' i kak s nei zhit'?" *Russkii Reporter*, October 6, 2010, http://arkada-ivanov.ru.

42. Aleksei Ivanov, "Pisatel' Aleksei Ivanov: 'Menia vosprinimaiut kak oligarkha ot gumanitarnoi sredy,'" *Izvestiia*, August 9, 2006, http://izvestia.ru/news/316118#ixzz351DzoajN.

43. Galina Rebel, "Iavlenie Geographa, ili zhivaia voda romanov Alekseia Ivanova," *Oktiabr'*, 4 (2006): 174.

44. Aleksei Ivanov, "Rossii nuzhny dvoinye standarty."

45. Aleksei Ivanov, "V global'nom mire tsenno tol'ko unikal'noe," *Stol'nik*, June 2011, http://www.ivanproduction.ru/intervyu/v-globalnom-mire-czenno-tolko-unikalnoe.html.

46. Lev Danilkin, "Geograf globus propil," *Afisha* (Moscow) May 2003, http://www.ivanproduction.ru/reczenzii/geograf-globus-propil1/posle-oshhetinivshejsya.html.

47. Aleksei Ivanov, *Geograf globus propil* (Moscow: ACT, 2007), 478–79.

48. The comment about how difficult yet necessary it is to love Russian nature accords with the tradition of positing the Russian landscape, uninviting and non-picturesque, as essential to patriotic sentiment. See Christopher Ely, *This Meager Nature: Landscape and National Identity in Imperial Russia* (DeKalb: Northern Illinois Press, 2002).

49. Ian Shenkman, "Message—myth. Dve knigi Alekseia Ivanova—'Bluda i Mudo' i 'Chusovaia,'" *Ogonek*, May 12, 2007, http://ivanproduction.ru/reczenzii/bluda-i-mudo/message-mif.html.

50. Lev Danilkin, "Famil'ony prosiat ognia." *Afisha*, May 2, 2007, http://ivanproduction.ru/reczenzii/bluda-i-mudo/familonyi-prosyat-ognya.html.

51. Aleksei Ivanov, *Bluda i Mudo* (St. Petersburg: Azbuka—klassika, 2007), 71–72.

52. Aleksei Ivanov, *Psoglavtsy* (St. Petersburg: Azbuka—klassika, 2013), 47.

53. Ibid., 61.

54. I. N. Ivanova, "Derevenskaia proza v sovremennoi otechestvennoi literature: konets mifa ili perezagruzka?" *Filologicheskie nauki: Voprosy teorii i praktiki* (Tambov) 6, no. 24 (2013): 93.

55. Aleksei Ivanov, *Psoglavtsy*, 61.

56. Ibid., 235.

57. Ibid., 61. The reference is to the mega-popular novels by Sergei Lukianenko, *Night Watch* (*Nochnoi Dozor*), *Day Watch*, and others, populated with witches, vampires, and other dark creatures.

58. Vadim Nesterov, "Ivanov na ostanovke." *Gazeta.ru*, April 11, 2012, http://www.ivanproduction.ru/reczenzii/komyuniti1/ivanov-na-ostanovke.html.

59. Aleksei Ivanov, *Kom'iuniti* (St. Petersburg: Azbuka—klassika, 2012), 59.
60. Ibid., 79.
61. Ibid., 139.
62. S. P. Gurin, "Provintsiia: potaennost' i sokrovennost'," *Topos*, September 15, 2009, http://www.topos.ru/article/6847.
63. Natal'ia Zemskova, *Gorod na Stikse* (Moscow: Arsis Books, 2013), 328.
64. Ibid., 339.
65. Ibid., 204-5.
66. Zakhar Prilepin, "Moskva dlia menia chto-to vrode offisa," *TimeOut* (Moscow), April 4, 2016, http://www.timeout.ru/msk/feature/458212/page/2.
67. Zakhar Prilepin, "Pis'mo iz provintsii luchshim liudiam," *Russkaia planeta*, March 28, 2016, http://rusplt.ru/views/views_129.html.
68. Zakhar Prilepin, *Ia prishel iz Rossii* (St. Petersburg: Limbus Press, 2008), 245-46.
69. Zakhar Prilepin, *Sankya*, trans. Mariya Gusev and Jeff Parker (Ann Arbor: DISQUIET, 2014), 27.
70. Ibid., 29.
71. Ibid., 85.
72. Ibid., 23.
73. Ibid., 135.
74. Ibid., 177.
75. M. V. Selemeneva, "Prostranstvennye obrazy romana Z. Prilepina 'San'kia,'" *Vestnik Gosudarstvennogo Leningradskogo Universiteta im. Pushkina* 3, no. 1 (2014): 70-71.
76. Zakhar Prilepin, "Na miagkoi perine, ili o stolitse," in Prilepin, *Ia prishel iz Rossii*, 167.
77. Ibid., 166.
78. Dmitrii Bykov, "Osoboe mnenie," *Ekho Moskvy*, October 15, 2012, http://echo.msk.ru/programs/personalno/935744-echo/.
79. Dmitry Bykov, "Mozharovo," in *Read Russia: An Anthology of New Voices*, ed. Elena Shubina (Read Russia, Inc. 2012), 261.
80. Ibid., 260.
81. Ibid., 261, 262.
82. Ibid., 269.
83. See introduction, n. 103.

Chapter 3. Film and TV

1. Nancy Condee, *The Imperial Trace: Recent Russian Cinema* (Oxford: Oxford University Press, 2009).
2. David MacFadyen, *Russian Television Today: Primetime Drama and Comedy* (London, New York: Routledge, 2008); Stephen Hutchings and Natalia Rulyova,

eds., *Television and Culture in Putin's Russia* (London, New York: Routledge, 2009).

3. Birgit Beumers, "The Serialization of Culture, or the Culture of Serialization," in *The Post-Soviet Russian Media. Conflicting Signals*, ed. Birgit Beumers, Stephen Hutchings, and Natalia Rulyova (London, New York: Routledge, 2009), 159–77.

4. David C. Gillespie, *Russian Cinema* (Harlow, New York: Longman, 2003); Birgit Beumers, *A History of Russian Cinema* (Oxford, New York: Berg, 2009); *Russia on Reels: The Russian Idea in Post-Soviet Cinema*, ed. Birgit Beumers (London, New York: Tauris, 1999); *Insiders and Outsiders in Russian Cinema*, ed. Stephen M. Norris and Zara M. Torlone (Bloomington: Indiana University Press, 2008); *The Post-Soviet Russian Media: Conflicting Signals*, ed. Birgit Beumers, Stephen Hutchings, and Natalia Rulyova (London, New York: Routledge, 2009); *The Russian Cinema Reader II*, ed. Rimgalia Salys (Boston: Academic Studies Press, 2013); Yana Hashamova, *Pride and Panic: Russian Imagination of the West in Post-Soviet Film* (Bristol, Chicago: Intellect, 2007); *Russia's New Fin de Siècle: Contemporary Culture between Past and Present*, ed. Birgit Beumers (Bristol, Chicago: Intellect, 2013); *Gender and National Identity in Twentieth-Century Russian Culture*, ed. Helena Goscilo and Andrea Lanoux (DeKalb: Northern Illinois University Press, 2006); *Russian Mass Media and Changing Values*, ed. Arja Rosenblum, Kaarle Nordenstreng, and Elena Trubina (London, New York: Routledge, 2010).

5. A. Popov, "Novyi fil'm Kirilla Serebrennikova Iur'ev den' vykhodit v prokat 18 sentiabria," *ProfiCinema*, September 10, 2008, http://www.proficinema.ru/news/detail.php?ID=37159; A. Plakhov, "An Ironical Collectivist Community (*sobornost'*)," *KinoKultura* 22 (2008); Mark Lipovetsky, "Living through a Loss," *KinoKultura* 22 (2008); Dusty Wilmes, "National Identity (De)construction in Recent Independent Cinema: Kirill Serebrennikov's *Yuri's Day* and Sergei Loznitsa's *My Joy*," *Studies in Russian and Soviet Cinema* 8, no. 3 (2014): 218–32; O. Zintsov, "Ee krepost'," *Vedomosti*, September 19, 2008, http://www.vedomosti.ru/newspaper/articles/2008/09/19/ee-krepost.

6. This ambiguity of positions is reflected even in such basic components as the identity of the main protagonists: the town's police investigator mistakes Liubov for a known criminal, Liudmila/Liusia, and before long she begins using that name herself; the police investigator turns out to be a former criminal; and for the purpose of finding her son, the heroine is constantly being asked to identify various people—that is, one could say that her son, too, has numerous incarnations.

7. This representation of the provinces speaks both to the uses of the provincial myth and to its imperial essence: "The provinces . . . is the capital's term for the marginal territories, the gaze (and edictal gesture) from the center, and from the top down. The term can be scornful, condescending and even moving to tears, [but] it doesn't alter the disposition of the relations. . . . After all, the

provinces are not tangible matter, but merely an attribute of the imperial spatial structure." "Liricheskuiu repliku Vitaliia Kapil'di 'Provintsiia kak fenomen kul'turnogo separatizma' obsuzhdaiut Vladimir Abashev, Viacheslav Rakov, Andrei Matveev, Dmitrii Kharitonov, Nikolai Koliada," *Ural'skaia Nov'* 1 (2000), http://magazines.russ.ru/urnov/2000/1/otklik.html.

8. Lipovetsky, "Living through a Loss."

9. Zintsov, "Ee krepost'."

10. S. Razor, "Bandits, Oligarchs, and Provincial Girls! Oh, My!" *KinoKultura* 20 (2008).

11. Naturally, the viewers noted these "mythical and grotesque provinces" that pop up in various films and remarked upon them in various internet forums. See, for example: https://www.kinopoisk.ru/film/271819/ord/rating/status/neutral/perpage/10/page/1/#list.

12. Razor, "Bandits, Oligarchs."

13. The unproductivity, and even the danger, of a "negative identity"—i.e., "self-construction on the basis of [one's] opposite"—is analyzed by Lev Gudkov thus: "[The] negative identity is formed only in contradistinction to a heterogeneous 'other' and in negative relation to one's own reality (one's social and economic situation, and the authorities). This type of social self-determination is characteristic of totalitarian societies." See his "K probleme negativnoi identichnosti," in Lev Gudkov, *Negativnaia identichnost': Stat'i 1997–2002* (Moscow: Novoe literaturnoe obozrenie VTSIOM-A, 2004).

14. Razor, "Bandits, Oligarchs."

15. Ibid.

16. Ian Buruma, Avishai Margalit, *Occidentalism: The West in the Eyes of Its Enemies* (New York: Penguin Press 2004), 5.

17. Ibid., 10.

18. Couze Venn, *Occidentalism: Modernity and Subjectivity* (London, Thousand Oaks, New Delhi: SAGE Publications 2000), 19.

19. Alastair Bonnett, *The Idea of the West: Culture, Politics, History* (New York: Palgrave Macmillan 2004), 7.

20. Ibid., 3.

21. Buruma and Margalit, *Occidentalism*, 16.

22. See Beumers, "To Moscow! To Moscow? The Russian Hero and the Loss of the Centre," in Beumers, *Russia on Reels*. See also Condee, *The Imperial Trace*; Hashamova, *Pride and Panic*.

23. Balabanov's city is never Moscow. From Leninsk to St. Petersburg to Chicago, it is described strictly according to Occidentalist logic as soulless, technological, and market-driven. Yet, Moscow, where the killer-hero supposedly goes at the end of *Brother*, remains absent and perhaps overly complex for a schematic representation.

24. Michael Bradshaw, "Globalization, Regional Change, and the Territorial Cohesion of the Russian Federation," in *Russia and Globalization: Identity, Security,*

and Society in an Era of Change, ed. Douglas W. Blum (Baltimore: Johns Hopkins University Press 2008), 104.

25. Vladimir Kaganskii, *Kul'turnyi landshaft i sovetskoe obitaemoe prostranstvo* (Moscow: Novoe literaturnoe obozrenie, 2001), 386.

26. Ibid., 389.

27. Buruma, Margalit, *Occidentalism*, 30.

28. Pyotr Bavin, "Moskva i regiony v predstavleniiakh rossiian (mart 2001)," in *Desiat' let sotsiologicheskikh nabliudenii*, ed. A. A. Oslon (Moscow: Institut fonda "Obshchestvennoe mnenie," 2003), 255–64.

29. In Vladimir Orlov's recent novel *Kamergerskii Lane* [*Kamergerskii pereulok* (2008), the narrator's favorite café—representing the "true" Moscow—has been replaced by a faceless version of a Western restaurant chain but can still be located and frequented by a few faithful customers on another plane of existence. The true Moscow, therefore, has merely been overlain and hidden, but not destroyed.

30. Beumers, "The Serialization of Culture."

31. Yuri Slezkine, "The USSR as a Communal Apartment, or How a Socialist State Promoted Ethnic Particularism," *Slavic Review* 53, no. 2 (1994): 414–52.

32. Birgit Beumers, "The Serialization of Culture, or the Culture of Serialization," in *The Post-Soviet Media: Conflicting Signals*, ed. Birgit Beumers, Stephen Hutchings, and Natalia Rulyova (London, New York: Routledge, 2009), 176.

33. Richard Taylor, "'But Eastward, Look, the Land Is Brighter': Toward a Topography of Utopia in the Stalinist Musical," in *The Landscape of Stalinism: The Art and Ideology of Soviet Space*, ed. Evgeny Dobrenko and Eric Naiman (Seattle: University of Washington Press, 2003), 201–18.

34. Beumers, "The Serialization of Culture," 167.

35. Taylor, "But Eastward, Look," 212.

36. Ol'ga Bogoslavskaia, "Moskva: Ot rastsveta do 'rastsveta,'" *Znamia* 3 (2009): 181–99.

37. Svetlana Stepanova, "Moia prekrasnaia palata No. 6," review of *Glianets*, dir. Andrei Konchalovskii, *russart.com*, August 27, 2007, http://ruskino.ru/review/141.

38. Thomas Elsaesser, "Tales of Sound and Fury: Observations on the Family Melodrama," in *Film Genre Reader III*, ed. B. K. Grant (Austin: University of Texas Press, 2003), 366–95; Kathleen Rowe, *The Unruly Woman: Gender and the Genres of Laughter* (Austin: University of Texas Press, 1995).

39. Official website of the actor Kirill Zhandarov, http://zhandarov.ru/cinema/provincial.

40. Rowe, *The Unruly Woman*, 99.

41. David MacFayden, *Russian Television Today*, 124.

42. Interview with Anna Gres', "So mnoi 'soidet i tak' ne prokhodit, pust' dazhe kto-to na eto i obizhaetsia," *Telekritika*, April 17, 2007, http://www.telekritika.ua/lyudi/2007-04-17/8729.

43. Yuri Lotman, *Culture and Explosion*, ed. Marina Grishakova, trans. Wilma Clark (Berlin, New York: Mouton de Gruyter, 2009), 171.

44. Julian Graffy, review of Boris Khlebnikov, *Free Floating* (*Svobodnoe plavanie*, 2006), *KinoKultura* 15 (2007).

45. See Aleksandr Etkind, "Russkaia literatura, XIX vek: Roman vnutrennei kolonizatsii," *Novoe literaturnoe obozrenie* 59 (2003): 103–24.

46. Mark Lipovetskii, "V otsutstvie mediatora—Siuzhet vnutrennei kolonizatsii," *Iskusstvo Kino* 8 (August 2003).

47. http://www.nashfilm.ru/modernserials/3016.html.

48. http://ruskino.ru/mov/forum/11353/2.

49. Homi K. Bhabha, *The Location of Culture* (London, New York: Routledge, 1994), 211.

50. Ibid., 209.

51. See, for instance, Andrew Horton and Michael Brashinsky, *The Zero Hour: Glasnost and Soviet Cinema in Transition* (Princeton: Princeton University Press, 1992).

52. Eliot Borenstein, *Overkill: Sex and Violence in Contemporary Russian Popular Culture* (Ithaca: Cornell University Press, 2008), 11.

53. Seth Graham, "*Chernukha* and Russian Film," *Studies in Slavic Cultures* 1 (2000): 23.

54. Seth Graham, "The New American Other in Post-Soviet Russian Cinema," in *Russia and Its Other(s) on Film*, ed. Stephen Hutchings (New York: Palgrave Macmillan, 2008).

55. Borenstein, *Overkill*, 13.

56. "'Novye tikhie'. Rezhisserskaia smena—smena kartin mira," *Iskusstvo kino* 8 (2011), http://kinoart.ru/archive/2011/08/n8-article4.

57. The obvious allusion to Sergio Leone's 1984 classic *Once upon a Time in America*.

58. One critic in particular mentioned the Chekhovian feel of the film: "this atmosphere of an endless *tristesse*, as in Chekhov's plays, but painted in a realistic manner and without any touch of melancholy." Klaus Eder, "Moscow 2008: The Center of the Province," *KinoKultura* 22 (2008). It would be fruitful to develop the allusion that I see as pointing to Chekhov's short story "In the Ravine": there is a similarity in village/town name—Ukleevo in Chekhov and Uletovo in the film, and in the all-permeating drunkenness, violence, and moral turpitude.

59. Gerald McCausland, "Katia Shagalova: *Once Upon a Time in the Provinces* (*Odnazhdy v provintsii*, 2008)," *KinoKultura* 24 (2009).

60. Klaus Eder, "Moscow 2008."

61. One is reminded also of Galia, the heroine of Konchalovsky's *Gloss*, who wears almost identical high-heeled white boots on the streets of Rostov before she leaves for Moscow.

62. Irina Makoveeva, "Ol'ga Subbotina: *Pro Liuboff* (*About Love*, 2010)," *KinoKultura* 33 (2011).

63. "Kinotavr-2012. Five Evenings: Avdotia Smirnova," *Seans*, June 9, 2012, http://seance.ru/blog/kinotavr-2012-smirnova/.

64. Lena Doubivko, "Avdot'ia Smirnova: *Kokoko* (2012)," *KinoKultura* 40 (2013).

65. Ibid.

66. Andrei Plakhov, "Nomenklaturnyi romkom," *Seans*, September 6, 2011, quoted in Doubivko.

Conclusion

1. Aleksei Ivanov, *Kom'iuniti* (St. Petersburg: Azbuka—klassika, 2012), 80. Emphasis added.

2. Colin Graham, "'... maybe that's just Blarney': Irish Culture and the Persistency of Authenticity," in *Ireland and Cultural Theory: The Mechanics of Authenticity*, ed. Colin Graham and Richard Kirkland (New York: St. Martin's Press, 1999), 8.

3. Jeff Karem, *The Romance of Authenticity. The Cultural Politics of Regional and Ethnic Literatures* (Charlottesville: University of Virginia Press, 2004), 2; Lothar Honninghausen, "The Old and the New Regionalism," in *"Writing" Nation and "Writing" Region in America*, ed. Theo D'haen and Hans Bertens (Amsterdam: Vrije Universiteit, 1996). 14.

4. Graham, "'... maybe that's just Blarney,'" 25.

5. William R. Handley and Nathaniel Lewis, "Introduction," in *True West. Authenticity and the American West*, ed. William R. Handley and Nathaniel Lewis (Lincoln: University of Nebraska Press, 2004), 6.

6. Scott Romine, *The Real South: Southern Narrative in the Age of Cultural Reproduction* (Baton Rouge: Louisiana State University Press, 2008), 1.

7. Drucilla Mims Wall, "Imagined Indians and Sacred Landscape from New Age to Nature Writing," in *True West: Authenticity and the American West*, 97.

8. Eugenia Demuro, "The Search for Cultural Uniqueness in the Narrative Fiction of Alejo Carpentier and Julio Cortázar," in *Latin America: Interdisciplinary Studies*, Volume 25: *Civilization and Authenticity* (New York: Peter Lang Publishing, 2012), xv.

9. Christa Salamandra, *A New Old Damascus: Authenticity and Distinction in Urban Syria* (Bloomington: Indiana University Press, 2004), 3.

10. Nicola Macleod, "Cultural Tourism: Aspects of Authenticity and Commodification," in *Cultural Tourism in a Changing World: Politics, Participation and (Re)presentation*, edited by Melanie K. Smith and Mike Robinson (Buffalo: Channel View Publications, 2006), 186.

11. Ibid., 147.

12. Mikhail Bakhtin, "Forms of Time and of the Chronotope in the Novel," in M. Bakhtin, *The Dialogic Imagination: Four Essays*, trans. Caryl Emerson and Michael Holquist (Austin: University of Texas Press, 1981), 148.

13. Nikolas V. Riasanovsky, *Russia and the West in the Teaching of the Slavophiles: A Study of Romantic Ideology* (Cambridge: Harvard University Press, 1952), 156.

14. Zaionts, "Russkii provintsial'nyi 'mif,'" 428.

15. Edith Clowes, *Russia on the Edge: Imagined Geographies and Post-Soviet Identity* (Ithaca: Cornell University Press, 2012), 2.

16. See, for instance, Birgit Beumers, "National Identity through Visions of the Past: Contemporary Russian Cinema," in *Soviet and Post-Soviet Identities*, 55–72; and Iuliia Liderman, "Kurs na patriotizm i otvet rossiiskogo kinematografa v 2000e gody. Novye biudzhety, novye zhanry, novye fil'my o voine," in *Sovremennye interpretatsii russkogo natsionalizma*, ed. Marlen Lariuel' [Marlène Laruelle] (Stuttgart: Ibidem-Verlag, 2007), 289–317.

17. V. Putin, "Address to the Federal Assembly," December 12, 2012, http://en.special.kremlin.ru/events/president/news/17118. This is the speech that introduced the now infamous phrase "the spiritual bonds."

18. Viatcheslav Morozov, *Russia's Postcolonial Identity: A Subaltern Empire in a Eurocentric World* (Basingstoke: Palgrave Macmillan, 2015), 131.

19. Richard Handler, "Authenticity," *Anthropology Today* 2, no. 1 (1986): 2.

20. On the role of Russian folk music and dance performances in the revival of nationalist feelings in Russia, see Laura J. Olson, *Performing Russia: Folk Revival and Russian Identity* (New York: Routledge Curzon, 2004).

21. Ivan Aksakov, "O znachenii oblastnoi Rossii i neobkhodimosti oblastnoi pechati," *Den'*, No. 15 (1865), http://dugward.ru/library/aksakovy/iaksakov_o_znachenii_oblastnoy.html.

Bibliography

Abalmasova, N. E., and E. A. Pain. "Symbolic Management in Creating Regional Identity." *Regional Research of Russia* 1, no. 3 (2011): 275–84.

Abashev, Vladimir. *Perm' kak tekst: Perm' v russkoi kul'ture i literature XX veka.* Perm': Izdatel'stvo Permskogo universiteta, 2000.

Abashev, Vladimir, Viacheslav Rakov, Andrei Matveev, Dmitrii Kharitonov, and Nikolai Koliada. "Liricheskuiu repliku Vitaliia Kal'pidi 'Provintsiia kak fenomen kul'turnogo separatizma' obsuzhdaiut Vladimir Abashev, Viacheslav Rakov, Andrei Matveev, Dmitrii Kharitonov, Nikolai Koliada." *Ural'skaia Nov'* 1 (2000), http://magazines.russ.ru/urnov/2000/1/otklik.html.

Akhapkina, Ia. E. "Provintsiia, periferiia—problemy nominatsii." In *Provintsiia kak real'nost' i ob"ekt osmysleniia*, edited by A. F. Belousov and M. V. Stroganov, 6–11. Tver': Tverskoi gos. universitet, 2001.

Akopov, Petr. "Russkie osoznaiut svoiu samostoiatel'nost'." *Vzgliad*, February 4, 2016, http://www.vz.ru/politics/2016/2/4/792395.html.

Aksakov, Ivan. "Ob obshchestvennoi zhizni v gubernskikh gorodakh." In *Ivan Aksakov, U Rossii odna edinstvennaia stolitsa*, edited by G. Chagin. Moscow: Russkii mir, 2006.

———. "O znachenii oblastnoi Rossii i neobkhodimosti oblastnoi pechati." *Den'*, No. 15 (1865), http://dugward.ru/library/aksakovy/iaksakov_o_znachenii_oblastnoy.html.

———. "Vozvrat k narodnoi zhizni putem samosoznaniia" (1861). In *Ivan Aksakov, U Rossii odna edinstvennaia stolitsa*, edited by G. Chagin. Moscow: Russkii mir, 2006.

Aksakov, Konstantin. "'No title,' *Molva* 9 (June 8) 1857." In Konstantin Aksakov, *Gosudarstvo i Narod*. Moscow: Institut russkoi tsivilizatsii, 2009.

Anderson, Benedict. *Imagined Communities: Reflections on the Origins and Spread of Nationalism*. London, New York: Verso, 2006.

Anholt, Simon. *Places: Identity, Image and Reputation*. Basingstoke: Palgrave Macmillan, 2010.

Ashcroft, Bill, Gareth Griffiths, and Helen Tiffin. *Post-Colonial Studies: The Key Concepts*. London, New York: Routledge, 2009.

Aslamova, Daria. "Uriupinsk—eto my!" In Daria Aslamova, *V liubvi kak na voine*, 236–43. Moscow: Olma Press, 2005.

Bakhtin, Mikhail. "Forms of Time and of the Chronotope in the Novel." In M. Bakhtin, *The Dialogic Imagination: Four Essays*, translated by Caryl Emerson and Michael Holquist. Austin: University of Texas Press, 1981.

Barthes, Roland. "Myth Today." In *Mythologies*, translated by Annette Lavers. New York: Hill and Wang, 1988.

Bavin, Pyotr. "Moskva i regiony v predstavleniiakh rossiian (mart 2001)." In *Desiat' let sotsiologicheskikh nabliudenii*, edited by A. A. Oslon, 255–64. Moscow: Institut fonda "Obshchestvennoe mnenie," 2003.

Belousov, A. F. "Simvolika zakholust'ia (oboznachenie rossiiskogo provintsial'nogo goroda)." In *Geopanorama russkoi kul'tury: Provintsiia i ee lokal'nye teksty*, edited by L. O. Zaionts, 457–80. Moscow: Iazyki slavianskoi kul'tury, 2004.

Berdiaev [Berdyaev], Nikolai. "O vlasti prostranstva nad russkoi dushoi." In *Sud'ba Rossii: Opyty po psikhologii voiny i natsional'nosti*. Moscow: Filosofskoe ob-vo SSSR, 1990.

———. "Tsentralizm i narodnaia zhizn'." In *Sud'ba Rossii: Opyty po psikhologii voiny i natsional'nosti*. Moscow: Filosofskoe ob-vo SSSR, 1990.

Beumers, Birgit. *A History of Russian Cinema*. Oxford, New York: Berg, 2009.

———. "National Identity through Visions of the Past: Contemporary Russian Cinema." In *Soviet and Post-Soviet Identities*, edited by Mark Bassin and Catriona Kelly, 55–72. Cambridge: Cambridge University Press, 2012.

———, ed. *Russia on Reels: The Russian Idea in Post-Soviet Cinema*. London, New York: Tauris, 1999.

———, ed. *Russia's New Fin de Siècle: Contemporary Culture between Past and Present*. Bristol, Chicago: Intellect, 2013.

———. "The Serialization of Culture, or the Culture of Serialization." In *The Post-Soviet Russian Media: Conflicting Signals*, edited by Birgit Beumers, Stephen Hutchings, and Natalia Rulyova, 159–77. London, New York: Routledge, 2009.

Beumers, Birgit, Stephen Hutchings, and Natalia Rulyova. *The Post-Soviet Russian Media: Conflicting Signals*. London, New York: Routledge, 2009.

Bezrogov, Vitaly. "'If the War Comes Tomorrow': Patriotic Education in the Soviet and Post-Soviet Primary School." In *Soviet and Post-Soviet Identities*,

ed. Mark Bassin and Catriona Kelly, 113–28. Cambridge: Cambridge University Press, 2012.
Bhabha, Homi K. *The Location of Culture*. London, New York: Routledge, 1994.
———. "Narrating the Nation." In *Nation and Narration*, edited by Homi K. Bhabha, 1–7. London, New York: Routledge, 1990.
Boele, Otto. "Boris Nemtsov—provintsial. K voprosu o politicheskom imidzhmeikerstve v postperestroechnoi Rossii." In *Russkaia provintsiia: Mif—tekst—real'nost'*, edited by A. F. Belousov and T. V. Tsiv'ian, 118–28. Moscow, St. Petersburg, 2000.
———. "'Polovoi vopros' i provintsiia v publitsistike nachala XX veka." In *Russkaia provintsiia: Mif—tekst—real'nost'*, edited by A. F. Belousov and T. V. Tsiv'ian, 75–84. Moscow, St. Petersburg, 2000.
———. Review of *Perm' kak tekst*, by Aladimir Abashev. *Slavic Review* 60 (winter 2001): 691.
Bogoslavskaia, Ol'ga. "Moskva: ot rastsveta do 'rastsveta.'" *Znamia* 3 (2009): 181–99.
Bondarenko, Vladimir. "Russkii lik patriotizma." *Gubernskii stil'* 1 (September 2006): 19–20.
Bonnett, Alastair. *The Idea of the West: Culture, Politics, History*. New York: Palgrave Macmillan, 2004.
Borenstein, Eliot. *Overkill: Sex and Violence in Contemporary Russian Popular Culture*. Ithaca: Cornell University Press, 2008.
———. "The Russia We Can't Find." In *Plots Against Russia*. February 15, 2016, http://plotsagainstrussia.org/eb7nyuedu/2016/2/15/ln58th5tzh526di36f71crsr9intb6.
Boym, Svetlana. *Common Places*. Cambridge: Harvard University Press, 1994.
———. *The Future of Nostalgia*. New York: Basic Books, 2001.
Bradshaw, Michael. "Globalization, Regional Change, and the Territorial Cohesion of the Russian Federation." In *Russia and Globalization: Identity, Security, and Society in an Era of Change*, edited by Douglas W. Blum, 79–110. Baltimore: Johns Hopkins University Press, 2008.
Buruma, Ian, and Avishai Margalit. *Occidentalism: The West in the Eyes of Its Enemies*. New York: Penguin Press, 2004.
Bykov, Dmitry. "Mozharovo." In *Read Russia: An Anthology of New Voices*, edited by Elena Shubina. Read Russia, Inc. 2012.
Cavanagh, Clare. "Idiotika." Review of *Lines of Fate*, by Mark Kharitonov, translated by Helena Goscilo. *New York Times*, August 11, 1996.
Cavender, Mary. *Nests of the Gentry: Family, Estate, and Local Loyalties in Provincial Russia*. Newark: University of Delaware Press, 2007.
Clark, Katerina. *Moscow, the Fourth Rome: Stalinism, Cosmopolitanism, and the Evolution of Soviet Culture, 1931–1941*. Cambridge: Harvard University Press, 2011.
———. *The Soviet Novel: History as Ritual*. Bloomington/Indianapolis: Indiana University Press, 2000.

Clowes, Edith. *Russia on the Edge: Imagined Geographies and Post-Soviet Identity.* Ithaca: Cornell University Press, 2012.

Condee, Nancy. *The Imperial Trace: Recent Russian Cinema.* Oxford: Oxford University Press, 2009.

———. "Tales Told by Nationalists." In *Soviet and Post-Soviet Identities,* edited by Mark Bassin and Catriona Kelly, 37–52. Cambridge: Cambridge University Press, 2012.

Cross, Anthony. "'Them': Russians on Foreigners." In *National Identity in Russian Culture,* edited by Simon Franklin and Emma Widdis, 74–92. Cambridge: Cambridge University Press, 2004.

Danilkin, Lev. "Famil'ony prosiat ognia." *Afisha,* May 2, 2007, http://ivanproduction.ru/reczenzii/bluda-i-mudo/familonyi-prosyat-ognya.html.

———. "Geograf globus propil." *Afisha,* May 2003, http://www.ivanproduction.ru/reczenzii/geograf-globus-propil1/posle-oshhetinivshejsya.html.

Demuro, Eugenia. *Latin America: Interdisciplinary Studies,* Volume 25: *Civilization and Authenticity: The Search for Cultural Uniqueness in the Narrative Fiction of Alejo Carpentier and Julio Cortázar.* New York: Peter Lang Publishing, 2012.

D'iachenko, G. V. "Dekonstruktsiia antitezy tsentr-provintsiia N. A. Berdiaevym." In *Zhizn' provintsii kak fenomen dukhovnosti: Mezhdunarodnaia nauchnaia konferentsiia 18–19 aprelia 2005 g.* 214–16. Nizhnii Novgorod, 2009.

Dickinson, Sara. *Breaking Ground: Travel and National Culture in Russia from Peter I to the Era of Pushkin.* Amsterdam, New York: Rodopi, 2006.

Diligenskii, G. "Druzhit' s Amerikoi." In *Desiat' let sotsiologicheskikh nabliudenii,* edited by A. A. Cherniakov, 430–31. Moscow: Institut Fonda Obshchestvennogo Mneniia, 2003.

Diment, Galya, and Yuri Slezkine, eds. *Between Heaven and Hell: The Myth of Siberia in Russian Culture.* New York: St. Martin Press, 1993.

Dinnie, Keith. "Introduction to the Theory of City Branding." In *City Branding: Theory and Cases,* edited by Keith Dinnie, 3–7. Houndmills, UK, New York: Palgrave Macmillan, 2011.

Dixon, Simon. "The Past in the Present: Contemporary Russian Nationalism in Historical Perspective." In *Russian Nationalism Past and Present,* edited by Geoffrey Hosking and Robert Service, 149–77. New York: St. Martin Press, 1998.

Domanskii, V. A. "Russkaia usad'ba v khudozhestvennoi literature XIX veka: kul'turologicheskie aspekty izucheniia poetiki." *Vestnik Tomskogo gos. universiteta,* 291 (June 2006): 56–60.

Dostoevsky, Fedor. *Winter Notes on Summer Impressions,* translated by Richard Lee Renfield. New York: Criterion Books, 1955.

Doubivko, Lena. "Avdot'ia Smirnova: *Kokoko* (2012)." *KinoKultura* 40 (2013).

Dyrdin, A. A. "Dukhovnaia zhizn' Rossii: provintsial'noe izmerenie." In *Dukhovnaia zhizn' provintsii. Obrazy, Simvoly, Kartina Mira. Materialy Vserossiiskoi nauchnoi konferentsii. Ul'ianovsk, 19–20 iiunia 2003 goda*, 5–8. Ul'ianovsk: Ul'ianovskii gos. universitet, 2003.

Eder, Klaus. "Moscow 2008: The Center of the Province." *KinoKultura* 22 (2008).

Elsaesser, Thomas. "Tales of Sound and Fury: Observations on the Family Melodrama." In *Film Genre Reader III*, edited by B. K. Grant, 366–95. Austin: University of Texas Press, 2003.

Ely, Christopher. *This Meager Nature: Landscape and National Identity in Imperial Russia*. DeKalb: Northern Illinois Press, 2002.

Etkind, Aleksandr. "Fuko i tezis vnutrennei kolonizatsii: Postkolonial'nyi vzgliad na sovetskoe proshloe." *Novoe literaturnoe obozrenie* 49 (2001): 50–73.

———. "Russkaia literatura, XIX vek: Roman vnutrennei kolonizatsii." *Novoe literaturnoe obozrenie* 59 (2003): 103–24.

Etkind, Alexander. *Internal Colonization: Russia's Imperial Experience*. Cambridge: Polity Press, 2011.

Evgen'eva, A. P. *Slovar' russkogo iazyka v 4-kh tomakh*. Moscow: Poligrafresursy, 1999.

Evtuhov, Catherine. *Portrait of a Russian Province: Economy, Society, and Civilization in Nineteenth-Century Nizhnii Novgorod*. Pittsburgh: University of Pittsburgh Press, 2011.

Fortunatova, V. A. "K istolkovaniiu semantiki provintsial'nogo." In *Zhizn' provintsii kak fenomen dukhovnosti. Mezhdunarodnaia nauchnaia konferentsiia 18–19 aprelia 2005 g.*, 3–10. Nizhnii Novgorod, 2006.

Gellner, Ernest. *Nations and Nationalism*. Ithaca, NY: Cornell University Press, 2006.

Gerovitch, Slava. *Soviet Space Mythologies: Public Images, Private Memories, and the Making of a Cultural Identity*. Pittsburgh: University of Pittsburgh Press, 2015.

Gillespie, David C. *Russian Cinema*. Harlow, NY: Longman, 2003.

Goscilo, Helena, and Andrea Lanoux, eds. *Gender and National Identity in Twentieth-Century Russian Culture*. DeKalb: Northern Illinois University Press, 2006.

Graffy, Julian. Review of *Free Floating*, by Boris Khlebnikov. *KinoKultura* 15 (2007).

Graham, Colin. "'. . . maybe that's just Blarney': Irish Culture and the Persistency of Authenticity." In *Ireland and Cultural Theory: The Mechanics of Authenticity*, edited by Colin Graham and Richard Kirkland, 7–28. New York: St. Martin's Press, 1999.

Graham, Seth. "*Chernukh*a and Russian Film." *Studies in Slavic Cultures* 1 (2000): 9–27.

———. "The New American Other in Post-Soviet Russian Cinema." In *Russia and Its Other(s) on Film*, edited by Stephen Hutchings. New York: Palgrave Macmillan, 2008.

Greenfeld, Liah. *Nationalism: Five Roads to Modernity*. Cambridge: Harvard University Press, 1992.

Gres', Anna. "So mnoi 'soidet i tak' ne prokhodit, pust' dazhe kto-to na eto i obizhaetsia." *Telekritika*, April 17, 2007, http://www.telekritika.ua/lyudi/2007-04-17/8729.

Grigorian, Bella. "'Figura blednaia, neiasnaia': Obraz pomeshchika v romanakh Goncharova." *Novoe literaturnoe obozrenie* 106 (2010): 117-29.

Groys, Boris. "Russia and the West: The Quest for Russian Self-Identity." *Studies in Soviet Thought* 43, no. 3 (1992): 185-98.

Gudkov, L., B. Dubin, and N. Zorkaia, eds. *Molodezh' Rossii*. Moscow: Moskovskaia Shkola Politicheskikh Issledovanii, 2011.

Gudkov, Lev. *Negativnaia identichnost': Stat'i 1997-2002*. Moscow: Novoe literaturnoe obozrenie VTSIOM-A, 2004.

Gurin, S. P. "Provintsiia: potaennost' i sokrovennost'." *Topos*, September 15, 2009, http://www.topos.ru/article/6847.

Handler, Richard. "Authenticity." *Anthropology Today* 2, no. 1 (1986): 2-5.

Handley, William R., and Nathaniel Lewis. "Introduction." In *True West: Authenticity and the American West*, edited by William R. Handley and Nathaniel Lewis, 1-19. Lincoln: University of Nebraska Press, 2004.

Hashamova, Yana. *Pride and Panic: Russian Imagination of the West in Post-Soviet Film*. Bristol, Chicago: Intellect, 2007.

Hutchings, Stephen, and Natalia Rulyova, eds. *Television and Culture in Putin's Russia*. London, New York: Routledge, 2009.

Honninghausen, Lothar. "The Old and the New Regionalism." In *"Writing" Nation and "Writing" Region in America*, edited by Theo D'haen and Hans Bertens, 3-20. Amsterdam: Vrije Universiteit, 1996.

Horton, Andrew, and Michael Brashinsky. *The Zero Hour: Glasnost and Soviet Cinema in Transition*. Princeton: Princeton University Press, 1992.

Hosking, Geoffrey. *Russia: People and Empire, 1552-1917*. Cambridge: Harvard University Press, 1997.

Hughes, Michael. "The Russian Nobility and the Russian Countryside: Ambivalences and Orientations." *Journal of European Studies* 36, no. 2 (2006): 115-37.

Iakovlev, Sergei. "Pis'mo iz Soligalicha v Oksford." *Novy Mir* 5 (1995).

Ignatiev, O. V., and O. V. Lysenko. "Kul'turnaia politika i strategiia konstruirovaniia imidzha territorii." *Labirint: Zhurnal sotsial'no-gumanitarnykh issledovanii* 1 (2015): 6-16.

Iudin, Aleksei. "Kontsepty 'provintsiia' i 'region' v sovremennom russkom iazyke." *Otechestvennye Zapiski* 5, no. 31 (2006): 26-40.

Ivanov, Aleksei. *Bluda i Mudo*. St. Petersburg: Azbuka—klassika, 2007.

———. *Geograf globus propil*. Moscow: ACT, 2007.

———. *Kom'iuniti*. St. Petersburg: Azbuka—klassika, 2012.

———. "Pisatel' Aleksei Ivanov: 'Menia vosprinimaiut kak oligarkha ot gumanitarnoi sredy.'" *Izvestiia*, August 9, 2006, http://izvestia.ru/news/316118#ixzz351DzoajN.

———. *Psoglavtsy*. St. Petersburg: Azbuka—klassika, 2013.

———. "Rossii nuzhny dvoinye standarty." *Profil'*, October 7, 2006, http://www.profile.ru/arkhiv/item/50930-items_19552.

———. "Rossiia: Sposob sushchestvovaniia. Gde iskat' natsional'nuiu identichnost' i kak s nei zhit'?" *Russkii Reporter*, October 6, 2010, http://arkada-ivanov.ru.

———. "V global'nom mire tsenno tol'ko unikal'noe." *Stol'nik*, June 2011, http://www.ivanproduction.ru/intervyu/v-globalnom-mire-czenno-tolko-unikalnoe.html.

Ivanova, I. N. "Derevenskaia proza v sovremennoi otechestvennoi literature: konets mifa ili perezagruzka?" *Filologicheskie nauki: Voprosy teorii i praktiki* (Tambov) 6, no. 24 (2013): 88–94.

Ivanova, Natalia. "Bandersha i sutener. Roman literatury s ideologiei: krizis zhanra." *Znamia* 5 (2000): 173–81.

———. *Russkii krest: Literatura i chitatel' v nachale novogo veka*. Moscow: Vremia, 2011.

Jackson, Linda A., Linda Sullivan, Richard Harnish, and Carole N. Hodge. "Achieving Positive Social Identity: Social Mobility, Social Creativity, and Permeability of Group Boundaries." *Journal of Personality and Social Psychology* 70, no. 2 (1996): 241–54.

Kaganskii, Vladimir. *Kul'turnyi landshaft i sovetskoe obitaemoe prostranstvo*. Moscow: Novoe literaturnoe obozrenie, 2001.

———. "Rossiia. Provintsiia. Landshaft." *Otechestvennye Zapiski* 5, no. 32 (2006): 244–315.

Karem, Jeff. *The Romance of Authenticity: The Cultural Politics of Regional and Ethnic Literatures*. Charlottesville: University of Virginia Press, 2004.

Kempton, Daniel R., and Terry D. Clark. *Unity or Separation: Center-Periphery Relations in the Former Soviet Union*. Westport: Praeger, 2002.

Kharitonov, Mark. *Izbrannaia proza*. Moscow: Moskovskii rabochii, 1994.

———. *Lines of Fate*, translated by Helena Goscilo. New York: The New Press, 1996.

Khumar'ian, Svetlana. "Sizif byl schastlivee, chem my dumaem." *Rossiiskaia provintsiia* 2 (1996): 38–47.

"Kinotavr-2012. Five Evenings: Avdotia Smirnova." *Seans*, June 9, 2012, http://seance.ru/blog/kinotavr-2012-smirnova/.

Kislov, A. G., and I. V. Shapko. "Sotsial'no-topologicheskoe opravdanie provintsii." *SOTsIS* 8 (2000): 118–22.

Klubkova, T. V., and P. A. Klubkov. "Russkii provintsial'nyi gorod i stereotipy provintsial'nosti." In *Russkaia provintsiia: Mif—tekst—real'nost'*, edited by A. F. Belousov and T. V. Tsiv'ian, 20–29. Moscow, St. Petersburg: Tema, 2000.

Kolodiazhnyi, Ivan. "Russkaia provintsiia kak Noev kovcheg." *Russkaia narodnaia liniia*. December 21, 2015, http://ruskline.ru/special_opinion/2015/12/russkaya_provinciya_kak_noev_kovcheg/.

Konfederat, O. V. "Identifikatsiia russkogo provintsiala v smeshannoi kul'ture." In *Chelovek v prostranstve kul'tury (tsentr—provintsiia, provintsiia—tsentr). Materialy mezhregional'noi nauchno-prakticheskoi konferentsii. 21 aprelia 2004 g.*, 29–38. Chelyabinsk, 2006.

Kornblatt, Judith. *The Cossack Hero in Russian Literature: A Study in Cultural Mythology*. Madison: University of Wisconsin Press, 1992.

Krylov, M. P. *Regional'naia identichnost' v evropeiskoi Rossii*. Vologda: Novyi khronograf, 2010.

Kukulin, Il'ia. "The Heroization of Survival: A Detailed Review of Aleksei Ivanov's Popular Historical Novels as Thinly Disguised Commentary on a Single Historical Period: The 1990s and the 2000s." *Russian Studies in Literature* 45, no. 2 (spring 2009): 42–74.

Kuptsova, I. A. "Russkaia provintsial'naia kul'tura i rossiiskaia tsivilizatsiia: sushchnost' i vzaimodeistvie." *Srednerusskii vestnik obshchestvennykh nauk* 4 (2008): 13–19.

Kuzmin, D., ed. *Nestolichnaia literatura: Poeziia i proza regionov Rossii*. Moscow: Novoe literaturnoe obozrenie, 2001.

Lariuel', Marlen [Laruelle, Marlène]. "Razmyshleniia na temu 'russkii natsionalizm' kak predmet issledovaniia." In *Sovremennye interpretatsii russkogo natsionalizma*, edited by Marlen Lariuel' [Marlène Laruelle], 7–14. Stuttgart: Ibidem-Verlag, 2007.

Laruelle, Marlène, ed. *Russian Nationalism, Foreign Policy and Identity Debates in Putin's Russia: New Ideological Patterns after the Orange Revolution*. Stuttgart: Ibidem-Verlag, 2014.

Leiderman, N., and M. Lipovetskii. "Zhizn' posle smerti, ili novye svedeniia o realizme." *Novy Mir* 7 (1993): 233–52.

Levesque, Jean. "Foremen in the Field: Collective Farm Chairmen and the Fate of Labour Discipline after Collectivization." In *Dream Deferred: New Studies in Russian and Soviet Labour History*, edited by Donald A. Filtzer, 243–64. Berne: Peter Lang AG, 2008.

Lewis, Martin W., and Karin E. Wigen. *The Myth of Continents: A Critique of Metageography*. Berkeley: University of California Press, 1997.

Liderman, Iuliia. "Kurs na patriotizm i otvet rossiiskogo kinematografa v 2000e gody. Novye biudzhety, novye zhanry, novye fil'my o voine." In *Sovremennye interpretatsii russkogo natsionalizma*, edited by Marlen Lariuel' [Marlène Maruelle], 289–317. Stuttgart: Ibidem-Verlag, 2007.

Likhachev, Viacheslav. *Natsizm v Rossii*. Moscow: Panorama, 2002.

Lipovetskii, Mark. "V otsutstvie mediatora—Siuzhet vnutrennei kolonizatsii." *Iskusstvo Kino* 8 (August 2003).

———. "Living through a Loss." *KinoKultura* 22 (2008).

Lotman, Yuri. *Culture and Explosion*, edited by Marina Grishakova, translated by Wilma Clark. Berlin, New York: Mouton de Gruyter, 2009.

Lounsbery, Anne. "Dostoevsky's Geography: Center, Peripheries, and Networks in *Demons*." *Slavic Review* 66, no. 2 (2007): 211–29.

———. "'No, this is not the provinces!' Provincialism, Authenticity, and Russianness in Gogol's Day." *Russian Review* 64 (April 2005): 259–80.
MacFadyen, David. *Russian Television Today: Primetime Drama and Comedy*. London, New York: Routledge, 2008.
Macleod, Nicola. "Cultural Tourism: Aspects of Authenticity and Commodification." In *Cultural Tourism in a Changing World: Politics, Participation and (Re)presentation*, edited by Melanie K. Smith and Mike Robinson, 177–90. Buffalo: Channel View Publications, 2006.
Maiantseva, Aleksandra. "Provintsialy ne liubiat moskvichei." *Komsomol'skaia Pravda*, August 31, 2013, http://www.msk.kp.ru/daily/26126/3018983/.
Maiorova, Olga. *From the Shadow of Empire: Defining the Russian Nation through Cultural Mythology, 1855–1870*. Madison: University of Wisconsin Press, 2010.
Makoveeva, Irina. "Ol'ga Subbotina: *Pro Liuboff (About Love*, 2010)." *KinoKultura* 33 (2011).
Malinova, Olga. "Obsession with Status and *Ressentiment*: Historical Backgrounds of the Russian Discursive Identity Construction." *Communist and Post-Communist Studies* 47 (2014): 291–303.
Martin, Terri. *The Affirmative Action Empire: Nations and Nationalism in the Soviet Union, 1923–1939*. Ithaca: Cornell University Press, 2001.
McCannon, John. *Red Arctic: Polar Exploration and the Myth of the North in the Soviet Union, 1932–1939*. New York: Oxford University Press, 1998.
McCausland, Gerald. "Katia Shagalova: *Once Upon a Time In the Provinces (Odnazhdy v provintsii*, 2008)." *KinoKultura* 24 (2009).
Meltzer, Bernard, and Gill Musolf. "Resentment and *Ressentiment*." *Social Inquiry* 72, no. 2 (2002): 440–55.
Mikhalin, O. "Est' li v Rossii demokratiia?" *Moscow Post*, June 15, 2010, http://www.moscow-post.com/politics/001252991497517/.
Miliugina, E. G., and M. V. Stroganov. "Tekst prostranstva. Fragmenty slovaria 'Russkaia provintsiia.'" *Labirint: Zhurnal sotsial'no-gumanitarnykh issledovanii* 3 (2012): 33–74.
Miller, Alexei. "The Empire and the Nation in the Imagination of Russian Nationalism." In *Imperial Rule*, edited by Alexei Miller and Alfred Rieber, 9–26. Budapest, New York: Central European University Press, 2004.
Milovanov, Iurii. "So stolitsei naravne. Zametki o perezhivaniiakh provintsial'noi intelligentsii." *Rossiiskaia provintsiia* 1 (1993): 47–50.
Moiseev, Nikita. "Ia printsipial'nyi opportunist." *Rossiiskaia provintsiia* 1 (1993): 80–81.
Moore, David Chioni. "Is the Post- in Postcolonial the Post- in Post-Soviet? Toward a Global Postcolonial Critique." *PMLA* 116, no. 1, Special Topic: Globalizing Literary Studies (2001): 111–28.
Morozov, Viatcheslav. "In Search of Europe: Russian Political Discourse and the Outside World." *Eurozine*, February 23, 2004, http://www.eurozine.com/articles/2004-02-18-morozov-en.html.

———. *Russia's Postcolonial Identity: A Subaltern Empire in a Eurocentric World*. Basingstoke: Palgrave Macmillan, 2015.

"Moskva i provintsiia." VTSIOM, September 4, 2012, 2016, http://wciom.ru/index.php?id=236&uid=113000.

Mozgovaia, O. "Moskva teper' provintsii po nravu. My ne razdrazhaem, nam ne zaviduiut." *Vecherniaia Moskva*, September 7, 2006.

Nelepov, A. Iu. "Prakticheskaia realizatsiia kontseptsii razvitiia regional'nykh brendov." *Sovremennaia ekonomika: Problemy i resheniia* 2, no. 2 (2010): 16–23.

Nemtsov, Boris. *Provintsial*. Moscow: Vagrius, 1997.

———. *Provintsial v Moskve*. Moscow: Vagrius, 1999.

Nemzer, Andrei. "Rasseiannye pomety na poliakh. Mark Kharitonov, Linii sud'by ili sunduchok Milashevicha." In Andrei Nemzer, *Literaturnoe segodnia: O russkoi proze. 90-e.*, 385–89. Moscow: Novoe literaturnoe obozrenie, 1998.

Nesterov, Vadim "Ivanov na ostanovke." *Gazeta.ru*, April 11, 2012, http://www.ivanproduction.ru/reczenzii/komyuniti1/ivanov-na-ostanovke.html.

Neumann, Iver B. *Uses of the Other: The "East" in European Identity Formation*. Minneapolis: University of Minnesota Press, 1998.

Nietzsche, Friedrich. *On the Genealogy of Morals*, translated by Walter Kaufmann. New York: Vintage Books, 1989.

Norris, Stephen M., and Zara M. Torlone, ed. *Insiders and Outsiders in Russian Cinema*. Bloomington: Indiana University Press, 2008.

"'Novye tikhie'. Rezhisserskaia smena—smena kartin mira." *Iskusstvo kino* 8 (2011), http://kinoart.ru/archive/2011/08/n8-article4.

Obrist, Amy Isaac. "The Russian Metahistorical Imagination and Russian Fiction of Perestroika." PhD Diss., University of Southern California, 2005.

Olson, Laura J. *Performing Russia: Folk Revival and Russian Identity*. New York: Routledge, 2004.

Ooi, Can-Seng. "Paradoxes of City Branding and Societal Changes. In *City Branding: Theory and Cases*, edited by Keith Dinnie, 29–41. Houndmills, UK, New York: Palgrave Macmillan, 2011.

Overing, Joanna. "The Role of Myth: An Anthropological Perspective." In *Myths and Nationhood*, edited by Geoffrey Hosking and George Schopflin, 1–18. New York: Routledge, 1997.

Pain, Emil'. *Mezhdu imperiei i natsiei. Modernistskii proekt i ego traditsionalistskaia alternativa v natsional'noi politike Rossii*. Moscow: Novoe izdatel'stvo, 2004.

Panarin, Aleksandr. "Rossiia mezhdu atlantizmom i evraziistvom." *Rossiiskaia provintsiia* 1 (1993): 142–44.

Parland, Thomas. *The Extreme Nationalist Threat in Russia: The Growing Influence of Western Rightist Ideas*. Abington, UK: Routledge Curzon, 2005.

Parthé, Kathleen. *Russian Village Prose: The Radiant Past*. Princeton: Princeton University Press, 1992.

Bibliography

Parts, Lyudmila. *The Chekhovian Intertext: Dialogue with a Classic*. Columbus: Ohio State University Press, 2008.
Pavliuk, Semen. "Chuvstvo mesta i nizovoi regionalizm." *Otechestvennye Zapiski (Anatomiia provintsii)* 5, no. 31 (2006): 104–13.
Plakhov, A. "An Ironical Collectivist Community (*sobornost'*)." *KinoKultura* 22 (2008).
Popadiuk, Sergei. "Sviiazhsk." *Rossiiskaia provintsiia* 5 (1995): 76–85.
Popov, A. "Novyi fil'm Kirilla Serebrennikova Iur'ev den' vykhodit v prokat 18 sentiabria." *ProfiCinema*, September 10, 2008, http://www.proficinema.ru/news/detail.php?ID=37159.
Popov, N. P. "Poiski natsional'noi idei Rossii prodolzhaiutsia." *VTSIOM* November 27, 2009, http://russkie.org/?module=fullitem&id=16991.
Prilepin, Zakhar. "Moskva dlia menia chto-to vrode offisa." *TimeOut* (Moscow), April 4, 2016, http://www.timeout.ru/msk/feature/458212/page/2.
——. "Na miagkoi perine, ili o stolitse." In *Ia prishel iz Rossii*. St. Petersburg/Moscow: Limbus Press, 2008.
——. *Sankya*, translated by Mariya Gusev and Jeff Parker. Ann Arbor: DISQUIET, 2014.
Putin, Vladimir. "Address to the Federal Assembly." December 12, 2012, http://en.special.kremlin.ru/events/president/news/17118.
Rabow-Edling, Susanna. *Slavophile Thought and the Politics of Cultural Nationalism*. Albany: State University of New York Press, 2006.
Raeff, Marc. *The Origins of the Russian Intelligentsia*. New York: Harcourt Brace, World, 1966.
Rasputin, Valentin. "Skazhite vsem, chto Rus' zhiva." *Rossiiskaia provintsiia* 1 (1996): 4–8.
Razor, S. "Bandits, Oligarchs, and Provincial Girls! Oh, My!" *KinoKultura* 20 (2008).
Razumova, I. A., and E. V. Kuleshov. "K fenomenologii provintsii." In *Provintsiia kak real'nost' i ob"ekt osmysleniia*, edited by A. F. Belousov and M. V. Stroganov, 12–25. Tver': Tverskoi gos. universitet, 2001.
Rebel, Galina. "Iavlenie Geographa, ili zhivaia voda romanov Alekseia Ivanova." *Oktiabr'* 4 (2006): 173–82.
Riasanovsky, Nikolas V. *Russia and the West in the Teaching of the Slavophiles: A Study of Romantic Ideology*. Cambridge, Harvard University Press, 1952.
Romine, Scott. *The Real South: Southern Narrative in the Age of Cultural Reproduction*. Baton Rouge: Louisiana State University Press, 2008.
Rowe, Kathleen. *The Unruly Woman: Gender and the Genres of Laughter*. Austin: University of Texas Press, 1995.
Rowley, Alison. *Open Letters: Russian Popular Culture and the Picture Postcard, 1880–1922*. Toronto: University of Toronto Press, 2013.
Rowley, David G. "Imperial vs. National Discourse: The Case of Russia." *Nations and Nationalism* 6, no. 1 (2000): 23–42.

Rozanov, V. V. "Embriony." In *Russkaia filosofiia: Konets XIX—nachalo XX v.*, edited by A. A. Ermichev and B. V. Emelianov. St. Petersburg: Izd-vo S.-Peterburgskogo universiteta, 1993.

Rosenblum, Arja, Kaarle Nordenstreng, and Elena Trubina, eds. *Russian Mass Media and Changing Values*. London, New York: Routledge, 2010.

Said, Edward. *Orientalism*. New York: Vintage Books, 1979.

Salamandra, Christa. *A New Old Damascus: Authenticity and Distinction in Urban Syria*. Bloomington: Indiana University Press, 2004.

Salys, Rimgalia, ed. *The Russian Cinema Reader II*. Boston: Academic Studies Press, 2013.

Sapelkin, Nikolai. "Chem Voronezh ne Parizh?" *Gubernskii stil'* 8–9 (spring-summer 2010): 51–58.

Savkina, Irina. *Provintsialki russkoi literatury (zhenskaia proza 30–40x godov XIX veka)*. Wilhelmshorst: Verlag F. K. Göpfert, 1998.

Selemeneva, M. V. "Prostranstvennye obrazy romana Z. Prilepina 'San'kia.'" *Vestnik Gosudarstvennogo Leningradskogo Universiteta im. Pushkina* 3, no. 1 (2014): 63–71.

Shenkman, Ian. "Message—myth. Dve knigi Alekseia Ivanova—'Bluda i Mudo' i 'Chusovaia.'" *Ogonek*, May 12, 2007.

Shevchenko, Maksim. "My ne Evropa? I slava Bogu! Rossiia—odin iz poslednikh oplotov cheloveka i chelovechestva." *Moskovskii Komsomolets*, #26160, February 11, 2013, http://www.mk.ru/politics/2013/02/10/810258-myi-ne-evropa-i-slava-bogu.html.

Shevelenko, Irina. "Reprezentatsiia imperii i natsii: Rossiia na Vsemirnoi vystavke 1900 v Parizhe." In *Tam vnutri: praktiki vnutrennei kolonizatsii v kul'turnoi istorii Rossii*, edited by A. Etkind, D. Uffelmann, and I. Kukulin, 413–46. Moscow: Novoe literaturnoe obozrenie, 2012.

Sibiriakov, I. V. "Tsentr i provintsiia v Rossii: Traditsiia tragicheskogo neponimaniia." In *Tsentr—provintsiia: istoriko-psikhologicheskie problemy: Materialy Vserossiiskoi nauchnoi konferentsii*, edited by S. N. Poltorak, 194–98. St. Petersburg: Nestor, 2001.

Slezkine, Yuri. "The USSR as a Communal Apartment, or How a Socialist State Promoted Ethnic Particularism." *Slavic Review* 53, no. 2 (1994): 414–52.

Smirniagin, Leonid. "Transformatsiia obshchestvennogo prostranstva Rossii." *Otechestvennye Zapiski (Anatomiia provintsii)* 5, no. 31 (2006): 114–23.

Smith, Anthony D. "The Golden Age and National Revival." In *Myths and Nationhood*, edited by Geoffrey Hosking and George Schopflin, 36–59. New York: Routledge, 1997.

———. *National Identity*. Reno, Las Vegas, London: University of Nevada Press, 1991.

Smith-Peter, Susan. "Bringing the Provinces into Focus: Subnational Spaces in the Recent Historiography of Russia." *Kritika: Explorations in Russian and Eurasian History* 12, no. 4 (2011): 835–48.

Sokolovskaia, Mariia. "Gubernskii stil' ot Pekina do Parizha." *Gubernskii stil'* 8–9 (spring–summer 2010): 46–50.
Solomin, Iurii. "Provintsiia khranit talant dobroty." *Rossiiskaia provintsiia* 1 (1996): 10–13.
Solovei, V. D. "Revoliutsiia russkoi identichnosti. Rossiia dlia russkikh?" *Monitoring obshchestvennogo mneniia* 4, no. 80 (2006): 51–67.
Spivak, M. L. "'Provintsiia idet v regiony': O nekotorykh osobennostiakh sovremennogo upotrebleniia slova provintsiia." In *Geopanorama russkoi kul'tury: Provintsiia i ee lokal'nye teksty*, edited by L. O. Zaionts, 503–15. Moscow: Iazyki slavianskoi kul'tury, 2004.
Stepanian, Karen. "Realizm kak zakliuchitel'naia stadiia postmodernizma." *Znamia* 9 (1992): 231–38.
Stepanova, Svetlana. "Moia prekrasnaia palata No. 6." Review of *Glianets*, dir. by Andrei Konchalovskii. *russart.com*, August 27, 2007, http://ruskino.ru/review/141.
Stesin, Anatolii. "Moskvichi priznalis', za chto nenavidiat provintsialov." *Maxpark*, September 24, 2011, http://maxpark.com/community/Rodina_Russia/content/810369.
Sutcliffe, Benjamin. *The Prose of Life: Russian Women Writers from Khrushchev to Putin*. Madison: University of Wisconsin Press, 2009.
Tajfel, Henri, and John C. Turner. "An Integrative Theory of Intergroup Conflict." In *The Social Psychology of Intergroup Relations*, edited by William G. Austin and Stephen Worchel, 33–47. Monterey, CA: Brooks/Cole, 1979.
Taylor, Richard. "'But Eastward, Look, the Land Is Brighter': Toward a Topography of Utopia in the Stalinist Musical." In *The Landscape of Stalinism: The Art and Ideology of Soviet Space*, edited by Evgeny Dobrenko and Eric Naiman, 210–18. Seattle, London: University of Washington Press, 2003.
Timofeev, M. Iu. "Goroda i regiony Rossii kak (post)industrial'nye brendy." *Labirint: Zhurnal sotsial'no-gumanitarnykh issledovanii* 5 (2013): 29–41.
Todorov, Tsvetan. *On Human Diversity: Nationalism, Racism, and Exoticism in French Thought*. Cambridge: Harvard University Press, 1993.
Tolz, Vera. "Forging the Nation: National Identity and Nation Building in Post-Communist Russia." *Europe-Asia Studies* 50, no. 6 (1998): 993–1022.
———. *Russia*. London, New York: Oxford University Press, 2001.
Trofimova, E. "Zhenskaia literatura i knigoizdanie v sovremennoi Rossii." *Obshchestvennye nauki i sovremennost'* 5 (1998): 147–56.
Umland, Andreas. "Tri raznovidnosti postsovetskogo fashizma. Kontseptual'nye i kontekstual'nye problemy interpretatsii sovremennogo russkogo ul'tranatsionalizma." In *Sovremennye interpretatsii russkogo natsionalizma*, edited by Marlen Lariuel' [Marlène Laruelle], 129–70. Stuttgart: Ibidem-Verlag, 2007.
Usitalo, Steven. *The Invention of Mikhail Lomonosov: A Russian National Myth*. Brighton: Academic Studies Press, 2013.

Vaiskopf, Mikhail. *Siuzhet Gogolia. Morfologiia. Ideologiia. Kontekst.* Moscow: Radiks, 1993.

Venn, Couze. *Occidentalism: Modernity and Subjectivity.* London, Thousand Oaks, New Delhi: SAGE Publications 2000.

Voronkov, V., and O. Karpenko. "Patriotizm kak natsionalizm (post)sovetskogo cheloveka." In *Sovremennye interpretatsii russkogo natsionalizma,* edited by Marlen Lariuel' [Marlène Maruelle], 81–128. Stuttgart: Ibidem-Verlag, 2007.

Walicki, Andrzej. *The Slavophile Controversy: History of a Conservative Utopia in Nineteenth-Century Russian Thought.* Oxford: Clarendon Press, 1975.

Wall, Drucilla Mims. "Imagined Indians and Sacred Landscape from New Age to Nature Writing." In *True West: Authenticity and the American West,* edited by William R. Handley and Nathaniel Lewis, 97–116. Lincoln: University of Nebraska Press, 2004.

Warnaby, Gary, and Dominic Medway. "Semiotics and Place Branding: The Influence of the Built and Natural Environment in City Logos." In *Toward Effective Place Brand Management: Branding European Cities and Regions,* edited by Gregory Ashworth and Mikhalis Kavaratzis, 205–21. Cheltenham, UK: Edward Elgar, 2010.

Wartman, Richard. *Scenarios of Power: Myth and Ceremony in Russian Monarchy from Peter the Great to the Abdication of Nicholas II.* Princeton: Princeton University Press, 2006.

Welch Larson, Deborah, and Alexei Shevchenko. "Shortcut to Greatness: The New Thinking and the Revolution in Soviet Foreign Policy." *International Organization* 57 (2003): 77–109.

Wilmes, Dusty. "National Identity (De)construction in Recent Independent Cinema: Kirill Serebrennikov's *Yuri's Day* and Sergei Loznitsa's *My Joy*." *Studies in Russian and Soviet Cinema* 8, no. 3 (2014): 218–32.

Wolff, Larry. *Inventing Eastern Europe: The Map of Civilization on the Mind of the Enlightenment.* Stanford: Stanford University Press, 1994.

Zamiatin, Dmitrii. "Geokul'turnyi brending territorii. Kontseptual'nye osnovy." *Labirint: Zhurnal sotsial'no-gumanitarnykh issledovanii* 5 (2013): 11–23.

Zamiatina, Nadezhda. "Avtoreprezentatsiia regionov (po ofitsial'nym saitam sub"ektov Rossiiskoi Federatsii)." *Otechestvennye Zapiski (Anatomiia provintsii)* 5, no. 31 (2006): 272–82.

Zaionts, L. O. "Istoriia slova i poniatiia provintsiia v russkoi kul'ture." *Russian Literature* 53 (2003): 307–30.

———. "Russkii provintsial'nyi 'mif' (k probleme kul'turnoi tipologii)." In *Geopanorama russkoi kul'tury, Provintsiia i ee lokal'nye teksty,* edited by L. O. Zaionts, 427–56. Moscow: Iazyki slavianskoi kul'tury, 2004.

Zemskova, Natal'ia. *Gorod na Stikse.* Moscow: Arsis Books, 2013.

Zholkovskii, A. K., and M. B. Iampol'skii. *Babel'/Babel.* Moscow: Carte Blanche, 1994.

Bibliography

Zintsov, O. "Ee krepost'." *Vedomosti*, September 19, 2008, http://www.vedo mosti.ru/newspaper/articles/2008/09/19/ee-krepost.

Zvereva, G. "Diskurs gosudarstvennoi natsii v sovremennoi Rossii." In *Sovremennye interpretatsii russkogo natsionalizma*, edited by Marlen Lariuel' [Marlène Maruelle], 15–80. Stuttgart: Ibidem-Verlag, 2007.

Zwejnert, J. "Conflicting Patterns of Thought in the Russian Debate on Transition: 2003–2007." *Europe-Asia Studies* 62, no. 4 (2010): 547–69.

Index

Abalmasova, N. E., 61, 71
Abashev, Vladimir, 11, 34
About Love (*Pro Liuboff*) (Subbotina; film), 40, 132–34
Akopov, Pyotr, 32
Aksakov, Ivan, 28, 144–45
Aksakov, Konstantin, 26
All-Russian Public Opinion Research Center (VTsIOM), 35
Anderson, Benedict, 16
Andrei (character in *Pro Liuboff*), 105–6
Anholt, Simon, 70–71
Anna Karenina (Tolstoy), 20, 160n7
Apatity, 95
authenticity: of capital, 21; cultural construction in, 143, 144; and Damasceneness, 141; as elusive, 140; ideology and, 144; intelligentsia quest for Russian spirit, 3; in intelligentsia vs. people binary, 137; in "irretrievable past," 141–42; marketing and, 144; modernity and, 143; and nation-ness, 140; provinces as imagined locale of, 4; provincial myth and, 125, 141, 142; and regionalism, 140–41; superiority of provinces and, 21; towns and, 21

Babel, Isaak, 76
Bakhtin, Mikhail, 141–42
Balabanov, Aleksei, 138; *Brother* (*Brat*), 111; *Brother 2* (*Brat 2*), 111; *Cargo-200*, 128
Barthes, Roland, 69
Beijing, 68, 69, 70
Berdyaev, Nikolai, 3–4, 142
Beumers, Birgit, 105, 114, 126
Bhabha, Homi K., 16, 34, 127
The Blessed (*Blazhennaia*) (Strausovsky; film), 117
Blok, Alexander, 107, 108
Bogoslavskaya, Olga, 115–16
Bondarenko, Vladimir, 65
Borenstein, Eliot, 50, 128
Boym, Svetlana, 77–78
branding: of cities, 39, 60–61, 63, 67, 68, 71; myth and, 71; of nations, 71; of places, 70–71; of provinces, 139–40, 143–44; regional, 60–61, 62, 71; regional specificity vs., 89; theory, 69; of towns, 62

Braveheart (film), 141
"Broad Is the Motherland" ("Shiroka strana"; song), 126
"Broad Is the River" ("Shiroka reka"; song), 126
Broad Is the River (*Shiroka reka*; TV series), 124–27
Brother (*Brat*) (Balabanov), 111
Brother 2 (*Brat 2*) (Balabanov), 111
Bulgakov, Mikhail, *Heart of a Dog*, 58
Bunin, Ivan, 63
Buruma, Ian, 110, 111
Bykov, Dmitri, 100–101; "Mozharovo," 40, 101–2, 103

capital: about, 17; authenticity of, 21; concentration of film industry in, 105; fragmentation of concept, and "capitals," 53–54; gravitation toward provinces, 145; as home to elite, 33; Lurkmore and, 54; measuring provincial city against, 69; Occidentalist view of, 34; as Other, 109–10; provincial imitations of, 62; and regional identity, 54, 57; and regional self-identification, 66; towns vs., 19, 21; use of term "provinces," 164–5n7; in West vs. Russia binary, 21. *See also* center; Moscow; St. Petersburg
capital vs. periphery. *See* center vs. periphery binary
capital vs. provinces (*stolitsa-provintsiia*) binary: attributes of provinces in, 83; and ceasing to measure provincial city against capital, 69; Cinderella trope, 115–23, 132–34; cultural representations and shifting meanings of, 19; cultural texts, and positive vs. negative of each, 9–10; and definition of periphery in negative terms, 7; dichotomies characterizing, 77; end of Soviet Union and, 4; in films, 104, 124; intelligentsia vs. people in, 134; Ivanov on, 91–92; in literature, 40, 73–74, 103; in "Mozharovo," 101–2; and national character, 21; in national identity creation, 108–9; in nineteenth-century literature, 20; in periodicals, 52–53; positive vs. negative aspects of provinces in, 139–40; post-Soviet reevaluation of, 71–72; *ressentiment* in, 127; and Russianness of provinces, 62; symbolic geography and, 72, 144; as synonymous with state vs. individuals, 78; TV and, 104, 124–27; West vs. Russia binary compared, 21, 36, 72. *See also* center vs. provinces binary
capital vs. towns binary, 19, 21, 125
capital vs. village/countryside (*stolitsa-derevnia*) binary: in *Community*, 94–95; in *The Dog-Headed*, 92–94; and sentimental pastoralism, 7
Cargo-200 (Balabanov; film), 128
Catherine II, 6, 61; "Charter of Nobility," 7
center: as within individual, 3; negative vs. positive connotations regarding provinces, 9–10; postcolonialism and ethnicities vs., 58–59; viability of concept of, 54. *See also* capital
The Center for Supplementary Fornication (*Bluda i Mudo*) (Ivanov), 40, 90–92
center vs. periphery binary: in Empire, 17; films depicting movement between, 115; in journalism, 38–39; and meaning of "center," 56–57; movement to center, and social ascent, 115; Occidentalism vs. Orientalism in, 127; Orientalism in, 126; as parasitical relationship, 109–10; provincial writers and, 73; *ressentiment* in, 109; severing of ties between, 111
center vs. provinces binary: colonization/postcolonialism and, 58–59; cultural myth of, 6; cultural vs. physical distance and, 20–21; in films, 4, 138; intellectual life compared, 9; Ivanov on, 89; in literature, 4, 20; in mass culture, 4; mutual *ressentiment*, 46–47; and outward vs. inward gaze from center, 33; porosity of boundaries/reconcilability of differences in, 127; privileging of center in, 4; and Russian "soul," 3–4; in *Russia's Provinces*, 48; social class in, 133; in TV series, 138; West vs. Russia compared, 112. *See also* capital vs. provinces (*stolitsa-provintsiia*) binary
Chef magazine, 66

Index

Chekhov, Anton, 167n58; "In the Ravine," 167n58; and noncapital space, 5–6; peasants in literature, 26; on provincial towns, 125; and small towns, 19
chernukha, 109, 128, 130
Chernyshevsky, Nikolai, *What Is to Be Done?*, 76
Chukhloma, 84
Churbanov, Vadim, 45–46
cinema. *See* films
Circus (film), 126
cities: branding of, 39, 60–61, 63, 67, 68, 71; in "Mozharovo," 101; as Occidental, 111; provincial, 61, 69, 71, 98, 99. *See also* capital; center; towns; *and names of individual cities*
City News (later *Ivanovo Provinces*), 52
The City on the Styx (Zemskova), 96–97
Clark, Katerina, 28
class, social: in center vs. provinces binary, 133; movement from center to periphery, and, 115. *See also* intelligentsia
Clowes, Edith, 142
Cold War, 32
colonialism/colonization: in intelligentsia vs. people binary, 136; intensification of interest in subordinate territories as, 10–11; internal, 149n25; and love triangle plot, 125
Community (*Kom'iuniti*) (Ivanov), 40, 92, 94–95, 102, 139–40
Condee, Nancy, 29–30, 33, 104
consumerism: in Moscow, 29, 94, 95; of West, 29; West vs. Russia binary and rejection of, 24–25
country estates, 7, 20, 63
Cultural Landscape and Soviet Inhabited Space (Kagansky), 111
cultural myth(s): articulation/transmission through texts, 144; *chernukha* vs., 128; in cinema, 105; and idealized Russianness of noncapital space, 6; ideology and, 5, 138, 140; intelligentsia and, 5; Moscow as, 36; and national identity, 14–15; and nationalism, 140; and nationalist discourse, 30; the people as, 26; and provinces, 6, 19; provinces at core of, 4; provincial myth compared, 11; provincial space within, 71; towns and, 5; West as, 18. *See also* provincial myth
Culture and Explosion (Lotman), 122–23

Dal, Vladimir, 8
Danilkin, Lev, 91
Dasha (character in *Pro Liuboff*), 132–34
democracy, 32, 35
Demons (Dostoevsky), 20
Dima (character in *Milkmaid*), 118, 120, 121–22
Dimitrovgrad, 54
The Dog-Headed (*Psoglavtsy*) (Ivanov), 40, 92–94, 95, 99, 102
Dondurei, Daniil, 129
Dostoevsky, Fyodor: *Demons*, 20; Pushkin speech, 23, 81; and tea drinking, 76; *Winter Notes on Summer Impressions*, 27
Doubivko, Lena, 135–36

Eco, Umberto, *The Name of the Rose*, 74
economy, 31–32
Eder, Klaus, 130, 131
elite(s): capital as home to, 33; cultural, 43, 105; and film industry, 105; and Moscow, 67; post-Soviet reevaluation of capital vs. provinces binary, 71–72; pride in provinciality, 43; and provinces as Other, 33–34; provincial, 67, 71–72; and ternary of provinces–capital–West, 72; and true Russianness of provinces, 43
Emancipation of the Serfs, 7
Embryos (Rozanov), 75, 76
Envy (Olesha), 58
Esenin, Sergei, 120
ethnic identity: and national identity, 16–17, 42; postimperial, 16; post-Soviet, 42
ethnicity: in fashion, 68, 71; in *Guberniia Style*, 64–65; postcolonial relationship between center and, 58–59; in provincial population, 58–59
Ethnomir (museum-park), 60
ethnonationalism: in *Guberniia Style*, 65; and patriotism, 65; rise in, 30–31

Etkind, Alexander, 10–11, 21, 59, 125, 149n25, 152n79
Europe: Eastern Others vs., 25; and Europeans vs. Russians, 102; influence on Russia/Russians, 20, 27, 61; and Latin America, 141; and Occidentalism, 110; Prilepin on, 97–98; Russia as "provincial" in, 19, 20, 84, 97–98; Russia as savior of, 23, 32; Russia as true center, vs., 85–86; Russian capital imitating, 20, 21; and Russian Europeans, 32–33; St. Petersburg modeled on, 61–62; traditionalism of, 85; in West, 18; and westernization of Russia, 18. *See also* West; West vs. provinces binary; West vs. Russia binary
Evtuhov, Catherine, 69

Fallen Leaves (Rozanov), 75
fashion, 12, 14, 67–69, 71
Fedotych, Frol (TV character), 125
feng-shui, 131, 132
films: about, 40–41; center vs. provinces in, 138; Cinderella trope in, 115–23, 132–34; clichés of provinces in, 124–32; cultural myth in, 105; dark naturalism in, 128–29, 130; depicting provincials setting out to conquer Moscow, 115; industry, 105; intelligentsia vs. people in, 134–38; Occidentalism in, 121, 126; opposition to regime of Putin's Russia in, 138; periphery in, 128; provincial myth in art-house vs. commercial, 105, 138; Putin era and, 114; scholarship on, 104–5; themes of 1990s, 128; themes of mid-2000s, 124, 127. *See also* TV serials/series
films, art-house: capital vs. provinces binary in, 124; center vs. provinces in, 4; Cinderella trope in, 117; content of, 104; and provinces as microcosm of Russia, 123–24; and provinces as "true" Russia, 105; provinces of myth in, 124
films, commercial/mainstream: capital vs. provinces binary in, 104; Cinderella trope in, 117–18; content of, 104
food, 57–58

Fortunatova, V. A., 153n88
Free Floating (Khlebnikov; film), 128

Galia (character in *Gloss*), 109–10, 167n61
Gellner, Ernest, 16, 25
The Geographer Drank Away the Globus (Ivanov), 89–90
geography/-ies: city branding vs., 67; as constructs, 67; imagined, 59, 142; in literature, 38, 39; metageography vs., 67; and privileging of cities/towns, 53; and provinces as state of mind vs., 80; regional identity vs., 90; and Russia as second rate, 87; of Russian soul, 3–4, 6, 11. *See also* symbolic geography/-ies
German, Aleksei, 138
Gibson, Mel, 141
Ginzburg, Lidia, 118
Gloss (*Glianets*) (Konchalovsky; film), 40, 109–10, 167n61
glubinka, 8, 142
Gogol, Nikolai: and Chichikovian troika, 23; Kharitonov compared to, 75; and N., 21, 61, 77; and noncapital space, 5; and provinces as backward/uniform, 61; and provinces as imitating capital, 20; and provinces-capital distinction, 21; on towns, 19, 125; and underdevelopment of regional tradition, 69
Golden Age. *See* utopia
Goscilo, Helena, 74
Graffy, Julian, 124
Graham, Colin, 140
Graham, Seth, 128
Great Russia: Geographical, Ethnographic, and Cultural Profiles of Contemporary Russia (encyclopedia), 10
Greenfeld, Liah, 22
Gres, Anna, *The Milkmaid from Khatsapetovka* (*Doiarka iz Khatsapetovki*), 40, 118–22
Groys, Boris, 22–23
guberniia, 6, 61
Guberniia Style (fashion festival), 12, 67–69
Guberniia Style (journal), 38, 43, 63–70
Gudkov, Lev, 25, 31, 35, 165n13
Gurin, Stanislav, 95–96

Index

Handler, Richard, 143
Hashamova, Yana, 105
Heart of a Dog (Bulgakov), 58
Heart of the Uplands (Ivanov), 87
hermetic national model, 5, 41, 52, 72, 103, 127, 138
Honninghausen, Lothar, 140
Hosking, Geoffrey, 17, 157n20
Hutchings, Stephen, 105

"I Came from Russia" (Prilepin), 98
identity: negative, 165n13; social, 23–24, 36. *See also* ethnic identity; national identity; provincial identity; regional identity
ideology/-ies: and authenticity, 144; and cultural myths, 138, 140; imperial vs. national, 17; in nationalist discourse, 15; and provincial myth, 11, 138
intelligentsia: and cultural myth, 5; escape into private sphere, 79–80; in *Lines of Fate*, 80; marginalized feelings of provincial, 46; and Occidentalism, 34, 111; provincial as true Russian people, 45; and provincial forms of art, 78; provincials' disenchantment with center, 46; quest for authentic Russian spirit, 3; retreat into private sphere/domain, 77–78; *Russia's Provinces* on, 45, 46; and West vs. provinces, 144–45; in *Yuryev Day*, 106
intelligentsia vs. people binary: in capital vs. provinces binary, 134; in films, 134–38; Orientalism in, 136, 137; and provincial myth, 138
"In the Ravine" (Chekhov), 167n58
Ivanov, Alexei: *The Center for Supplementary Fornication* (*Bluda i Mudo*), 40, 90–92; *Community* (*Kom'iuniti*), 40, 92, 94–95, 102, 139–40; *The Dog-Headed* (*Psoglavtsy*), 40, 92–94, 95, 99, 102; *The Geographer Drank Away the Globs*, 89–90; *Heart of the Uplands*, 87; and Kalitino, 103; *The Rebellion's Gold*, 87; "Russia: A Mode of Existence," 88
Ivanova, Natalia, 33, 80, 93
Ivanovo Provinces (formerly *City News*), 52

journalism, 38–39. *See also* newspapers; periodicals

Kadysheva, Natalia, 126
Kagansky, Vladimir, 148n12; *Cultural Landscape and Soviet Inhabited Space*, 111
Kalitino (fictional village), 93–94, 103
Kamerģerskii Lane (*Kamerģerskii pereulok*) (Orlov), 166n29
Karaganov, Sergei, 24–25
Karamzin, Nikolai, 45; peasants in literature, 26; "Poor Liza," 26
Karem, Jeff, 140
Kasatkin, Aleksandr, *Listening to Silence*, 117
Katia (character in *Milkmaid*), 118–22
Kharitonov, Mark: *Lines of Fate, or Milashevich's Trunk*, 39, 74–83, 86, 97; and Nechaisk, 103; *Prokhor Menshutin*, 74; *Provincial Philosophy*, 74
Khatsapetovka, 118–19, 120, 122
Khlebnikov, Boris, 138; *Free Floating*, 128
Kirill (character in *Dog-Headed*), 92–93, 94
Kirill (character in *Kokoko*), 136, 137
Kokoko (Smirnova; film), 40, 134–38
Kolia (character in *Once Upon a Time in the Provinces*), 130
Koltsov, Aleksei, 63
Konchalovsky, Andrei, *Gloss* (*Glianets*), 40, 109–10, 167n61
Konfederat, O. V., 78
Kornblatt, Judith, 18
Koviazin (fictional town), 91–92
Krylov, Mikhail, 55
Kukulin, Il'ia, 87
Kul'tura, *Provincial Museums of Russia*, 12
Kunstkamera Museum, St. Petersburg, 135–36

Latin America, and Europe as Other, 141
Leiderman, Naum, 74–75
Lena (character in *Once Upon a Time in the Provinces*), 131–32
Leontyev, Konstantin, 157n21
Letter from Soligalich to Oxford (Yakovlev), 39–40, 84–87
"Letter from the Provinces to the Best People" (Prilepin), 98

Letters from the Provinces (documentary journalism series), 12
Levada-Center, 25
"Level with the Capital: Notes on the Worries of the Provincial Intelligentsia" (Milovanov), 46
Leviathan (Zvyagintsev; film), 128
Likhachev, Dmitri, 51
Lines of Fate (*Linii sud'by*) (Meskhiev; TV series), 40, 112–14, 129
Lines of Fate, or Milashevich's Trunk (Kharitonov), 39, 74–83, 86, 97
Lipovetsky, Mark, 74–75, 108, 125
Lisa (character in *Kokoko*), 134–38
Listening to Silence (Kasatkin; film), 117
literature: capital vs. provinces binary in, 4, 20, 40, 73–74, 103; Europe vs. Russia in, 20; as metafictional/metahistorical, 75; negative image of provinces in, 4; the people in, 26–27; provinces in, 4, 9; provincialism in, 20; provincial myth in, 39–40; provincial writers and center-periphery dynamic, 73; Putin era and, 114; Russian national identity in, 74, 103; and ternary of provinces-capital-West, 20; towns in, 61; use of terms "provinces/provincial" in titles of academic works, 12–13; and village as abode of peasant, 28
Little Motherland (*malaia Rodina*), 55, 60
Liubov (character in *Pro Liuboff*), 105–9, 129
Live (Sigarev; film), 128
Lizavin, Anton Antonovich (character in *Lines of Fate*), 75–76, 77, 78–80
Lotman, Yuri, *Culture and Explosion*, 122–23
Lounsbery, Anne, 19, 20, 21, 61, 143
Lukianenko, Sergei, 97; *Night Watch* (*Nochnoi Dozor*), 94, 162n57
Lurkmore, 54

MacFadyen, David, 105
Macleod, Nicola, 141
magazines. *See* periodicals
Makoveeva, Irina, 133
Malinova, Olga, 24
Mandelstam, Osip, 63
Margalit, Avishai, 110, 111

Markedonov, Sergei, 65
marketing: and authenticity, 144; use of terms "provinces/provincial," 12. *See also* branding
Martin, Terri, 17
Maslennikova, S., 51
McCausland, Gerald, 130, 131
Melikian, Anna, *Mermaid*, 117
Menshov, Vladimir, *Moscow Doesn't Believe in Tears*, 115–16
Mermaid (Melikian; film), 117
Meskhiev, Dmitri, *Lines of Fate*, 40, 114
Middle East, reinvention of traditions, and self-definition, 141
Mikhalkov, Nikita, 57–58
Milashevich, Simeon (fictional character), 75–77, 78–80, 84
The Milkmaid from Khatsapetovka (*Doiarka iz Khatsapetovki*) (Gres; TV series), 40, 118–22
Milovanov, Yuri, "Level with the Capital: Notes on the Worries of the Provincial Intelligentsia," 46
modernity: and authenticity, 143; and nationalism, 143; Occidentalism vs., 110, 111; provincial Cinderella trope and, 119
Moiseev, Nikita, 46–47
Moore, David Chioni, 59
Morozov, Viatcheslav, 59, 143
Morzhov, Boris (character in *Center for Supplementary Fornication*), 91–92
Moscow: as center of Stalinist utopia, 115; as city-colonizer, 111; in *Community*, 94–95; consumerism in, 94, 95; as cultural myth, 36; cultural paternalism of, 46; dual nature of, 112; erosion of authority of, 53, 54, 65–66, 70; as existential city, 95; and food, 57–58; *Guberniia Style* on, 65–66; as imperial vs. Occidental city, 127; and interregional inequality, 111; Koviazin compared to, 91–92; in *Letter from Soligalich to Oxford*, 84, 86; in *Lines of Fate*, 112–14; in national identity creation, 108–9; negative view of, 65–66; non-Russians peopling, 98; nostalgic vision of "true," 112; Occidentalism and, 67, 110, 112, 121, 123, 127, 128;

Index

as Other, 36, 108–10, 112; Prilepin and, 97, 98; provinces as microcosm of Russia vs., 124; provincial elite and, 67; provincial girls in, 115–23, 132–34; provincials in, 38, 111, 113–14, 115–23; provincial towns vs., 125–26, 128; public opinion regarding, 35–36; regional identity projects vs., 57; and *ressentiment*, 110, 112; Russianness outside, 4; *Russia's Provinces* on, 46–47; in *Sankya*, 99; as Soviet utopia, 127; symbolic border between Paris and, 122; and theater, 57, 58; Voronezh compared, 63; westernization of, 29, 121, 127. *See also* capital; capital vs. provinces (*stolitsa-provintsiia*) binary; capital vs. towns binary; capital vs. village/countryside (*stolitsa-derevnia*) binary

Moscow Doesn't Believe in Tears (Menshov), 115–16

"Mozharovo" (Bykov), 40, 101–2, 103

Mukhosransk, 119

myth(s): about, 141–42; Russian national, 17–18. *See also* cultural myth(s); provincial myth

"Nadenka" (Zhukova), 20

The Name of the Rose (Eco), 74

Nastia (film character), 129–30, 131

Nasybulin, Artem, *The Provincial Girl* (*Provintsialka*), 116–17

national idea: cultural myth of provinces and, 74; *Lines of Fate* and, 81; Other and, 144; provinces and, 13–14; provincial discourse and, 82; provincial myth and, 37–38; repetition of "Russian," 50–51; *ressentiment* and, 144; Russian Europeans and, 33; Russianness of provinces in, 144; towns and, 4; West vs. Russia and, 22–23, 24–25

national identity: appropriation of rhetoric by provincial elites, 72; capital vs. provinces in creation of, 108–9; components of positive, 6; and creative reevaluation of advancement concept, 24; cultural myths and, 14–15; culture and, 30; and ethnic identity, 16–17; in *Guberniia Style*, 64–65; hermetic national models and, 103; in *Lines of Fate*, 74; in literature, 74, 103; nationalism vs., 16; in nationalist discourse, 50–51; nationalist discourse and, 4–5; otherness and, 25; in periodicals, 52–53; post-Soviet, 42; provinces and, 139–40; provinces as central in, 19; provincial myth and, 102–3; Russian people vs. West in, 27–28; shift from temporal to spatial focus, 142; Soviet, 17; and symbolic geography, 144; and ternary of provinces–capital–West, 19–20, 122; "us vs. them" vs. "us vs. us," 37; West vs. Russia and, 4–5, 22

nationalism: about, 15–16, 31; commodification and, 141; cultural myths and, 140; culture and, 16; ethnic identity and, 17, 42; extremism in, 31; liberal thinkers and, 15; modernity and, 143; and modernization, 31–32; national identity vs., 16; Other and, 25, 34; the people and, 26; provinces and, 4–5, 33; and provincial myth, 15; and *ressentiment*, 24; of *The Russian Provinces*, 49; Scottish, 141; and Slavophilia, 27; state, 31; and symbolic geography, 62; village-provinces distinction, 28; and West vs. Russia, 32

nationalist discourse: in "Broad Is the River," 126; and creative reevaluation of advancement concept, 24; defined, 15; ideology in, 15; Iron Curtain and, 24; lack of specificity in, 50–51; Moscow vs. provinces in, and redirection from West, 112; myth and, 30; national identity in, 50–51; nature of, 29–30; Occidentalism and, 110; Other and, 24, 25, 34; political/ideological stances, 15; provinces and, 4–5, 13, 14–15, 33, 62, 70, 81, 100–101; provincial focus in identity and redirection from West, 4–5; provincial myth and, 6, 83–84, 138; *ressentiment* in, 50, 65; and Russian national identity, 4–5; in *The Russian Provinces*, 50; in scholarship on cinema, 105; as temporal and spatial, 142; ternary structure and, 123; TV serials and, 115–16 nation-building: Moscow's dual nature and, 112; and myth of past vs. change/becoming, 127; nation branding and, 71; provincial Russian role in, 38

nation-ness: authenticity and, 140; provincial myth and, 143

Nazikian, Arminiak, *The Provincial (Provintsial)*, 116–17

Nazirov, Stanislav, *Wide Is the River*, 40

Nechaisk (fictional town), 77, 103

Nemtsov, Boris, 12, 44

Nemzer, Andrei, 75, 76, 77

The New Provinces (weekly newspaper), 51–52

newspapers: inaugural issues, 51–52; local markers in titles of, 56; neutral designations used by Soviet Union in, 8–9; regional coverage in, 56; usage of words "province/provincial," 11–12, 43, 44

New York Times, on *Lines of Fate*, 74

Nietzsche, Friedrich, 23

Night Watch (*Nochnoi Dozor*) (Lukianenko), 94, 162n57

Nizhniy Novgorod, 97; capital of the Volga Region program, 53–54

nostalgia: and passéism, 10, 11; of post-Soviet culture, 81; provinces and, 81; and provincial myth, 11; and true Moscow, 112; villages and, 28–29

Occidentalism: about, 34; of capital, 34; capital as negative in, 65–66; defined, 110; in films, 121, 126; intelligentsia and, 34, 111; modernity vs., 110, 111; and Moscow, 67, 110, 112, 121, 127, 128; nationalism and, 65; Orientalism vs., 34, 38, 110, 127; Other and, 110; *ressentiment* in, 65; in TV series, 124, 126; in Voronezh's image-making, 63; on West, 65

Olesha, Yuri, *Envy*, 58

Once Upon a Time in the Provinces (Shagalova; film), 40, 127–32

One Day in the Life of Ivan Denisovich (Solzhenitsyn), 58

Orientalism: about, 34; and capital vs. towns binary, 125; colonialism and, 11; and exotic in periphery vs. capital, 126; and Golden Age, 36; in intelligentsia vs. people binary, 136, 137; Occidentalism vs., 34, 38, 110, 127; in provincial Cinderella-in-Moscow trope, 119–20, 121; Russian populism as, 10–11

Orlov, Vladimir, *Kamergerskii Lane* (*Kamergerskii pereulok*), 166n29

Other(s)/otherness: capital as, 109–10; collective identity and definition of, 31; construction of image for identity formation, 18; Latin America, and Europe as, 141; Liubov (film character) as, 107; Moscow as, 36, 109–10, 112; and national idea, 144; and national identity, 25; nationalism and, 25; nationalist discourse and, 24, 34; in Occidentalism, 110; Orientalism and, 121; the people as, 136, 152n79; provinces as, 34, 36, 72, 102; provinces vs. West as, 5, 52–53; repetition of "Russian" and, 51; *ressentiment* and, 47, 110, 144; in *Russia's Provinces*, 47, 48; superimposition by *chernukha* onto Self, 128; and values, 25; West as, 18, 72, 109; in West vs. Russia binary, 23, 65

Oxford, 85, 86

Ozhegov dictionary, 8

Pain, Emil A., 30, 61, 71

Panarin, Alexsandr, 47

Paris: geography vs. metageography of, 67; in *Milkmaid*, 122; Soligalich compared to, 84; Voronezh compared to, 66–70

passéism: defined, 10; and idealization of provincial life, 109; nostalgia and, 10, 11; and Orientalism, 11; post-Soviet focus on provinces compared, 19; and provinces, 10; and significance of capital vs. provinces in national identity creation, 109; and symbolic geography, 43

patriotism: definition of, 65; ethnonationalism and, 65; in history of Russian nation, 31; in Ivanov's novels, 40; local tourism promotion and, 60; provinciality and,

Index

98, 101; in regional identity, 55; "Russia-as-savior" discourse and, 81; Russian Europeans/global Russians and, 33; traveling and, 70

Pavliuk, Semyon, 56

peasantry, 26-27

people, the: about, 26; apophatic definition, 136; intelligentsia vs., in films, 134-38; nationalism and, 26; as Other, 136, 152n79; provincial girl as representative of, 135; public vs., 26; in *The Russian Provinces*, 49-50; Stalin's toast to, 49-50; in West vs. Russia binary, 27-28. *See also* intelligentsia vs. people binary; provincials

perestroika, 56, 58, 80, 112, 128, 130

periodicals: advertisements in, 60; inaugural issues, 44-45; renaming to include provincial references, 43; response to local/regional media needs, 59-60; tourism promotion, 49; two categories of, 44-45. *See also* newspapers

periphery: defined, 148n12; negative connotations of, 9; replacement of provinces by, 8; as terrible place in films, 128. *See also* center vs. periphery binary

Perm, 53, 87, 88, 90, 96, 97

The Perm Period (journal), 53

Peter the Great, 6

Platonov, Andrei, 63

Poltoratskaya, Daria, *Wide Is the River*, 40

"Poor Liza" (Karamzin), 26

Popadiuk, Sergei, 48

Popov, N. P., 35

Posad, Sergiev, *The Provincial Woman (Provintsialka)*, 52, 57

postcolonialism, 58-59, 110, 149n25

Prilepin, Zakhar, 97-98, 100, 103; "I Came from Russia," 98; "Letter from The Provinces to the Best People," 98; *Sankya*, 40, 98-100

private sphere: as alternative to political opposition, 77-78, 79-80; home as, 86

Prokhor Menshutin (Kharitonov), 74

provinces (*provintsiia*): attributes in cultural discourse, 82-83; autonomy of, 43; as both real and symbolic, 77; branding of, 139-40, 143-44; capital gravitation toward, 145; collapse into noncapital space, 29; commercial aspect to rhetoric, 49; definition of, 6-10, 148n12; and economic independence, 82; history of term, 6, 7; homogeneity of, 39, 48, 62; idealization of, 6, 14-15, 138; as idealized repository of Russianness, 6; as imagined, 7; intellectual life in, 9; in *Lines of Fate*, 77; as microcosm of Russia, 124, 129; as middle ground between people and educated society, 28; as mythologeme within symbolic geography, 7; and national character, 84, 109; and national idea, 13-14; and national identity, 19, 139-40; nationalism and, 4-5, 33; and nationalist discourse, 4-5, 13, 14-15, 62, 70, 81, 100-101; negative vs. positive connotations of, 5-6, 8-9, 14-15, 41, 61, 62, 139-40; and nostalgia, 81; Orientalist view of, 34; as Other, 34, 36, 40, 72; passéism and, 43; peasant commune compared, 27; perception from perspective of center, 9-10; periphery as replacing, 8; as philosophy, 74-84; positive connotations of village absorbed into, 29; post-Soviet focus on, 19, 82; Prilepin and, 98-100; provincialism of, 33; and provinciality vs. "people," 28; redefinition of, 10-15; rhythm of life, and national tradition, 77-78; Rousseauistic representation, 77; Russianness of, 4, 6, 43, 47-48, 62, 70, 73-74, 97-98, 105, 127, 132, 143-44; as sacral place, 95-96, 97; as savior of Russia, 82; self-definition, 43, 55; and Slavophilia, 27; Soviet official language and, 8; as state of mind, 80; and symbolic geography, 4, 5, 11; as synonym for villages, 29; as text, 5; as uniform, 61; usage of word in mass media, 43-44; utopia and, 81; vs. West as Other, 52-53. *See also* capital vs. provinces (*stolitsa-provintsiia*) binary; center vs. provinces; West vs. provinces binary "provinces (*provintsiia*)" / "provincial (*provintsial'nyi*)": history of *provintsial* as term, 6, 7; increasing use of terms, 11–12, 43–44; use of terms in newspaper titles, 11–12, 43; use of terms in titles of academic works, 12–13

The Provinces Are the Soul of Russia (Viatskoe history museum), 12

The Provincial (*Provintsial*) (TV serial) (Nazikian), 116–17

The Provincial Chronicles (newspaper), 52

Provincial Colleague (Sotrudnik provintsii) (bookstore), 10

provincial discourse: and *Guberniia Style*, 64; and local tourism promotion, 60; and national idea, 82

Provincial—Express (newspaper), 52

A Provincial Gal (*Provintsial'naia devchonka*; album), 12

The Provincial Girl (*Provintsialka*) (Nasybulin; TV serial), 116–17

provincial identity: Ivanov and, 88–89; in journals, 51; regional identity and, 55

provincialism / provinciality: cult of, 101; and hope, 21–22; in nineteenth-century literature, 20; as Other, 102; and patriotism, 98; the people vs., 28; Prilepin and, 98; of provinces, 33; in Russian vision of position in world, 143; of Russia's self-identity in Europe, 19

Provincial Museums of Russia (TV series) (Kul'tura), 12

provincial myth: about, 18, 69; abstraction of, 39; and authenticity, 70, 125, 141, 142, 144; Bykov on, 100–101; capital vs., 62; and capital-province relationship, 17; cultural myth compared, 5–6, 11; in films, 105, 124, 138; and idealization vs. demonization of provinces, 130–31; ideology and, 11, 138; imperial essence of, 164-5n7; intelligentsia vs. people binary and, 138; Ivanov on, 89–90; in *Lines of Fate*, 81; in literature, 39–40; and national idea, 37–38, 74; nationalism and, 15; nationalist discourse and, 6, 83–84, 138; national myths vs., 18; and nation-ness, 143; negative connotations of, 61, 62; nostalgia and, 11; as Other, 102; provinces as Other and, 72; provincial Cinderella trope and, 117; real places vs., 125; and Russian identity, 102–3; *Russia's Provinces* on, 45–46; symbolic geography and, 17, 43, 74; usefulness to politicians / business people, 71–72; and vertical axis, 142; in *Yuryev Day*, 106-7

Provincial News, 57–58

Provincial Philosophy (Kharitonov), 74

provincials: Cinderella trope, 115–23, 132–34; girls, 38, 115–23, 132–38; male protagonists in TV serials, 116–17; migrants vs., 155n117; in Moscow, 38, 113–14, 115–23; in St. Petersburg, 134–38. See also people, the

Provincial Thought (newspaper), 52

Provincial Woman (*Provintsialka*) (Sergiev Posad), 52, 57

The Provincial Word (newspaper), 52

Provintsiia (publishing house), 12

Pushkin Speech (Dostoevsky), 23, 81

Putin, Vladimir, 21, 63, 71, 114, 138, 142–43, 157n21

Rasputin, Valentin, "Tell Everyone That Russia Is Alive," 47

The Rebellion's Gold (Ivanov), 87

Red Coffin, or Eloquence Lessons in the Russian Provinces (Solntsev), 133–34

regional identity: about, 55; capital and, 66; "capital" designation and, 54; center-periphery relationship and, 56–57; food and, 57–58; inferiority complex and, 89; Ivanov and, 88–89; and Little Motherland, 55, 60; perestroika and, 56; of Perm, 88; in post-Soviet period, 55; and provincial self-definition, 55; and reevaluation / redefinition of provinces, 60; regional branding and, 60–61; and regional centers, 55; and sense of place, 56; similarity of projects, 57; Soviet identity vs., 55–56; Soviet Union collapse and, 56

Index

regionalism, 87, 140–41
regions: branding, 60–61, 62, 71, 89; as euphemism for areas removed from capital, 9; hierarchy of, 6, 7; study of, 5
ressentiment: in capital vs. provinces binary, 127; in center vs. periphery binary, 109; in center vs. provinces binary, 46–47; defined, 23; Dostoevsky's *Notes* and, 27; in *Gloss*, 109–10; in *Guberniia Style*, 65; Moscow and, 36, 110, 112; mutual, 41, 46–47; and national idea, 144; nationalism and, 24; in nationalist discourse, 50, 65; Other(s) and, 47, 110, 144; and relationship to West, 32; Russia-as-savior discourse and, 81–82; Social Identity Theory and, 23–24; in today's Russia, 31; toward West, 105; in West vs. Russia binary, 22–23, 105, 114; in *Yuryev Day*, 105–9
The Return (Zvyagintsev; film), 128
Rio de Janeiro, 125
Rita (character in *Pro Liuboff*), 132, 133
Robsky, Oksana, 133
Romine, Scott, 140
Rousseau, Jean-Jacques, 7, 77, 124–25
Rowe, Kathleen, 117
Rowley, Alison, 61
Rozanov, Vasili: *Embryos*, 75, 76; *Fallen Leaves*, 75
Rulyova, Natalia, 105
Ruslanova, Lidia, 137
Russia: architectural metaphors, 85–86; Prilepin on ideal, 100; provinces as, 97–98, 124, 129; provinces as savior of, 82; as provincial in West vs. Russia binary, 84; revolution, 8, 28; in *Sankya*, 99–100; as self-contained entity, 114; towns as microcosm of, 130; West as cultural/economic colonizer of, 111. *See also* West vs. Russia binary
"Russia: A Mode of Existence" (Ivanov), 88
Russia-as-savior discourse, 81–82
Russian Academy of Sciences, Institute of Scientific Information on the Social Sciences, 53–54
Russianness: and imperial pathos/past, 127; intelligentsia and quest for, 3; and internal Orientalism vs. Occidentalism, 127; in nationalist discourse, 50–51; noncapital space as idealized repository of, 6; and otherness, 51; the people and, 26; of provinces, 4, 132; provinces, and "true," 43, 62, 70, 73–74, 98, 105, 143–44; "Russian" (word) and, 50–51
Russian Olden Times (*Russkaia starina*; magazine), 10
The Russian Provinces (*Russkaia provintsiia*; journal), 12, 38, 43, 45, 49–51, 52, 63–64
"The Russian Provinces in the Context of Culture and History," 68
Russia's Provinces (*Rossiiskaia Provintsiia*) (journal), 12, 38, 43, 45–49, 52, 63–64
Russia vs. West binary. *See* West vs. Russia binary

Said, Edward, 11, 34
Salamandra, Christa, 141
Sankya (Prilepin), 40, 98–100
Sapelkin, Nikolai, 64–65, 66, 68, 69–70, 71
Saransk, 54
Savkina, Irina, 20
Selemeneva, M. V., 99–100
sense of place, 56
Serebrennikov, Kirill, 130, 138; *Yuryev Day* (*Iur'ev Den'*), 40, 105–9, 117
Shagalova, Katia, 138; *Once Upon a Time in the Provinces*, 40, 127–32
Shevchenko, Maxim, 32, 102
Sigarev, Vasili: *Live*, 128; *Spinner*, 128
Slavophiles, 24, 26–28, 141, 142
Slezkine, Yuri, 113
Sluzhkin, Viktor (character in *Geographer*), 90
Smirniagin, Leonid, 55–56
Smirnova, Avdotia, *Kokoko*, 40, 134–38
Smith, Anthony D., 16–17, 30
Snob, 33
Socialist Realist Kolkhoz Novel, 28
Soligalich, 84–87, 103
Solntsev, Roman, *Red Coffin, or Eloquence Lessons in the Russian Provinces*, 133–34
Sologub, F., 6, 10

Solomin, Yuri, 47
Solzhenitsyn, Alexander, *One Day in the Life of Ivan Denisovich*, 58
Soviet literature: hero as revolutionary worker, 28; Village Prose, 28–29
Soviet Union: identity, 55–56; neutral designations in newspapers, 8–9; newspapers during, 56; and private sphere as form of opposition, 78; provinces in official language, 8; sameness in, 62; sense of place during, 56; and Soviet identity, 17; temporal focus in ideology, 142
Soviet Union, collapse of: and capital vs. provinces, 4; and emphasis on space vs. time, 142; and loss of empire, 42; and national identity, 42; and peripheries as independent states, 17; and provinces in topical discourse, 11; and reconfiguration of symbolic geography, 43; and regional identity, 56
Spinner (Sigarev; film), 128
Spivak, Monica, 43–44
Stalin, Josef, 115; "Toast to the Russian People," 49–50
Stalinist musical, 115
Staro Tugolukovo (TV town), 124–25
Stepanova, Svetlana, 116
Stolbenets (fictional town), 77
St. Petersburg: in *TheCity on the Styx*, 96; Gogol's N. compared to, 21; intelligentsia in, 134; in *Lines of Fate*, 76, 78; Prilepin on, 98; provincial girls in, 116, 134–38; towns modelled after, 61; in TV serials, 116
Strausovsky, Sergei, *The Blessed* (*Blazhennaia*), 117
Subbotina, Olga, *About Love* (*Pro Liuboff*), 40, 132–34
symbolic geography/-ies: and capital vs. provinces binary, 72, 144; in center vs. provinces binary, 4; cultural myth of provinces and, 74; defined, 11; in literature, 74, 100; and national identity, 144; nationalism and, 62; passéism and, 43; and postmodernism, 67; post-Soviet reconfiguration of, 43; provinces and, 5, 11; provinces as mythologeme within, 7; and provincial myth, 17; provincial town and country estate in, 7; in Russia vs. West binary, 4, 144; and ternary of provinces–capital–West, 37, 72; and Voronezh compared with world capitals, 67; West vs. provinces and, 21–22; West vs. the people in, 27–28

Tajfel, Henri, 23–24
Taylor, Richard, 115
tea: drinking, 76; in *Letter from Soligalich to Oxford*, 86; and raspberry jam, 76, 78, 86
"Tell Everyone That Russia Is Alive" (Rasputin), 47
ternary of provinces–capital–West: about, 33; in *The City on the Styx*, 96; creation of/amalgamation of binaries into, 19–20; and creation of noncontentious national model, 123; equality within, 122; familiarity of, 122; in *Gloss*, 109; hermetic national model and, 138; Ivanov and, 87; in *Letter from Soligalich to Oxford*, 39–40, 84, 86–87; Moscow as Other in, 108–9; and national identity, 19–20; and nationalist discourse, 123; nineteenth-century literature and, 20; provincial elites and, 72; *ressentiment* in, 109–10; and reversing of hierarchies in binaries, 21, 122; and Russian identity, 122; switch from binary models to, 122–23; in symbolic geography, 37, 72; "us vs. us" model and, 138; in *Yuryev Day*, 109
Tiazhenko, Gleb (character in *Community*), 94–95, 139
"Toast to the Russian People" (Stalin), 49–50
Todorov, Tsvetan, 25
Todorovsky, Valeri, 114
Tolstoy, Leo: *Anna Karenina*, 20, 160n7; country estate, 63; peasants in literature, 26; and tea drinking, 76
Tolz, Vera, 17
tourism, 49, 60, 70
towns: associations with boredom/crudeness, 7; authenticity of, 21; branding, 62; and cultural myth, 5; cultural representations of, 19; dark portrayal in films,

Index

128; European influence on, 61; and government support, 35; Ivanov on, 91–92; in *Lines of Fate*, 76–77; in literature, 61, 73, 77, 103; as microcosm of Russia, 130; Moscow vs., 125–26, 128; and national idea, 4; negative connotations of, 9; negative vs. positive images of, 4; in nineteenth-century literature, 61; regional identity and, 55; in TV series, 124–25. *See also* capital vs. towns binary; cities; villages; *and names of individual towns*

traveling, 70

True West, 140

Turgenev, Ivan, 101; peasants in literature, 26

Turner, John C., 23–24

TV serials/series: about, 40–41; capital vs. provinces binary in, 104; center vs. provinces in, 138; content of, 104; nationalist discourse in, 115–16; Occidentalism in, 126; and post-Soviet situation, 105; provincial Cinderella trope, 115–16, 118; "sweet and sentimental" cliché of provinces, 124–27; use of terms "provinces/provincial," 12

uezd, 6, 61

Uletovo (filmic town), 129–31

Ulyanovsk, 54

United States: American Indian, 140–41; in concept of "West," 18; as cultural/economic colonizer of Russia, 111; mythology of Old West, 140; "real" South, 140; regionalism in, 140–41; Russian moral core vs., 25

Ural region, 87, 88, 90

Uriupinsk, 118–19

Ushakov dictionary, 8

"us vs. them" model, 5, 37

"us vs. us" model, 5, 37, 72, 138

utopia: fairytale in, 115; Golden Age myth and, 30, 36, 98; Moscow as Soviet, 127; peasant commune and, 26; pre-Petrine, 26, 141; provincial soul and, 81; provincials as embodying, 36; Stalinist musical and, 115; villages as, 98

"Valenki" (song), 137

Vasiliev (character in "Mozharovo"), 101–2

Venn, Couze, 110

Vera (character in *Once Upon a Time in the Provinces*), 129, 130, 131

Vika (character in *Kokoko*), 134–38

Village Prose, 28–29, 98, 141

villages: as abode of peasants in classics, 28; as alien to rest of country, 94; collapse into noncapital space, 29; degradation of, 93–94, 99; in *The Dog-Headed*, 92–93; as Golden Age, 98; in "Mozharovo," 101; and nostalgia, 28–29; provinces as absorbing positive connotations of, 29; in *Sankya*, 98–100; as synonym for provinces, 29; whole of Russia as, 98. *See also* capital vs. village/countryside (*stolitsa-derevnia*) binary; towns

Voronezh: about, 39; and "Bomb Voronezh," 63; as capital of Black Soil Region (*Chernozem'e*), 54; characteristics, 63; ethnic-style fashion in, 68, 71; Guberniia Style held in, 67–69; Identification project, 69–70; Paris compared to, 66–70; and provincial fashion, 12; World Tour (*Voronezhskaia krugosvetka*), 70, 71

Wall, Drucilla Mims, 141

West: anti-Americanism and, 30–31; and anti-Westernism, 21, 32–33; as both model and rival, 22; colonization of Russia, 32; consumerism of, 29; contrast to image of, in *Yuryev Day*, 107; as cultural myth, 18; as cultural/economic colonizer of Russia, 111; idea of nationality, 22; inability to serve as model, 31–32; intelligentsia and, 144–45; negative traits, 35; Occidentalism vs. modernity of, 110; as Other, 18, 109; provinces as Other vs., 52–53; and rationalism, 23; values corrupting Moscow, 121. *See also* Europe

West vs. provinces binary: and intellectuals and provincial forms of art, 78; in *Lines of Fate*, 81; and national character, 21; and symbolic geography, 21–22

West vs. Russia binary: anti-American rhetoric in, 114; architectural metaphor, 85–86; capital vs. provinces compared, 21, 36; center vs. provinces binary and, 4; common ownership vs. individualism in, 26; and definition of patriotism, 65; Dostoevsky and, 23, 27; Gogol and, 23; in journalism, 38; Liubov (film character) and, 108; moral aspects, 25; Moscow vs. provinces compared, 112; nationalism and, 32; and national philosophy, 22–23; and national self-definition, 22; and national sovereignty/national discourse, 24–25; in nineteenth-century literature, 20; otherness in, 23, 65; the people and, 27–28; popular opinion regarding, 35; positive vs. negative in, 19; in post-perestroika Russia, 24; provinciality and, 19; and rejection of consumerism, 24–25; *ressentiment* in, 22–23, 105, 114; Russia as provincial in, 84; Russia vs. provinces binary as replacing, 82; Russia vs. provinces replacing, 82; Russian capital and, 21; and Russian civilization as challenge to Western, 65; and Russian national identity, 4–5; symbolic geography and, 144; and ternary of provinces–capital–West, 19; "us vs. us" model compared, 72; and West as Other, 72

What Is to Be Done? (Chernyshevsky), 76

Wide Is the River (Poltoratskaya, Nazirov; TV "limited series"), 40

Winter Notes on Summer Impressions (Dostoevsky), 27

xenophobia, 30–31

Yakovlev, Sergei, 97; *Letter from Soligalich to Oxford*, 39–40, 84–87; and Soligalich, 103

Yudin, Aleksei, 9

Yuryev Day (*Iur'ev Den'*) (Serebrennikov; film), 40, 105–9, 117, 123–24, 127, 129

Zaitsev, Viacheslav, 68
Zamiatin, Dmitri, 67
Zamiatina, Nadezhda, 56–57, 66
Zayonts, Lyudmila, 6, 10
Zemskova, Natalia, *The City on the Styx*, 96–97
Zhukova, Maria, "Nadenka," 20
Zvyagintsev, Andrei, 138; *Leviathan*, 128; *The Return*, 128
Zwejnert, J., 154n102

www.ingramcontent.com/pod-product-compliance
Lightning Source LLC
Chambersburg PA
CBHW070843160426
43192CB00012B/2282